Flute FOR DUMMIES®

by Karen Evans Moratz

WILEY

John Wiley & Sons, Inc.

Flute For Dummies®

Published by
John Wiley & Sons, Inc.
111 River St.
Hoboken, NJ 07030-5774
www.wiley.com

WILEY

About the Author

Karen Evans Moratz is Principal Flutist with the Indianapolis Symphony Orchestra and Associate Professor of Flute and Artist in Residence at the School of Music/Jordan College of Fine Arts at Butler University.

Having a passion for teaching, Karen has served on the faculty of the Grand Teton Festival Orchestral Seminar and the Aria International Summer Academy. She also served as Visiting Professor at Indiana University/Bloomington and the University of Illinois/Champaign-Urbana. Her students have won a number of prestigious flute and piccolo competitions (including the National Flute Association's Young Artist Competition), and many have gone on to successful musical careers in teaching and music administration as well as performance.

Karen holds a bachelor's degree from the Peabody Conservatory and a master's degree from the Musikhochschule Freiburg im Breisgau. She has studied with Britton Johnson, Tim Day, Mark Sparks, and William Bennett and has recorded for NPR, Koss, London/Decca, and Arabesque. Her cadenzas for Mozart's Flute Concerto in G major, K.313 have been published by Southern Music.

She has performed with many notable conductors, including Raymond Leppard, Leonard Bernstein, John Williams, Marvin Hamlisch, and Michael Tilson Thomas, with whom she worked during the inaugural season of the New World Symphony. Ms. Moratz has also had the joy and privilege of playing with such diverse artists as Jean-Pierre Rampal, Paula Robison, William Bennett, Sir James Galway, Yo-Yo Ma, Joshua Bell, André Watts, Ray Charles, Bobby McFerrin, Judy Collins, The Moody Blues, Dave Brubeck, Art Garfunkel, and a host of others.

Karen is a former coordinator for the NFA's Young Artist Competition and regularly performs and presents at NFA Conventions. She is a founding member of the Greater Indianapolis Flute Club (Indyflute) and of the Indianapolis Baroque Orchestra. She gives recitals and masterclasses nationwide and continues to teach privately from her home studio in Indianapolis, Indiana.

Dedication

To Wibb, for his immense talent, profound insight, expert guidance, and boundless inspiration, and to my parents, Anna and Hermann Moratz, for the love and support they have given me all these years.

Author's Acknowledgments

I'd like to thank Kristin DeMint for recommending me for this project, as well as acquisitions editor Michael Lewis for giving me the chance to write this book. Thanks also to my always helpful and efficient project editor, Kelly Ewing, to Alicia South, art coordinator, and to Matt Bowen, photographer, for making the images in my head a reality. My gratitude also goes to all the other folks at Wiley Publishing whom I haven't had the privilege of meeting, but without whom this book could not have been completed.

A special thank-you goes to Julia Johnston, the manager at Indy Flute Shop, and to Barbara Kallaur, Visiting Assistant Professor of Music at Indiana University, who let me borrow the instruments you see in many of the photographs in this book, and also shared important insights and experiences that made it possible. I am most grateful to Victoria Jicha, Eva Kingma, and Valerie Simosko for providing photos for use in this book. Thanks also to Sharon Possick Lange for appearing as my resident oboist in Chapter 2. Many thanks to Emily McKay, technical editor and expert flutist and teacher, for her knowledge, perspective, and sage advice. Cyndee Giebler's arrangements and pianistic talents as well as Kent Vernon's engineering prowess made recording the CD at The Utility Room artistically gratifying and enjoyable.

My eternal gratitude goes to Becky Arrensen for her invaluable advice, to Loretta Contino for sharing her expertise, to Lainie and Bob Veenstra for their counsel and encouragement, and to all my friends and family who have also given me such fantastic support all the way through this project. (Thanks for the Red Bull, Jilly!)

I'd also like to extend my appreciation to all my students, who have taught me more than I can say.

And finally, my biggest thank-you goes to George H. Evans III: "my husband the writer," my best friend, my in-house editor and writing coach, and the love of my life. A & F.

Publisher's Acknowledgments

We're proud of this book; please send us your comments at http://dummies.custhelp.com. For other comments, please contact our Customer Care Department within the U.S. at 877-762-2974, outside the U.S. at 317-527-3993, or fax 317-572-4002.

Some of the People who helped bring this book to market including the following:

Acquisitions, Editorial, and Media Development

Project Editor: Kelly Ewing

Acquisitions Editor: Michael Lewis

Assistant Editor: Erin Calligan Mooney

Editorial Program Coordinator: Joe Niesen

General Reviewer: Dr. Emily McKay

Media Development Assistant Project Manager: Jenny Swisher

Media Development Associate Producer: Doug Kuhn

Media Development Quality Assurance: Marylin Hummel

Senior Editorial Manager: Jennifer Ehlrich

Editorial Supervisor and Reprint Editor: Carmen Krikorian

Editorial Assistant: Jennette ElNaggar

Art Coordinator: Alicia B. South

Cover Photos: © Getty Images/Hemera Technologies

Photographer: Matt Bowen

Cartoons: Rich Tennant (www.the5thwave.com)

Composition Services

Project Coordinator: Patrick Redmond

Layout and Graphics: Nikki Gately, Joyce Haughey

Proofreader: Shannon Ramsey

Indexer: Steve Rath

Special Help: W.R. Music Service, Kent Vernon

Publishing and Editorial for Consumer Dummies

Kathleen Nebenhaus, Vice President and Executive Publisher

David Palmer, Associate Publisher

Kristin Ferguson-Wagstaffe, Product Development Director

Publishing For Technology Dummies

Andy Cummings, Vice President and Publisher

Composition Services

Debbie Stailey, Director of Composition Services

Contents at a Glance

Table of Contents

Introduction

• •

The flute is a universally popular instrument that's been around for thousands of years. And, of course, it's popular: Who wouldn't want to play the flute? It's a beautiful instrument, visually and sonically. It looks as exquisite as a piece of fine jewelry, especially when it's crafted from silver, gold, or platinum. (See Chapter 3 for more on materials used in flutemaking.) It produces a pure sound that's perfect for playing slow, languid melodies, but it has the capability to execute rapid virtuosic passages at lightning speed. Its classical repertoire represents all periods of music, from early Baroque to Contemporary. (See Chapter 14 for more on periods in classical music.) It's at home with jazz, rock, and many other musical styles. And it's eminently portable, to boot. No wonder so many people play the flute. And with this book, you get expert guidance so that you can hone your flute-playing skills and enjoy making music for many years to come.

About This Book

Flute For Dummies takes you through everything you need to know to prepare for and play the flute, from buying your first instrument to how-tos on playing, practicing, ensemble playing, and caring for your instrument. Whether you're new to the flute or you've played before and want to brush up on your skills, this book is for you. No previous experience is required; I take you through everything you need to know, step by step, from before you even open your flute case through playing even the most challenging music in the flute repertoire. I share lots of handy insider tips, many of which you'll find useful even if you've already been playing for some time. No matter what your level of experience, I give you lots of helpful advice on everything from sound production and your practice routine to finger technique and choosing the right exercises and pieces for your level of playing.

Here's a brief overview of what you'll find throughout this book:

✔ **Step-by-step instructions:** Whenever you're learning a new skill or trying out an exercise to build on what you already know, I give you clear, numbered steps to follow, with plenty of understandable, jargon-free language so that you can be sure that you're getting the most out of this experience.

✔ **Photos:** In telling you about using good posture, breathing, making a sound, and holding the flute, I give you photos that illustrate exactly and clearly what to do while you're following the written instructions.

✔ **Fingering charts:** When I introduce you to a new note, I give you the note name, the note as it appears on the staff in musical notation, and a fingering chart telling you how to produce the note on your instrument. At the back of the book, in Appendix A, you find a collection of fingering charts, all in one place as a quick and ready reference for you. (I also explain how to read the fingering charts in Chapter 8 and in Appendix A.)

✔ **Sound production tips:** As you learn new notes, I give you tips on getting the best possible sound out of your instrument, whether you're playing high, low, or in between. I also include a whole chapter on sound production (Chapter 12) so that you can discover your very own beautiful sound.

✔ **Play-along CD:** On the CD included with this book, I give you flute and keyboard reference tracks as well as keyboard accompaniment tracks, both of which allow you plenty of opportunity to play along. You can listen to me playing first to give you an idea of correct tempo, rhythm, and notes and then try your own hand at making some music! Individual tracks on the CD also feature every single new note you learn so that you can compare your pitch to mine to make sure that you're playing it correctly, right from the start.

Conventions Used in This Book

Flute For Dummies is centered around learning how to play the western, Boehm system, concert C flute with a closed G♯ key. This is the flute that you'll find in school bands and orchestras, concert halls, and band instrument shops throughout the United States. (For more on Boehm's key system, closed versus open G♯, and other such technical stuff, see Chapter 2.)

I use standard music notation throughout this book. For a quick overview (or review) on how to read music, see Chapter 4.

I use the terms *flutist* and *flute player* interchangeably, but I don't use the word *flautist*. (See Chapter 2 for the reasons.)

What You're Not to Read

In some instances, I get a little carried away and include more information than you may need right at the moment — I get into the why's and where-fores of things, for example. A Technical Stuff icon appears before information that may seem superfluous at first, but that you may find interesting and — dare I say? — even enriching, the more you immerse yourself in your flute. Feel free to skip over it if you just want to get on with things for now — you can always come back to find out more later.

The same holds true for the gray sidebars you find throughout this book. They contain information that you don't necessarily need in order to play the instrument, but that can enhance your experience along the way. Read it all now or come back to the fun, fascinating material in the sidebars at a later time. This is your book, your time, so use it as you will. And enjoy.

Foolish Assumptions

You know what they say: "When you assume, you make. . . ." Oh, never mind; you know what I mean. Allow me to make at least a few simple assumptions about you, dear reader: You want to play the flute, and you want to do it right the first time around so that you don't have to waste time trying to get rid of accumulated bad habits later on. That's why I give you the most practical, straightforward advice that will work for you, whether you're a beginner or an intermediate to advanced flutist. (But never fear: If you've been playing for a while and have somehow already picked up some bad habits, I tell you how to get rid of them as quickly as possible!)

I'm also assuming that you've read musical notation at some time or other. But if not (or if you need a quick review session), turn to Chapter 4 to get up and running on the musical staff, clef, notes, and rhythms you'll need in order to make sense of the musical examples used throughout this book.

I don't assume that you're going to go through this book cover to cover, although I've designed it so that you can use it as a traditional method from beginning to end, if you're so inclined. But you can use the Table of Contents and the Index to flip directly to the information you want. I also include plenty of cross-references within each chapter, so that you can quickly and conveniently look up related information in other chapters.

How This Book is Organized

Flute For Dummies is organized so that you can quickly and easily get the information you want. The book contains six parts, each covering a different aspect of flute playing. Here's an overview of all the different parts in *Flute For Dummies*.

Part I: A Prelude to Flute Playing

In Part I, I introduce you to the flute and all its various parts, and you find out a little bit about how it works. You also get a comprehensive buyer's guide so that you can make informed choices about acquiring your very own instrument. I also include a chapter on reading music notation.

Part II: Playing the Flute: Just Wiggle Your Fingers and Blow!

After a brief (but important) discussion on breathing and posture, you start making flute sounds. You start by playing on a bottle and then progress through making sounds on various parts of the instrument. Finally, you put it all together for your very first breakthrough: making a sound on an actual flute! I tell you about holding the whole instrument, and you start to play your first notes. Before you start to play higher notes in the second octave, I tell you how to slur the notes together or play them separately by tonguing. With each chapter, you get simple tunes to play with the CD accompaniment so that you can explore your new skills at every turn.

Part III: Above and Beyond: Essential Intermediate Techniques

This part is where you get to refine your flute playing and develop skills that will have you sounding like you know what you're doing in no time. I give you a chapter that targets sound production so that you can produce a big, beautiful, resonant sound. Then you add the higher notes in the third octave to your repertoire, as well as vibrato, trilling, and more tonguing techniques so that you can articulate at lightning speed. As in Part II, I give you musical examples along the way so that you can hone each newfound skill. I also give you complete pieces written by classical composers that you can play with the CD accompaniment, along with a list of pieces that you can get a hold of and learn on your own.

Part IV: Darn Tootin': An Accompaniment to Your Growing Skills

If you're ready to spend more time in the practice studio and tackle some more challenging repertoire, this part is for you. I take you through the various components that make up an advanced practice session, which allows you to really take your playing and crank it up a few notches. This part also includes information on finding a teacher, playing in ensembles, performing, auditioning, and connecting to the burgeoning flute community locally and globally via flute clubs, publications, and e-mail chat groups. Finally, and most importantly, I give you tips on how to determine when your flute needs fixing and where to find a reliable repair technician.

Part V: The Part of Tens

The Part of Tens appears in every *For Dummies* book, with good reason: It gives you a lot of useful information in a convenient, easy-to-navigate format. Here, I give you lists of ten: ten bad habits you should avoid, ten inspiring flutists you need to hear, and ten different types of flutes. (In the ten types of flutes, the piccolo is first on the list because it's the "other" flute you're most likely to want to play after the C flute.)

Part VI: Appendixes

I include two appendixes in this part. Appendix A is chock-full of fingering charts that you'll want to refer back to regularly: They cover basic and alternate fingerings, trills, specialty fingerings for the C♯ trill key if you have one (find out more about the C♯ trill key in Chapter 3), and tremolos. Appendix B tells you how to use the play-along CD that accompanies this book — a handy lexicon of which tracks go with which musical examples my friend Cyndee Giebler and I play for you.

Icons Used in This Book

Consider these icons signposts along your journey as you read this book. When you see one in the margin, you'll know what kind of information awaits you. Depending on which icon you see, you may want to zoom right in and read that particular section, or you may decide to simply return to it later. Either way, it'll be easy to find.

When you see this icon, it's telling you that the information you're reading is going to be important to remember every time you pick up your instrument.

The Tip icon appears wherever I give you useful pointers to clarify and/or simplify the task at hand.

This is where I get a little carried away and tell you more than you may want to know — you can skip over these sections if you like. Or you may find the explanations fascinating and find that it helps you grow as a flutist and musician. Either way, when you see the Technical Stuff icon, you'll know what's coming.

Pay attention whenever you see this icon and don't skip over the important information that follows. By reading these sections carefully, you can avoid damage to your instrument, your ears, and/or your ego (which, if you're like me, is probably the most fragile of the three).

This icon shows you when you can listen to an example of the written material on the CD included with this book.

This icon alerts you to favorite recordings I mention in this book. Check them out by buying, borrowing, or downloading (if appropriate) a copy for your listening pleasure. They'll enhance your flute-playing experience and hopefully inspire you to be the best player you can possibly be.

Where to Go from Here

You don't have to read this book from beginning to end in order to get all its benefits. If you know exactly what you're looking for, just peruse the Table of Contents and/or the Index and flip right to the information you need. This book is set up so that you can skip around among the various sections to your heart's content without missing a beat.

If you've never played the flute before and don't know a thing about the instrument, turn to Chapter 1 and start right at the beginning. (It's a very good place to start. I'm told.) If you already have a good idea about how the instrument works, you know how to read music, and you're ready to start playing, go to Chapter 5 (and be sure to read the section on breathing and posture). If you've been playing for a while and are just looking for some guidance, start at Part III, although I recommend taking in Chapter 11 in Part II first so that you can get some pointers on what to do with your lips and jaw as you play up and down the range of the instrument.

Part I
A Prelude to Flute Playing

The 5th Wave   By Rich Tennant

Part I

A Prelude to Flute Playing

In this part . . .

The longest journey begins with a single step. In Part I of *Flute For Dummies,* I give you the fundamental information you need to start your own journey off on the right foot. First, you get to know the flute and its various parts, as well as variations on a theme, which, when considered together, can help you make informed choices when selecting and purchasing a new or used instrument. Finally, I include a primer on music notation so that you'll have no trouble deciphering the musical examples provided for you in the rest of this book.

Chapter 1

So You Want to Play the Flute

In This Chapter

▶ Understanding the nature of this magical instrument

▶ Appreciating the flute's great legacy

▶ Getting started with flute playing

I came to the flute in a pretty roundabout way — when I was 10 years old, the obligatory question came as to which instrument I'd like to play. I had played the recorder when I was six or so, and I had really enjoyed that, so I figured that woodwinds, such as the flute or the clarinet, would be my instruments of choice. They looked a little like the recorder, anyway, so I suppose that I found some comfort in that similarity. Well, my parents got a hold of two used instruments to try out: a flute and a clarinet. We took the instruments to a woodwind repair technician, who informed us that the clarinet was in a pretty bad state of disrepair, but the flute was in perfect condition. Hence, my musical future was decided for me.

I didn't know how a flute worked — I thought you were supposed to blow into the end of it, like a recorder. I wondered whether the flute wasn't broken, after all — until a neighbor kid who played the flute showed me that you were supposed to blow *across* the hole, not directly into it. Talk about an "aha" moment. From that point on, I gradually grew more and more obsessed with playing the flute. After a while, my parents couldn't get me to *stop* practicing. Before I knew it, I was majoring in music in college.

Maybe you've still got a flute that you used to play in high school, and you'd like to dust it off and start playing again. Maybe you've attended concerts or listened to recordings, and you've fallen in love with the way the flute sounds. Or maybe you just stumbled upon it like I did when I was a kid. Whatever brings you to the flute, I'd like to welcome you to this exciting and rewarding instrument and the adventures it promises — I hope you enjoy playing as much as I do, and that it brings you years of joy and accomplishment.

What, Exactly, Is a Flute?

For the purposes of this book, I'm talking about the instrument generally called the *western concert C flute*, shown in Figure 1-1, which is the same one that you see in any band or orchestra. (For an overview of flutes other than the western concert C flute, see Chapter 22.) This flute is based in the key of C, is usually made of metal, and is made up of three separate sections that you put together. (I talk more about the different parts of the flute in Chapter 2.)

Figure 1-1:
The flute.

Basically, a flute is a hollow tube that produces sounds when the player makes the air inside of it vibrate by blowing across a hole, hitting the opposite edge of the hole to split the airstream. (If you've ever tried to get a sound by blowing across the top of a pop bottle, you already have a pretty good idea of what I'm talking about.) All flutes make sounds according to this simple principle.

The modern Boehm system flute, which is just another name for the western concert C flute, has holes in the tube and keys on top of those holes. (See Chapter 2 for more about Theobald Boehm and the modern key system.) The flutist can play many different pitches by depressing or lifting the keys. (I talk more about the keys' function in changing the pitches in the section about the harmonic series in Chapter 2.)

The flute's range is about three and a half octaves. The notes you play most of the time, though, are within about a three-octave range. (I include all the notes within the flute's full range in the basic fingering chart, which you can find in Appendix A.)

The Legacy of the French Flute School

The way flutists play today is largely the product of something called the French Flute School, which was centered around the Conservatory in Paris, France (*Paris Conservatoire*). French flutist and teacher Paul Taffanel (1844–1908) gets much of the credit for being the driving force behind the French Flute School, but other flutists and teachers who had preceded him had also set the stage for the proliferation of flute-playing style and discipline that followed. Around the beginning of the 20th century, Taffanel and his students at the Paris Conservatoire were doing some groundbreaking things with the Boehm system flute. They practiced to play the challenging new pieces being written for them by creating many different scale and arpeggio exercises that flutists still use today. (See more about scales, arpeggios, and the Taffanel–Gaubert *Daily Exercises* (Leduc) in Chapter 17.)

Expressive, beautiful playing was an important part of Taffanel's approach as a flutist and teacher. People who heard him play said that no one had ever matched the beauty of his sound. In Taffanel's teaching studio, demanding technical exercises were essential to playing the repertoire, but expression and communication, governed by the flutist's breath and sound, were paramount. And thanks to Taffanel's writings and his teaching legacy, this distinctive style and feeling for the music itself is still at the heart of what flutists strive for today.

Playing the Flute

One of the many reasons that people are attracted to the flute is that it's fairly easy to start playing it. After you get comfortable with producing a sound (see Chapter 6), you can start working on the fingerings, and you'll be able to play quite a few notes in pretty short order (see Chapters 8 and 9).

The tricky part isn't just playing the flute — it's playing the flute *well.* And why bother playing it badly when, by putting in just a little bit more time and effort, observing the advice I give you in this book, and using powers of self-observation, you can ultimately get a far more pleasurable result?

Although you may be tempted to skip the sections on breathing and posture in Chapter 5 or my advice on balancing the flute in Chapter 7, read through these sections anyway, whether you've played the flute before or not. If you're a beginner, these points are absolutely essential to your playing. And if you're not a beginner, these points are absolutely essential to your playing — you may think you already know what you're doing with breathing, posture, and holding the flute to some extent, but I give you a few tricks that I'm willing to bet will be new to you.

If you already have some playing experience, you may want to skip ahead to Part III after you review the basics in Chapters 5 and 7. But go ahead and review the information on overblowing to the next octave in Chapter 11 as well. Here, I give you some important hints about how to maintain a good sound quality as you go up to the higher notes.

Once you've been playing for a couple of years, you'll find the advanced practice techniques in Part IV helpful. But don't shy away from Part IV if you're not an advanced flutist yet — in Chapters 18 and 19, you get lots of information on finding a teacher, playing in ensembles, performing, and (last but not least) maintaining and caring for your instrument.

Gathering the Tools of the Trade

What does it take to play the flute, besides just the desire to do it? Well, in Chapter 5, I give you a list of tools you need besides your flute to get started. I also recommend a couple of other necessary prerequisites that you don't have to go out and buy:

- ✔ **Passion:** Passion goes along with the desire to play the flute, of course. In order to have the motivation to practice daily, you've really got to *want* to do it. Of course, life is full of distractions, and you won't feel like getting the flute out of the case every single day, but if you have a general, unflagging passion for the flute and for music, it sure makes it a lot easier to devote your time to practicing, even on days when you're not really in the mood.

- ✔ **Commitment:** In order to progress on the flute, or on any instrument, for that matter, you've got to dedicate a certain amount of uninterrupted time to it each day. Carving out practice time isn't always easy to manage, but you need to do it if you want to keep getting better. (See Chapter 5 for more on practice time.) If you commit to playing the flute, schedule your practice time, and set realistic goals you can follow through on, you're well on your way.

- ✔ **Your ears:** Use them every time you practice or play and really listen to yourself carefully. Let your ears be your teacher!

- ✔ **Talent:** A little talent goes a long way. I define *talent* as innate ability. Some people seem to have that special "something" when it comes to music. But believe it or not, talent can actually be a hindrance — if an enormously talented person thinks that talent can substitute for daily practice, that person can crash, burn, and burn out pretty readily. Consider the famous Thomas Edison quotation: *"Genius is 1 percent inspiration, 99 percent perspiration."* Substitute "talent" for "inspiration" and "practice" for "perspiration," and you've got about the right ratio for success in mastering a musical instrument.

Marcel Moyse, one of Taffanel's star pupils, wrote this bit of advice in his book, *De la Sonorité* (Leduc): *"It is a matter of time, patience, and intelligent work."* (For more on Taffanel, see the section "The Legacy of the French Flute School," earlier in this chapter.) Moyse's student and well-known teacher Trevor Wye refers to this quotation time and time again in his *Practice Books for the Flute* (Novello). I find myself quoting it to my students regularly, and I'm sure many other teachers do the same. It's a simple concept, but incredibly important to remember during your musical travels. (For more on Marcel Moyse and Trevor Wye, see Chapter 17.)

Chapter 2

Getting to Know the Flute

. . . .

In This Chapter

▶ Answering the most frequently asked flute-related question

▶ Understanding the unique nature of your chosen instrument

▶ Identifying the various parts of the flute

. . . .

*I*n this chapter, you get to know the flute. Not only does this chapter introduce all of a flute's parts, you also discover the basic workings of the
instrument and how it's different from other woodwind instruments, such as
the clarinet and the oboe. You find out why the flute's immense popularity is
so well deserved. You also discover how to answer the ubiquitous question
that will likely be tossed your way at your next social gathering as soon as
people know that you play the flute: Are you a flutist or a flautist?

Flutist or Flautist: Which Term Is Correct, Anyway?

"Is it *flutist* or *flautist*?" is the most frequently asked question about the flute.
You'd best be prepared for it if you're going to be a flutist, or a flautist, or
whatever.

Although both terms are technically correct, the central issue surrounding the use of *flautist* versus *flutist* is that the former sounds overly formal,
whereas the latter is more down-to-earth. After all, in plain English, you do
play the flute, not the *flaut*. Those who ask the question in the first place tend
to be worried about appearances and correctness, which is admirable, but
unnecessary. Just say *flutist*. The word is friendly, straightforward, and
unaffected.

Flute or *flaut*: A historical perspective

The word *fluter* was in use in 15th-century Europe, a few hundred years before either *flutist* or *flautist*, and I find it quite charming. *Flute-player* has also been a popular term all along, but of course that term is much too logical to gain widespread acceptance, and probably doesn't do justice to the skill it takes to play the instrument even marginally well.

The word *Flutist* came into use around the 17th century, more than 200 years before the word *flautist* began to pop up in the middle of the 19th century.

Like many other words in the English language, such as *bravo*, *graffiti*, and *spaghetti*, the word *flautist* comes directly from the Italian language. *Flauto* is Italian for flute, and the Italian word for someone who plays the flute is *flautista*. So the word *flautist* comes from the Italian.

As a general rule, *flautist* is more commonly used in British English, whereas *flutist* is the American version. (At one of the National Flute Association Annual Conventions, someone once circulated a button that read, "Real Americans Don't Play *Flaut*." Actually, I've never met anyone in either the U.S. or the U.K. who plays a *flaut*.)

Standing Out from the Woodwind Crowd

Because of the flute's status as the highest-pitched of the woodwind instruments, the flute part usually sits on the top line in any musical score. (The flute's baby cousin, the piccolo, plays even higher than the flute — see Chapter 22 for more on the piccolo.) Most flutes today are made of precious metals, such as silver, gold, or platinum, so they stand out visually as well as sonically—the instruments are shiny and beautiful to behold.

But the flute also is different from other woodwind instruments in ways that aren't quite as obvious.

"Reed" my lips!

The flute, oboe, clarinet, bassoon, and saxophone make up the woodwind family of instruments. Not surprisingly, most of the woodwinds were made out of wood at some point (with the exception of saxophones, most of which are made out of brass, and which were invented much later than all the other woodwinds anyway). The diverse sounds produced by the different woodwind instruments are a result of the instruments' varying sizes, shapes, and materials, as well as the differences in how the sound is produced.

Unlike the flute, the saxophone, clarinet, oboe, and bassoon use different types of reeds to make their respective sounds. *Reeds* are small, thin, flexible pieces of either cane or synthetic material that vibrate when blown, creating the sound. If you've ever gotten a sound by blowing on blades of grass held between your fingers, you've played on a primitive reed. On modern reed instruments, you can attach reeds directly to the instrument or via a mouthpiece or other connecting piece. The player's top and bottom lips always rest on the reed to some degree, wrapped around either the mouthpiece or the reed itself.

The flute is the only member of the woodwind family that doesn't use a reed. The instrument rests on the player's lower lip and chin, and the player blows the air across the mouthpiece, rather than into it, to make the sound.

Figure 2-1 illustrates the differences between the oboe, a reed instrument, and the flute, the only woodwind instrument without a reed.

If you're coming to the flute after having played another woodwind instrument, you can expect it to feel drastically different because of the lack of resistance against the air being blown. When you're playing on a reed, you're blowing against something—it's a little bit like blowing through a straw to make bubbles in a milkshake. The smaller and more resistant the reed, the thicker the milkshake, and as a result, the harder you have to work just to get your air through the instrument. If you play the oboe, which uses a small double reed, it'll feel like you're trying to blow bubbles into a very thick milkshake using a cocktail straw. Playing the flute, by contrast, would be like a regular size straw just blowing into air, without anything to blow against.

Figure 2-1:
A flutist and
an oboist
playing their
instruments.

The trouble with reeds

Playing an instrument that doesn't use a reed has distinct advantages. Reed instrument players are forever fussing with their reeds. Because reeds are made of wood, they change over time, especially if temperature and humidity are volatile. Travel and altitude can be major factors in reed changes, too. Clarinetists and saxophonists use a *single reed,* one piece of commercially processed cane that's attached to the mouthpiece of the instrument. Professional clarinetists shape their reeds with reed knives to suit their own particular style of playing. Oboists and bassoonists have it the worst, because they have to buy the unprocessed cane and craft it into *double reeds,* two pieces of cane tied together on a small tube that vibrate perfectly against each other. Making double reeds is a painstaking and time-consuming process. Professional players devote many hours per day just to making their reeds. (You can buy commercially finished reeds, but they're typically not as good as the homemade ones.) Reeds have a short shelf life, too. As soon as the player has finished gouging, soaking, shaving, and scraping to craft the perfect reed, it starts disintegrating. Therefore, new ones always need to be fed into the production process in order to replace the ones that are wearing out. I have to say that as a flutist, I am perfectly happy not to have to mess with reeds!

This difference in resistance means that flutists have to handle their air differently from reed players. Flutists must consciously and actively control the air before it leaves the body in order to be able to play the length of a phrase. Even if you're a master at breath control, you'll have to breathe a little more often than other woodwind players. Oboists regularly have to exhale at the end of a phrase before they inhale again, while flutists often have to use their last bit of air just to get to the next possible place to breathe in the music. That's why working on your breathing at the outset is important. (I address breathing techniques in Chapter 5.)

The harmonic series: The making of a pitch

Where does a musical sound originate, and why is it different from the everyday noises we hear? Why aren't the noises the garbage truck makes at 6 a.m. music to our ears? The answer has to do with the *sound frequencies* (and, of course, it would help if the garbage truck could wait until at least 8 a.m.). I won't bore you with the exact science of it, but the bottom line is that what we know as musical pitches correspond with precise mathematical formulas. This math is present whether we are aware of it or not, and it affects a lot of things in music. It also explains why different instruments have different *timbres,* or sound qualities.

The frequencies of different pitches are mathematically related to each other. For example, all the notes with the name A sound very similar; in fact, any two As sound almost like the same note when played together, no matter how high or low they are. The relationship between one note and the next higher or lower note of the same name is called an *octave*. If you take any note higher by one octave, you'll multiply its frequency by exactly 2, if you're playing in tune. The one frequency number that's important to remember is A=440. This means that the note A above the flute's low C has the frequency of 440 cycles per second, or Hertz (Hz). This is what is known as the standard *tuning A* in the United States and many other countries. (I expand on tuning in Chapter 15.)

When you play a low C on the flute and then blow harder without moving your fingers, you get another C, but one that's an octave higher. If you continue to blow higher without changing your fingers, you get a G, another C, an E, another G, an A sharp, and a high C. Theoretically, you could also get the high D and high E above that, but you'd be blowing pretty hard to get there. This progression of notes is called the *harmonic series*. The first note, here the low C, is called the *fundamental:* It's the lowest note in the series, and the entire sequence is based on it. You can repeat this progression starting on any note on the flute, or on any other instrument, and you'd get the same relationship between the notes — that is, the same mathematical relationship between the frequencies of those notes.

The flute's fingerings, the mechanics of playing all instruments, and indeed all of Western tonal music, is based to some degree on the harmonic series. When all the holes on your flute are closed, the tube that you're playing on is the full length of your instrument. When you open the holes from the bottom up, one at a time, you're effectively shortening the tube. In other words, when you lift a key in sequential order from the bottom up, it will have the same effect on pitch as if you'd lopped off the end of the instrument at that point. (The sound also comes out of the flute in slightly different places as you shorten and lengthen the tube, although most of the sound still emanates from the end of the instrument.) The pitch frequency changes in relation to the length of the tube. Picture a pipe organ — the long pipes sound extremely low when the air is pumped through them, and the short ones make the little tinkly-sounding notes on top. You're just making your one tube longer and shorter to change the pitches. The fingerings for the flute's highest notes are based on the higher partials in the harmonic series, although they vary slightly from the fingerings of the fundamental notes in order to get the best sound quality.

You may sometimes wonder exactly what it is that makes different instruments vary so widely in the way they sound. A flute and a clarinet playing the same note in the same octave at the same volume, for example, don't sound alike at all. The answer to this question lies in the harmonic series. One note played on any instrument is made up of several different pitches from the corresponding harmonic series. Most people can't hear the separate notes sounding within that one note, but the effect that these harmonics have on sound is easily discernible: A clarinet has more harmonic tones in its sound than a flute does, which is why they sound completely different. Of all the woodwind instruments, the flute has the fewest harmonics in its sound; in fact, it has fewer harmonics than most other instruments as well. For that reason, musicians often refer to the flute as the instrument with the purest sound.

Versatility: The flute as style chameleon

The flute is the most versatile of the woodwind instruments. It can execute just about any style of music, from classical to jazz to rock. Other woodwinds like the oboe and bassoon don't play much jazz or rock, although they have a lot of classical repertoire. The clarinet and saxophone are more often heard in jazz than the oboe or bassoon, but their classical repertoire is more limited than the flute's because they were invented later — the clarinet around the early 18th century and the saxophone in 1841. Classical composers have been writing for the flute since the 17th century, and to this day, they're writing music that stretches the flute's capabilities. Many flutists like to explore the boundaries of the instrument, which further inspires the composers, so new music is constantly being written.

The flute is best known for playing classical music. It has been a popular solo instrument since the 17th century, so there is an astonishingly large repertoire for flute alone, flute and keyboard, solo flute with orchestra, and chamber music in various forms. The flute's repertoire includes numerous sonatas, concerti, salon pieces, and other types of music from the Baroque, Classical, Romantic, Impressionist, and Contemporary eras. (For more on musical periods and styles, see Chapter 14.) In other words, it's a veritable flute smorgasbord!

The flute plays a major part in many Broadway-style musicals. Shows like *Miss Saigon* and *The Lion King* even feature multiple flutes. The *Lion King* score includes no fewer than 15 different types of flutes (more on different types of flutes in Chapter 22). Only one flutist plays in the *Lion King* pit orchestra, and that person must rapidly switch around among those 15 flutes during the entire show.

Music in the movies often features the flute. The flute is one of the lead instruments in the theme from *Titanic*. The final scene from *E.T.* wouldn't be the same without the "farewell" piccolo solo. And if you haven't seen *Anchorman*, rent it immediately. The scene in which Will Ferrell "plays" an extended jazz flute solo is simply hilarious. And don't even get me started on the flute-related hijinks in *American Pie!*

Jazz greats Herbie Mann and Hubert Laws brought the flute into new territory in the 1960s and '70s, and today countless jazz flutists are following suit. Rather than doubling on a handful of woodwind instruments such as clarinets and saxophones, many jazz players are now specializing in flute. The flute lends itself well to jazz because it plays fast scales readily, it slides around on pitches easily, and it lends itself nicely to special effects such as flutter tonguing (see Chapter 16) and percussive sounds (see Chapter 17). It's also relatively easy to amplify, which is often necessary in jazz venues.

In pop music, you can often hear the flute in mellow, singing lines. Who could ever forget the beautifully placid flute solo in the 1970 hit song "Colour My World" performed by the band Chicago? Unless you're too young to remember it, in which case, don't tell me — I don't really need to know about it.

Speaking of the '70s, Ian Anderson gave the flute a voice in rock and roll via his band, Jethro Tull. The band's breakthrough albums from the early '70s include *Aqualung* and *Thick as a Brick,* on which Anderson gives the flute some serious attitude by singing into it and making cool growling noises on it. The well-known album *Songs from the Wood,* with a slightly more folk/acoustical feel, came out a few years later. (These three Jethro Tull albums are all available on the Capitol Records label.) Jethro Tull's music has withstood the test of time. The band has explored rock, folk, blues, Medieval, Classical, and Far East genres of music. Ian Anderson's unique approach has also inspired a number of classical composers to incorporate his modern flute sounds into their music.

The latest innovation in flute playing styles is *beatboxing,* a style of vocal percussion associated with hip-hop music, pioneered by Greg Pattillo on YouTube. (Just type his name into the YouTube search box, and get ready for a big surprise!) Pattillo manages to transform the flute into a melodic percussion instrument that you've got to hear to believe.

The flute can accomplish just about any task the player sets for it. It is an amazingly versatile instrument. You never know which way the wind will blow next!

Getting to Know the Flute Repertoire

The flute has a vast classical repertoire from as far back as the 1600s. Even if you don't end up playing every major work in the catalog of flute literature, you'll want to get to know some of the most widely performed flute music. These pieces are essential listening for every flute player — they're generally considered to be central to the repertoire and will inspire you as well as show you some of the wonderful things the flute can do. I indicate the approximate level of technical difficulty (in parentheses) on a scale of 1–5, 1 being the easiest and 5 being the most advanced. I also recommend my favorite editions in case you want to buy the sheet music. However, I'm not suggesting that you necessarily attempt to play any of these pieces as a beginning flutist — many of them are quite challenging. I would never claim that this list is exhaustive;

it's merely a starting point of works you'll want to get to know, at least on a cursory level, if you play the flute. Recordings of these pieces are widely available. Listen to them sometime; I'm sure you'll enjoy all of them. (A few movements and excerpts of these pieces are on the CD that accompanies this book. I've indicated those pieces on this list.)

✔ Georg Friedrich Handel: *Sonatas* (2) (Bärenreiter)

You can hear the first movement of Handel's *Sonata in F Major* on Track 59 of the CD, and you can find the flute part in Chapter 12 so that you can play along with the CD accompaniment track (Track 60).

✔ Georg Philipp Telemann: *Fantasies for Solo Flute* (3) (Musica Rara), *Methodical Sonatas* (3) (Bärenreiter)

✔ Johann Sebastian Bach: *Six Sonatas BWV 1030-1035 & 1020* for flute and keyboard /continuo (3) (Breitkopf/Kuijken), *Partita (Sonata) in A minor, BWV 1013* (3) for solo flute (Breitkopf / Kuijken)

You can hear the second movement of Bach's *Sonata in E♭ Major* on Track 61 of the CD, and I include the flute part in Chapter 12 so that you can play along with the CD accompaniment track (Track 62).

You can hear the second movement of Bach's *Sonata in C Major* on Track 79 of the CD, and I include the flute part in Chapter 16 so that you can play along with the accompaniment track (Track 80).

✔ Carl Philipp Emanuel Bach: *Sonata in A minor, Wq. 132 (3)* for solo flute (Little Piper or Universal), *Hamburger Sonata in G, Wq. 133* for flute and continuo (3) (Schott)

✔ Wolfgang Amadeus Mozart: *Concerto #1 in G Major, K.313 (3)*, *Concerto #2 in D Major, K. 314 (3)*, and *Andante in C Major, K.315* (2) (Bärenreiter or Novello)

You can hear an excerpt from Mozart's *Andante in C Major, K.315,* on Track 86 of the CD that accompanies this book, and I include the flute part in Chapter 16 so that you can play along with the CD accompaniment track (Track 87).

✔ Franz Schubert: *Introduction and Variations*, op. 160 (4) (ed. Bärenreiter, Breitkopf & Härtel, or Henle)

✔ Carl Reinecke: *Sonata "Undine" op. 167* (3) (International or Boosey & Hawkes)

✔ Various composers: *Flute Music by French Composers* (3) (Schirmer). This book, a collection of pieces by French Romantic composers, includes the classic works *Concertino op. 107* by Cecile Chaminade, *Cantabile et Presto* by Georges Enesco, *Fantasie op. 79* by Gabriel Fauré, *Andante et Scherzo* by Louis Ganne, *Nocturne et Allegro Scherzando* by Philippe Gaubert, and *Andante Pastoral et Scherzettino* by Paul Taffanel, among others.

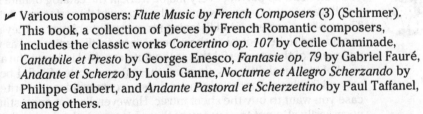

You can hear excerpts from Fauré's *Fantasie* (Tracks 34 and 35) as well as Ganne's *Andante et Scherzo* (Track 88) on the CD that accompanies this book. The Fauré excerpt appears in Chapter 10, and the Ganne excerpt in Chapter 16.

✔ Albert Franz Doppler: *Fantasie Pastorale Hongroise, op. 26* (3+) (Little Piper or Schott)

You can hear an excerpt from Doppler's *Fantasie Pastorale Hongroise* on Track 66 of the CD that accompanies this book. The Doppler excerpt appears in Chapter 14.

✔ Francis Poulenc: *Sonata* (3) (Chester)

✔ Claude Debussy: *Syrinx* (2+) (Jobert)

✔ Paul Hindemith: *Sonata* (3) (Schott)

✔ Sergei Prokofiev: *Sonata in D Major, op. 94* (4) (Hal Leonard)

The flute's status at the top of the woodwinds, along with its silvery, pure tone quality, prompts many composers to feature it as a solo instrument within the orchestra. Orchestral flutists have the pleasure of performing some of the most beautiful and challenging solos in the repertoire. These masterpieces also make for enjoyable listening and will give you an idea of the flute's role in the orchestra. Here are some of the most famous orchestral pieces that feature the flute:

✔ Johann Sebastian Bach: *Suite in B minor*

✔ Ludwig van Beethoven: *Symphony #7*

✔ Johannes Brahms: *Symphony #4*

✔ Nikolai Rimsky-Korsakov: *Scheherazade*

✔ Claude Debussy: *Prelude to the Afternoon of a Faun*

✔ Maurice Ravel: *Daphnis and Chloe, Suite #2*

In orchestral works about the animal kingdom, the flute is almost always called upon to represent the bird, as in these classical gems:

✔ Camille Saint-Saëns: *Carnival of the Animals (Volière)*

✔ Sergei Prokofiev: *Peter and the Wolf*

The Flute's Rise in Popularity

The flute is an overwhelmingly popular instrument. Who wouldn't want to play the flute? It's relatively easy to start playing, it produces a gorgeous, pure sound, it's small and easy to carry, you don't have to fuss with reeds, and you have lots of flute music and styles to choose from. And it looks beautiful and shiny, to boot. The flute has actually seen a rise in popularity in the last 50 years or so. Two flutists in particular are responsible for this surge in status.

Jean-Pierre Rampal

In the 1960s, French flutist Jean-Pierre Rampal (1922–2000) took the music world by storm. His unparalleled skill and on-stage charisma put him in a category with the world's best violinists, cellists, and pianists as a sought-after soloist who could sell out big venues.

Before Rampal, the idea of a recital of solely flute music was unheard of; when flute music was featured, it was usually on varied programs including other instruments. The flute's reputation previous to these events was as a *salon instrument,* one that was pretty and fun to play in someone's living room or in a small recital hall, but that couldn't hold its own as a solo instrument in a big concert hall setting.

Everything changed when Rampal hit the scene. He made it his mission to prove that the flute could hold its own as a major solo instrument and consequently started programming big flute recitals in France. Before anyone knew what was happening, Rampal was cranking out recordings and touring internationally. He was unearthing old flute music that hadn't been performed in centuries and putting it on recitals. He also commissioned new flute music from contemporary composers.

Rampal's career was a real milestone for the flute. People who went to his recitals and bought his numerous recordings appreciated the flute and its music, and they also became interested in playing the instrument themselves.

I had the privilege of performing a duet with Jean-Pierre Rampal in 1990, which was an incredibly inspiring experience for me. At that point, he had already been performing all over the world for more than three decades; he was obviously still having the time of his life making music on the flute.

Here are a couple of classic Jean-Pierre Rampal recordings:

- Jean-Pierre Rampal: *The Great Flute Concertos* (Sony)
- Jean-Pierre Rampal, Robert Veyron-Lacroix: *The Art of the Flute* (CreateSpace)

James Galway

After Rampal had paved the way, Irish flutist James Galway (now Sir James Galway after he was knighted by Queen Elizabeth II in 2001) followed suit and became a popular flute soloist as well. After a stint as Principal Flute with the world-famous Berlin Philharmonic (1969–1975), he decided to launch a solo career and quit the most prestigious orchestra in the world to do so. Galway blew everybody away (literally) with his unbelievable technique and unique, voluminous sound, and his warm, at times amusing, stage presence was disarming.

The 1980s saw Galway rise to stardom — he was (and still is) one of the top classical artists in the world.

Younger than Rampal, he was clearly the heir to the solo flutist's legacy. Like Rampal, he commissioned many great new works for flute. Rampal and Galway were both in great demand around the world for two decades. The classical music business had room for not just one but two major flute soloists!

Here are just a few of Galway's many excellent classical recordings:

- James Galway: *Flute Sonatas- Franck, Prokofiev, Reinecke,* with Martha Argerich and Philip Moll (RCA Victor Europe)
- James Galway: *Mercadante Flute Concertos,* with I Solisti Veneti, Claudio Scimone (RCA)
- *James Galway Plays Khachaturian,* with the Royal Philharmonic, Myung-Whun Chung (RCA)

Crossing over

Rampal and Galway were both crossover artists, though Galway did a bit more of this genre. Rampal had broken ground with his bestselling recording of the charming *Suite for Flute and Jazz Piano Trio* by Claude Bolling. He was one of the first classical artists to experiment with other styles of music. Galway recorded with many popular artists, including Cleo Laine, Henry Mancini, and the Chieftains. More than 30 years after its premiere, Galway also re-invented Bolling's *Suite for Flute and Jazz Piano Trio* with the Cuban jazz group, Tiempo Libre, on the *O'Reilly Street* album.

Here are some of Rampal's and Galway's most popular crossover recordings:

- Jean-Pierre Rampal, Lily Laskine: *Japanese Melodies for Flute and Harp* (Sony)
- Jean-Pierre Rampal, Claude Bolling, Max Hediguer, Marcel Sabiani: *Bolling: Suite for Flute and Jazz Piano Trio* (Fremeaux & Assoc. Fr)
- James Galway and Tiempo Libre: *O'Reilly Street* (Red Seal)
- *James Galway & the Chieftains in Ireland* (RCA)
- *James Galway: Greatest Hits* (RCA)

The legacy

More audiences than ever before were exposed to the flute through Rampal's and Galway's successful careers, which raised the profile of the flute like nothing before ever had. People were flocking to the flute in droves.

Today, we're still seeing the results of what Jean-Pierre Rampal and Sir James Galway did for the flute. More flutists are out there than ever. The National Flute Association has about 6,000 members, and local flute clubs are on the rise throughout the country. (See Chapter 18 for more about flute clubs.)

It's nice to know that flutists have a lot of company, but it's also a double-edged sword: Because so many are out there, flutists also face serious competition. At auditions for local ensembles, you can bet that you'll always see more flute players trying out than oboists or bassoonists. In the professional music world, advertised orchestral flute openings typically receive hundreds of resumes from applicants hoping to get an audition. On the plus side, the increased level of competition means that the general level of flute playing is quite high these days as well. You'll hear some fine flutists in recital halls throughout the country.

Anatomy of the Flute

The flute's design is really pretty simple, but it can be daunting to look at when you see it for the first time. The first flute was likely a hollowed-out bone with some holes punched into it, and a few millennia later, it had graduated into a wooden tube with holes carved into it. The silvery, complicated-looking thing of beauty you see today is merely a higher-tech version of its simpler precursors.

The real beauty of the modern key system is that, although the instrument now looks more complicated, it's actually easier to play than its simpler primordial cousins. The modern C flute has a cylindrical bore; that is, approximately the same width from top to bottom, and it is divided into three main sections:

- Headjoint
- Body
- Footjoint

The headjoint

The *headjoint,* shown in Figure 2-2, is aptly named because it's not only the top of the instrument, it's also the part of the flute that sits closest to your head — right on your lower lip, as a matter of fact. The sound of the flute originates at the headjoint when the player places the chin and lower lip on the *lip plate* and blows across the *embouchure hole.* The lip plate is attached to the tube by means of a metal ring called a *riser.* The shaping of the lip plate and embouchure hole largely determines how a flute plays and what it sounds like.

A small, decorative-looking metal piece called the *crown* sits at the top of the headjoint. The crown is screwed into the cork assembly (see Figure 2-3), which is lodged into the top of the headjoint tube and is usually made of cork or synthetic material. The basic function of the cork is to keep the air going in the right direction — that is, into the body of the flute and not out the top. The cork fits tightly into the top of the headjoint and is measured carefully when it goes into the flute during manufacturing to ensure proper tuning.

Embouchure hole

Crown   Riser   Lip plate   Tube   Tenon

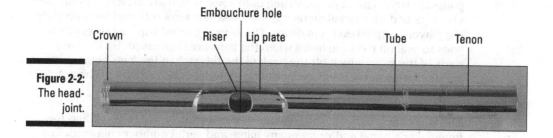

Figure 2-2:
The head-
joint.

Figure 2-3:
A crown
and cork
assembly.

The bottom of the headjoint, or the headjoint *tenon,* fits into the body of the flute for assembly, but it also has another purpose: to adjust the overall pitch of the instrument for tuning. When you pull the headjoint slightly up out of the body, the whole instrument gets slightly larger, which means that the overall pitch gets a little lower. When you push the headjoint into the body, the flute gets that much smaller and the overall pitch rises slightly.

The body

The *body* is the middle of the flute (see Figure 2-4). It's the largest of the three main flute parts and also has the most visible gadgetry on it. The most obvious difference between the headjoint and the body is the presence of keys on the body.

The function of the keys is to cover or uncover the *tone holes,* which are strategically placed on the metal tube of the body. Contrary to what you might think, the tone holes aren't just holes. The holes in the body actually have metal *chimneys* attached to them, which extend out of the body to meet the pads and keys. The keys are strung onto rods, which are attached to the tube via posts and ribs. Small metal springs make the keys rebound back up after the player has pushed them down. The keys are fitted with felt or synthetic pads to seal off the tone holes when the keys are depressed. On the back parts of the keys, which hit the back of the tube when the keys come down, are tiny strips of cork, felt, or synthetic material called *bumpers.* These act as mufflers, keeping any clicking noises to a minimum.

The body has a *barrel* at the top end — that's usually where you'll find the flutemaker's name and/or company name and serial number engraved. The headjoint fits into the barrel via the tenon and can be pulled out or pushed in for tuning purposes. The bottom part of the body also has a tenon: the thin metal extension that fits right into the footjoint.

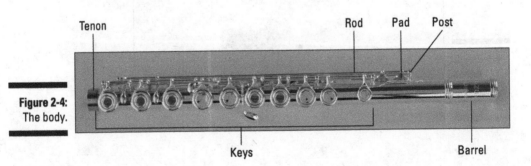

Figure 2-4:
The body.

Tenon   Rod   Pad   Post

Keys   Barrel

Theobald Boehm and the modern flute

The flute didn't always have as many keys as it does today. In fact, at one time, it had no keys at all. From 1660 until Theobald Boehm's (1794–1881) key system gained popularity, the flute's keys grew in number from one to eight. Most earlier flutes had no footjoint, so their lowest note was usually a D.

Boehm invented the modern flute's key system back in 1832 and continued to improve on it until 1847. Basically, it's still the system in use today. Boehm's system offered the player easier fingerings, more accurate intonation, and homogeneity of sound. Today's Boehm system concert C flutes can have anywhere from 17 keys to 23 and above, depending on the extra keys and specific variations in key systems. Because flutists don't normally have 17 or more fingers to work all those keys, Boehm devised a way that some keys could be connected by a rod so that the flutist could depress more than one at the same time with just one finger.

Theobald Boehm, aside from being a master flutemaker and acoustician, was also known as a virtuoso flutist and a prolific composer in his day. He has left an amazing legacy for flutists everywhere.

The footjoint

At the top end of the footjoint (see Figure 2-5) is a thick metal ring called the *socket,* which fits onto the tenon at the bottom end of the flute body. The footjoint is set up the same way as the body, with tone holes, posts, ribs, keys, pads, and springs.

Without the footjoint attached to the end, the lowest note on the flute would be a D. Most flutes on the market today have either a low C or low B footjoint. The footjoint extends the range of the instrument and, with the use of the D#/Eb key, provides an extra note above D as well. All of the keys on the footjoint are commanded by your right pinky finger. Without the D#/Eb key at the top of the footjoint, your right pinky would also have nowhere to sit in order to balance the flute (see Chapter 7 for more on balancing the flute). Most of the time, your right pinky sits on the D#/Eb key, but to hit the lowest notes and to accomplish other various and sundry tasks, it's jumping around on the various other footjoint keys.

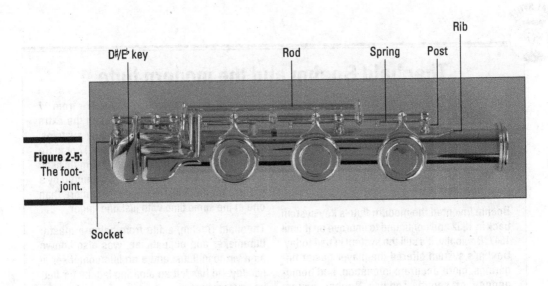

D#/E♭ key   Rod   Spring   Post   Rib

Figure 2-5:
The foot-
joint.

Socket

Chapter 3

Choosing Your Instrument

· ·

· ·

Where do I start?" you may ask. Good question! With the flute's incredible popularity, flute manufacturing has become a booming industry. Demand is greater than ever, and the resulting profit is a big incentive for the dozens of flute manufacturers operating in the world today to make the best quality flutes at the lowest possible prices. The competition is good news for the flute buyer: You can choose from a wide range of prices and options and shop around for a good deal. However, the highest quality, top-of-the-line handmade flutes are always expensive, so get ready to shell out the big bucks if you want one.

Before the flute boom (which, coincidentally began around the same time as the Post–WWII Baby Boom ended), you could pretty much walk into your local music store and tell them you wanted to buy a flute, and you wouldn't get too many questions like "Would you like a split E, C♯ trill, offset or half-offset G, high G♯ facilitator, synthetic or traditional pads, and by the way, have you considered a navigation system or a satellite radio?" Anyone can get confused. The most important thing to remember is that you're still just talking about a metal tube with holes in it — a pricey piece of plumbing, as it were. Those elaborate-sounding extras were designed to make your life easier, not to baffle you. In this chapter, I tell you all about the astonishing array of options available on the market today.

Parting with Your Hard-Earned Cash

Flutes come in basically three price ranges:

- Student model flutes for beginning and intermediate flutists
- Conservatory model flutes for advanced students and college-bound music majors
- Professional model flutes, for aspiring to seasoned professionals

That's not to say, however, that you're not allowed to purchase a professional model flute if you're a beginner. The better the flute you buy, the better you'll sound, and the more subtleties you'll be able to get out of your instrument. You probably won't be able to appreciate the subtler differences in the top-end flutes, though, until you're a few years into your studies. And by then, you may find that you would have preferred different options than what you bought before you could really get around on the instrument. It would be a little like buying a Ferrari before you've taken your driver's test. (You're not in much danger of wrecking a flute, though.)

Whatever model you choose, ask a relatively experienced flutist to test-drive it for you, especially if you're a beginner. Make sure that the flute you're considering is solidly built and a pleasure to play. The tips and advice in this chapter are a good place to start.

Where I list actual dollar amounts for the price ranges, do keep in mind that prices go up, usually on a yearly basis. (Unfortunately, they never seem to go down.) Also, note that these are approximate prices and your actual experience may vary.

Many band instrument retailers, which cater to local school music programs, offer instrument rentals or rent-to-own deals. This option can be useful if you're not sure you want to commit to playing the flute, but would like to give it a try to see how it goes. On average, beginning student model silver-plated flutes rent for $25 to $40 per month. You may also find student models with solid silver headjoints, bodies, and plated or solid silver keys available at around $55 to $100 per month.

Student models: The most basic option

Generally, the biggest differences between the three price ranges are in materials and construction. The quality of mass-produced instruments is getting better and better all the time, resulting in pretty darn good instruments for the price in the student model category.

Buying options: Brick-and-mortar versus online

If you know exactly which make and model of student model flute you'd like to buy, you can get some great deals from online stores, which generally tend to charge less than your local band instrument shop — you can usually save somewhere between $100 to $300 by buying online, depending on the make and model. Keep in mind, however, that the opportunity to try several different models side by side has its advantages, provided that your local shop has a good selection of flutes. With a brick-and-mortar store also comes person-to-person customer service, which can be invaluable if problems arise after purchase. If you buy online, you'll be shipping the instrument back to the dealer or the manufacturer for warranty work, whereas in some cases your local dealer can make small adjustments right in the shop.

Most beginning models are usually made of silver-plated nickel silver and are entirely machine-made. Beginning student model flutes range from about $400 to $900. To keep the cost down, manufacturers take the following steps:

✔ Sometimes the ribs on the flute tube are eliminated, and the posts are attached directly to the tube. This type of construction is less solid than posts and ribs (also called *ribbed construction*), but it's much less labor-intensive to manufacture and therefore makes for a much less expensive flute. Sometimes manufacturers also make just one rib instead of multiple ribs.

✔ Springs on a beginning flute will usually be made of stainless steel, rather than a pricier metal.

✔ A beginner's student model flute won't include a lot of options. Some manufacturers include an extra key option here or there, but it's not common. (For more on extra keys, see the upcoming section "Bells and Whistles: Making Sense of Those Extra Keys.")

✔ The headjoints on some beginning model flutes feature an embouchure hole that has been cut by hand (instead of being punched out by a machine) so that it can mimic the sound quality of a more expensive instrument. (For more on hand-cut headjoints, see "The All-Important Headjoint: The Soul of the Flute," later in this chapter.)

✔ The most interesting option on a beginner's flute is the addition of a curved headjoint, shown in Figure 3-1. Curved headjoints effectively make the flute shorter without changing anything about the body or footjoint (though some manufacturers leave out the C and B footjoints to lighten the instrument) so that younger folks can be more comfortable playing. Just a generation ago, this option did not exist, so children had to be around age nine or ten in order to start playing the flute. Now, with the advent of curved headjoints, kids are picking up the flute as young as five years of age. Some beginning models include both styles of headjoints.

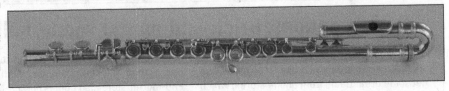

Figure 3-1:
Student
model flute
with curved
headjoint.

The intermediate level student flutes, also called *step-up flutes,* graduate from silver-plated nickel silver to richer-sounding solid silver, and an increasing number of parts on them are hand-assembled for greater precision. White gold springs, which facilitate a lighter touch from the player, begin to appear as well, along with more key options and gold-plated lip plates. (Gold-plated lip plates are mostly cosmetic at this stage, but the kids love 'em!) The price range on intermediate student flutes is approximately $1,000 to $2,000.

Conservatory models: The preprofessionals

After you're sufficiently frustrated by the clunky feel of machine-made flutes, but not ready to shell out the big bucks for a custom professional handmade flute, it's time to look at conservatory model flutes, also known as *preprofessional flutes.*

Preprofessional flutes are relatively new to the market. In the 1980s and '90s, high-end flutemakers had waiting lists that were several years long, and the prices kept going up due to demand and rising material costs. The soaring prices and lack of availability created a gap in the market between intermediate and professional model flutes, so flute manufacturers started racing to fill it around the mid-1990s. Many manufacturers have come out with handmade flutes that cut corners here and there on materials. The result is a professional-feeling and -sounding instrument at about half the cost of the high-end professional models.

Conservatory models go by various monikers, but you can identify them by the fact that they're mostly or entirely handmade and fall into the $2,500 to $9,000 price range, considerably less than the top-of-the-line handmade flutes. These preprofessional models tend to include most of the features and options present on top-of-the-line flutes, but they don't offer the most labor-intensive custom features. Manufacturers have come up with some brilliant ways to keep the cost down on these handmade conservatory models:

- ✔ They make the body out of silver-plated nickel silver, but include a hand-cut headjoint, either made of solid silver or featuring a silver plated tube and a solid silver lip plate.

- ✔ Because the metal used on the keys has no effect on the flute's sound, they make a solid silver body with silver-plated keys.

- They use less expensive stainless steel springs, but carefully adjust them by hand.

- They extrude the tone holes out of the flute tube instead of soldering them on. (See the section "Tone holes: Drawn versus soldered," later in this chapter.)

- They strategically choose the hand-cut headjoints that are sold with the conservatory models. Companies that make both conservatory and professional models usually have only a small number of people hand-cutting all of their headjoints. The best ones tend to be reserved for the professional model flutes. The ones that turned out "just okay" might go onto the conservatory models. That way they don't have to melt them down and start over, which saves on the company's overall labor costs. (More on hand-cut headjoints in the section, "The All-Important Headjoint: The Soul of the Flute" later in this chapter.)

You'd think that buying the instrument made from the highest quality materials would be the best way to go when buying a flute. But the deciding factor in how a flute will play, and hold up over time, is *how* it's put together. Building a flute painstakingly by hand is an incredibly precise process that a machine could never possibly replicate. Flutemakers are artisans as well as craftsmen, and they work to more exacting standards than the finest Swiss watchmakers. Building a flute by hand is extremely labor-intensive, which is why it adds so much to the cost of an instrument. If you offered me a choice of two flutes to play, a machine-made one of entirely 18K gold or a silver-plated handmade one, I would choose the handmade silver-plated one without reservations.

Professional models: Going all-out

This category is Flute Nirvana. High-end flutemakers pull out all the stops in materials and labor where their top-of-the-line professional model flutes are concerned. You can buy them from a specialized dealer or order them to your specifications from the manufacturer.

It takes a few months to build one of these flutes, but manufacturers' waiting lists can be one to three years long. Typically, these companies employ very few workers, and sometimes one person builds the whole flute for you.

Choosing your specifications for a custom-built flute is a fascinating and awe-inspiring process. You choose the material, usually silver, gold, or platinum; the wall thickness of the tube (which affects the sound); and extra keys. Some companies even have custom key configurations available to enhance your flute-playing comfort. Engraving is also often an option. If you can visit the company, you usually get to hand-pick your own headjoint from a selection they have available. Most companies also have a generous exchange policy on headjoints (usually one year) so that you can find the perfect headjoint to suit your needs.

Where it's made: Countries of origin

Most flute manufacturing these days occurs in the United States, Japan, or China. Japan was a leader in mass-production of student model flutes in the 1980s and '90s, and China caught on a few years later. Some U.S. companies that are best known for their handmade flutes are now even contracting some of their work out to China to have their newer lines of step-up and conservatory model flutes machine-made there (Verne Q. Powell's *Sonare* line and Wm. S. Haynes's *Classic* line are two examples).

Check into the flute's country of origin, just to be in the know. Flutemakers in the United States are known globally as the leaders in top-quality handmade flutes, and many of these flutemakers are located in the Boston, Massachussetts area (Brannen Brothers Flutemakers, Burkart, Miguel Arista, Nagahara, Verne Q. Powell, Wm. S. Haynes, and quite a few others.) Elkhart, Indiana, is a hotbed for student model flute manufacturing: The Armstrong, Avanti (Conn-Selmer), and Gemeinhardt flute companies all reside there. Japan has generally enjoyed a great reputation for turning out extremely reliable instruments, and Japanese companies pioneered machine production of high-quality instruments. One Japanese company often makes many different models, in both machine- and handmade varieties. The most prevalent example is Yamaha; however, companies such as Altus (Azumi) and Miyazawa (Lyric) also carry both handmade and machine-made lines The work done in China is less of a known quantity. Some excellent flutes, along with a few lemons, come out of China,. However, you can get a great deal on a Chinese-made flute if you know what to look for.

Of course, good flutes can be made anywhere, as long as the company exercises good quality control. For example, if an American company has its own factory in China, said company probably has a good idea of what is going on with regards to production. If, however, the American company is farming out to a large flute manufacturing plant in China that cranks out flutes for X number of companies, the quality of each instrument is tougher to control. It pays to do a bit of research into a company's business practices. Always ask around if you're not sure — online flute groups are a great place to start. (See Chapter 18 for details on flute-related e-mail chat groups.)

Having your instrument custom-built is a really cool thing, and that's how I like to buy my flutes. But every flute is a little different, and you take the small chance that you won't like your own flute as much you liked the demo model when you order a custom instrument. You'll have to pay for your flute before it goes into production, so you buy it sight unseen, although you're encouraged to try any available demo models. Some flutists prefer to buy from specialty dealers because they can try out the exact same flute they're going to buy (because it's not technically custom-built for the flutist at that point, there may be a limited number of options to choose from). Prices in this category start at around $10,000 for silver flutes and go up to about $40,000 for gold flutes, depending on your options. All bets are off on platinum flutes — the brochures usually tell you to contact the company for pricing, which is based on the current market value of platinum.

If you're a professional flutist or aspiring to be one, the professional model is the kind of flute you'll need to succeed in the highly competitive field of flute performance. The beauty, subtlety, and ease of playing you get on these instruments is unsurpassed.

If you're a novice flute buyer, be sure to ask an experienced flutist to try the instrument you're considering. If you're buying used or have an extended trial period on a new flute, you can even get a repair technician to take a look at it before you buy (You can read about how to find a repair technician in Chapter 19).

When you get an instrument on trial, the company selling the instrument will usually want to take your credit-card number. Some companies charge the full amount of the instrument to the credit card for the period of the trial and then refund the money once you return the instrument. Other companies just hold the credit-card number and don't make a charge until you're ready to buy.

Buying a used flute

You may want to consider saving a few bucks by purchasing a used instrument. But, as with purchasing cars, buying used can be tricky. Local band instrument shops and flute specialty retailers often carry used flutes, and a few companies actually specialize in used flutes. Used flute dealers operate in two different ways: buying/selling outright or selling on consignment. Either way, a middle man marks up the retail price, but it can be comforting to deal with a company rather than just an individual selling a flute. Do check into warranty policies, however: they'll vary wherever you go.

You can also check classified listings. I like the Flute Network (www.flutenet.com), but you can also find many other used flute newsletters with classified ads and used flute Web pages out there. With no middle man and no consignment fees, buying a used flute directly from another flutist via an ad can be an excellent way to get a good deal, but only if you know exactly what you're looking for.

Because instrument trials involve shipping charges, they're not cost-effective for student model flutes, so people usually only place classified ads for conservatory or professional model flutes. Trials involve a level of trust: The buyer and seller make all the transactions, and trials usually entail the seller shipping the flute across the country for the buyer to try, while the buyer sends the seller a check for the full amount of the asking price. The check remains uncashed until the buyer agrees to the purchase. If it's no deal, the buyer ships the instrument back to the seller, and the seller either mails the check back or shreds it. Many flutists know each other, so this process isn't as scary as it sounds — most flutists don't want to risk their good reputation by ripping off an unsuspecting buyer.

Silver in 19th-century Paris

Some mystique surrounds the antique flutes made by French flutemaker Louis Lot (1807–1896). He used seamed silver tubing to make his flutes, which is different from the extruded tubing mostly in use today. The theory is that rolling and seaming preserves the molecular structure of the silver, whereas extruding actually stretches the material into a tube shape.

Many of today's professional flutists have bought the old Louis Lot flutes, have tweaked their tone hole sizes for tuning, and play on them exclusively. Some flutemakers have even devised a way to make the old-style seamed tubing, which they claim makes for a slightly denser silver.

Insuring your flute against loss or theft is essential. If you buy a conservatory or professional model flute, it's unlikely that you can cover it under regular homeowner's insurance. To insure your flute, you need to look into instrument insurance. One way get this type of insurance is through the National Flute Association. The NFA offers special discounted rates to all its members through Clarion, an insurance company specializing in musical instruments. For more details, go to www.nfaonline.org.

Sorting Out Your Material Choices

Flutemakers have constructed instruments using many different types of materials, including a dizzying array of metals and metal alloys, wood, and even carbon fiber. The difference in sound between the metals and most other materials is readily apparent, even to the untrained ear.

The difference between metals themselves is more subtle (though the difference in price tag is not). Scientific studies have shown no discernible difference in sound with different metals, but flutists and flutemakers tell a different story. Many flutists have strong allegiances to their metal of choice. I know that I can differentiate between silver and gold instruments blindfolded because I tried headjoints while blindfolded one afternoon several years ago, with fascinating results.

Flutes come in seemingly infinite combinations of metals: a gold flute with silver keys, for example, or a silver headjoint with a gold lip plate and platinum riser. These combinations purport to combine the best qualities of each metal. If you're thinking of buying anything other than a silver-plated flute, take your time and get to know the materials little by little.

For me, flute shopping is a little bit like a trip to the perfume counter: It's fascinating and fun, but if I try more than two or three at a time, I go on sensory overload. As with fragrance, flute materials are a highly personal choice.

Others may have a valid opinion, but you're the one who is going to be playing the instrument, so it comes down to your own preferences.

You have several options for your flute's material:

- **Nickel silver** is the most common metal used for beginning level student model flutes because it's less expensive than solid silver. Nickel silver is actually not silver at all, but an alloy of copper, nickel, and other metals. Flutes made of nickel silver are usually plated with real silver.

- **Solid silver,** a resonant metal, is the top choice for most flutists. Flute manufacturers use it to build student model up to professional level flutes. Precious metals used in flutemaking are almost always *alloys* — mixtures of two or more metals — because the pure metals would be too soft (and therefore fragile) for everyday use. (I have seen flutemakers use pure silver as well, albeit rarely.) Silver alloys are anywhere between 92.5 to 95.8 percent silver, so the percentage of pure silver is quite high, unlike most alloys of other precious metals, such as gold or platinum. When it comes to silver flutes, some flutists believe that the alloys higher in silver create a more beautiful sound.

- Due to its warm quality, many flutists feel that **gold** affords the most pleasing of flute sounds. Gold is so soft that it needs to be combined with copper and other metals for practical use. These gold alloys come in many forms, and flutemakers use just about all variants of them: yellow gold in 10K, 14K, 18K, 20K, and (rarely) even 24K. They also use white gold, rose gold, and even green gold. The different colors of gold are due to the varying percentages of other metals present in the alloy. Personally, I prefer silver to gold, and my banker thanks me!

- Some flutists are passionate about playing on **platinum.** Platinum is the most dense of the precious metals, although flutemakers usually still alloy it with other metals. Platinum flutes produce a big, heavy, intense sort of sound.

- Flutemakers are always experimenting with **variants on traditional metal alloys** in an effort to create an instrument that combines the best features of several metals . You'll find many variations, such as silver/copper alloys and gold/silver alloys in various combinations. You'll also find flutes that are made of bonded materials, such as a tube made of gold and silver fused together in equal amounts — you'll see silver on the outside of the tube and gold on the inside, for example. Aurumite, made by Powell, is a popular result of such a gold/silver fusion process.

- **Wood** has recently experienced a resurgence. Flutemakers have embraced the trend, offering more and more wooden flutes and headjoints. Because the flute originally was made of wood (hence the inclusion in the woodwind family of instruments), and because historical instruments are also going more mainstream (see Chapter 22), flutists enjoy trying the modern Boehm system flutes made from wood as well. Composers wrote much of the flute's earlier repertoire with the sound of a wood flute in mind, so it makes sense to consider playing at least those pieces on wood.

Wood has a soft, warm, round sound that many flutists find refreshing after they've been playing on metal. The combination of wooden headjoints with metal flutes is becoming more common, as well.

One caveat about wood: It requires more care than metal. Wood is sensitive to temperature changes, and it's prone to cracking, especially when the instrument is new. Makers of wooden flutes give specific care instructions, and their advice must be followed to the letter in order to avoid cracking and other potential damage.

✔ **Carbon fiber** is a real wild card. Only Matit, a Finnish company, makes carbon-fiber flutes. Extraordinarily light and strong, this high-tech material is most often used in high-performance applications, such as in bicycles, racing cars, helmets, and other sports equipment. The Matit flute's keywork is also quite high-tech, using magnets, ball bearings, and other innovative techniques. The sound on these flutes is light and pleasing, and as they're quite light and seemingly indestructible, they make great travel flutes. Who knows? Carbon-fiber flutes may just catch on.

In addition, flutemakers have used various nonprecious metals, such as aluminum and titanium, to make experimental flutes. Flutists are always searching for the perfect instrument and, in their quest for the Holy Grail of flutes, are willing to experiment with many different materials, styles, and configurations. Flutemakers are only too happy to oblige. Some wonderfully useful things have come from such experimentation. Who knows what they'll think of next?

With the higher-end flute models, the buyer can often choose the wall thickness, which is the thickness of the flute tube. Most often this option will exist with silver, but sometimes also with other metals (though often gold and platinum thicknesses come standard). The choices in wall thicknesses are usually given in increments of .02 inches: .012, .014, .016, or .018. These may seem like small differences, but they make a big difference in how a flute feels and sounds. As a rule, the heavier the wall, the darker and richer the flute sounds and the more resistant feel it provides to the player. The most popular wall thicknesses are .014 and .016 inches. If the manufacturer doesn't give a choice for wall thickness, the standard one is usually .015 inches.

A very expensive flute

The late William Kincaid (1895–1967), longtime principal flute with the Philadelphia Orchestra, bought a platinum flute made by Verne Q. Powell (1879–1968) in 1939 and played on it for the rest of his life. Kincaid's platinum flute sold at auction in 1986 for $187,000.

Under Your Fingers: Keys, Pads, and Tone Holes

The modern flute is a wonder of modern engineering and precision construction. A novice might get intimidated by what looks like some pretty fancy gadgetry. This section breaks the mechanism down into distinct parts, each of which have several options available to the flute buyer. Take your time with this section and get to know these options now — all this information may seem a bit overwhelming at first, but you'll want to know your way around these details before you start trying instruments.

Keys: Closed versus open holes

The flute's keys are either *closed* (also called *plateau style*), meaning that they're flat metal discs, or *open (French style)*, with holes in the middle (see Figure 3-2). The holes are only present on keys that are directly operated by your fingers.

Because the open hole flute is less forgiving of poor finger position (notes won't respond well if the holes aren't completely sealed), the closed hole keys are ideal if you're a beginner and usually come standard on all beginning model flutes. If you're interested in buying an open hole flute, key plugs can help ease the transition from closed hole keys. Most advanced and professional flutists play on open hole flutes, though it's a matter of personal preference.

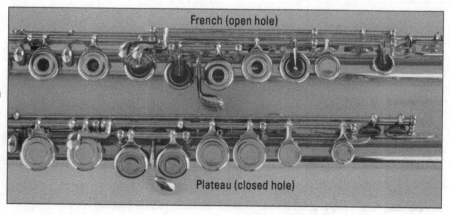

French (open hole)

Plateau (closed hole)

Figure 3-2:
Closed (plateau) versus open (French) style keys.

The hybrid flute

I currently own a Brannen Brothers flute that has closed hole keys in the left hand (upper) part of the flute, and open hole keys in the right hand (lower) part. It combines the nice, resonant low register of an open hole flute with the darker high notes of a closed hole flute. It also plays very well in tune — I really love it. This style is available via custom order from a few flutemakers (Brannen Brothers calls it their *orchestral model flute*).

Closed hole and open hole keys affect sound and intonation differently. Good flutemakers make adjustments in how the tone holes are placed so that they can produce a flute that plays in tune, whether open or closed hole. Closed hole keys muffle the sound a bit, whereas open hole keys, logically, open up the sound.

The other quandary you'll face regarding key styles is whether to choose pointed, or French-style key arms or the plainer looking Y arms, so named because the arm that connects the key to the rod forms a Y shape. (see Figure 3-3.) Pointed key arms only appear on the keys that you don't depress with your fingers.

The difference is purely cosmetic, although some argue that the construction of the pointed key arms puts the pressure more in the center of the key. Regardless, pointed key arms are more labor-intensive (and therefore more expensive) to produce because they require the hand-soldering of parts. You'll generally find pointed arms on handmade flutes and Y arms on machine-made student models, with a lot of variations in between.

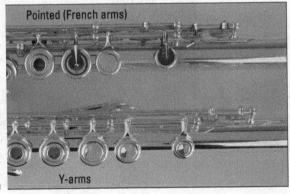

Figure 3-3:
Y-arms
versus
pointed
(French) key
arms.

The flute and France

Some features on flutes labeled French style or having French names like *plateau* or *embouchure hole* are holdovers from the time of Louis Lot and the rest of the French flutemakers of the 19th and early 20th centuries. Before flutes were made in the United States, the New York Philharmonic and Boston Symphony flutists, some of whom had immigrated from France themselves, were performing on French flutes. The flutemakers who began working in Boston were copying the Louis Lot flutes that were brought over to the United States from France. So today's American flutes have a strong French heritage. Vive la flute!

Tone holes: Drawn versus soldered

Tone holes have evolved tremendously since the time of the earliest bone, bamboo, and wood flutes. While tone holes still are just basically holes in a tube with chimneys attached, the science of discovering the correct placements and sizes of the various holes has been the subject of an infinite amount of research. As a result, flutists have the luxury of playing on flutes that are better in tune than ever before. Because of the competition in the flute market and also because flutemakers tend to be perfectionists, new configurations, or flute scales, keep coming out.

The main choice you need to make when buying a flute is what type of tone hole to go with:

- *Drawn tone holes* are made by extruding the metal right out of the flute tube. Drawn tone holes, just by the nature of the extruding process, don't add any extra material to the flute, so they leave the flute feeling and sounding lighter.

- To produce *soldered tone holes* flutemakers leave the tube alone and solder the metal chimneys onto the tube. Compared to drawn tone holes, soldered tone holes add the slight weight of the separately made tone holes and the metal alloy used in soldering. The extra weight gives the flute a slightly darker sound and more resistant feel when played. The soldering process makes for a more expensive flute, but just because a flute costs more doesn't necessarily mean it's a better instrument.

Your budget may make this decision for you because, as a rule, student and conservatory models use drawn tone holes, which are less labor-intensive to make. However, some professional models are also made with drawn tone holes rather than soldered. It's a matter of preference.

There has been some controversy about drawn versus soldered tone holes, particularly about how well each type of tone hole holds up over time. Some say that the drawn tone holes, by nature thinner than the soldered ones, are more fragile. But the soldering material can develop tiny leaks, depending on the particular alloy used and how thoroughly the flutemaker completes the fusing process. No one process is better than the other. It's a matter of how carefully each individual flute is made, and in the end, it comes down to the player's personal preference.

Sometimes high-end flutemakers offer certain modifications in tone hole design other than just the flute's scale. These modifications usually involve special shaping of the tone holes, which affects the sound and feel of the instrument. Make sure that you try demo models with and without whatever modifications are being offered so that you know what the differences are before you choose.

One important pioneer of tone hole measurements on the flute was British flutemaker Albert Cooper (1924–2011). He developed his flute scale mathematically and with the advice of professional flutists. Cooper overhauled the measurements and placement of tone holes on the modern flute and developed the most important innovation since Theobald Boehm invented the modern key system. (You can read more about Theobald Boehm in Chapter 2.)

The *Cooper scale* (sometimes also referred to as the *modern scale*) enabled flutists to play much better in tune than with the older traditional scale flutes and with less effort. It became popular with flute manufacturers in the 1970s and '80s, and most flutemakers still use some version of it today. Thanks to the Cooper Scale, most flutes on the market today are much easier to play in tune than their predecessors.

If you're considering buying a used flute over 25 years old, be sure that you know whether it was built using traditional or modern Cooper-style scale. You'll definitely struggle less with pitch on a modern scale flute.

Pads: Traditional versus synthetic

The function of the *flute pad* is to cover the tone hole and seal it completely when a key is depressed. This job isn't as simple as it sounds, however. The pad has to seal tightly all the way around the tone hole when touched relatively lightly by the player's finger; otherwise, you end up with some really funny noises instead of the desired notes. Padders of professional model flutes routinely work in .001 to .004-inch tolerances.

Many different kinds of flute pads are on the market today. Traditional-style pads are basically made of bladder (animal skin)-covered felt. The softness or hardness of the felt varies according to the model of flute.

- *Soft pads* are used on student model flutes, because when a flutemaker is working with softer traditional-style pads, getting a good seal all the way around the tone hole is pretty easy. Softer pads, though, don't hold adjustments for long, and the player has to push on the keys fairly hard to make sure that they're sealing all the way around.

- Harder *professional-style pads* are less forgiving in the padding process, so it takes a highly skilled technician to get them exactly right. However, they do hold adjustments better than the soft student model pads. Even the harder professional-style traditional felt pad, though, gets a little squirrely when a big weather change occurs. Felt absorbs water, so if the humidity rises drastically on a day of rain, traditional felt pads swell up. At that point, you can forget about the .001-inch tolerances — your pads may or may not seal, and your notes may or may not come out right.

- The synthetic-based *Straubinger Pad* was introduced in 1985 and has been widely touted as the gold standard for flute pads ever since. The process of installing and working on Straubinger Pads is quite different from that of traditional pads — flutemakers and repair technicians need to take a course with David Straubinger himself in order to be certified to use them. At last count, 257 flutemakers and repair technicians all over the world are certified Straubinger technicians.

- Other innovative types of pads are also available, some made entirely out of synthetics, some with a gold film on top, and some even made with kangaroo skin.

Some flutists still prefer traditional pads — usually because they feel that the harder synthetic pads tend to brighten the sound of the flute. To that end, some custom flutemakers offer the buyer a choice among several different types of pads.

Synthetic-based pads cost more than traditional pads, but if installed correctly, they can save you endless frustration and countless trips to the repair shop. Previously reserved only for professional model flutes, less expensive versions of synthetic-based pads like Straubinger's new Phoenix Pad are also becoming available on intermediate to conservatory model flutes.

The Straubinger Pad saves the day

As an instrument repair person, David Straubinger was frustrated when working on flutes, finding that the adjustments he was making with tremendous care one day were virtually gone the next. After four years of extensive research, he came up with the Straubinger Pad, a synthetic-based pad. This pad still used some organic materials, but placed synthetic materials under and around them in order to stabilize the whole setup. It turned out that this new type of pad was much more stable and long-wearing than traditional flute pads. This was the answer many flutemakers were waiting for.

Bells and Whistles: Making Sense of Those Extra Keys

Choosing the options always seems like the most daunting part of buying a flute. But if you're aware of your options before you start shopping, you'll know what you're getting into, and you're less likely to be overwhelmed.

In the following sections, I list all the options currently on the market. The offerings vary by manufacturer. Generally, the more expensive the flute, the more options you have available to you.

Customizing your flute

The standard tuning A in the United States is A=440 Hz. However, in some areas of the United States and other countries, the standard A is a slightly higher pitch. Some professional American orchestras tune to A=442, and in Germany, the pitch can range from A=442 to A=445.

Pitch tends to rise over time. Just a generation ago, standard pitch in the U.S. was closer to A=438, so musicians were playing everything slightly lower then. Custom flutemakers offer a few different pitch options, especially because they often ship flutes overseas. In the United States, a recent trend is to purchase flutes at A=442, just to make sure that the player can get up to a higher pitch than A=440, if necessary. Most flutes in the United States are pitched to A=440 or A=442.

The *inline* or *offset G* option refers to the G key, which is the fifth key counting down from the top (barrel end) of the flute. It can be configured inline, in a straight line with the other keys. Alternatively, it can be configured offset, which means that it's skewed slightly toward the player's left hand (see Figure 3-4).

Beginning student models almost always come with an offset G as standard to accommodate a child's small hands. Professional model flutes used to come with inline G as a rule, but these days it's just another custom option. If you have small hands, you'll likely be more comfortable with an offset G. Conversely, if your hands run large, you may prefer an inline G; however, it really is a matter of what's most comfortable for you. Some manufacturers provide specific hand measurements to determine which style suits you best, but the only effective way to decide is to try both styles to see which one feels better to you. A few manufacturers are now also offering a *half-offset G* option, which puts the G key about halfway in between the inline and offset placements. This option is designed to cater to the player's comfort and preferences.

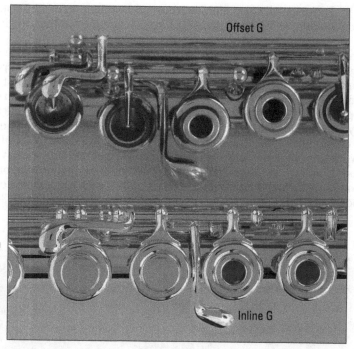

Figure 3-4:
Inline
versus
offset G
keys.

Your choice of footjoint determines the lowest note on your flute. The two most common options for the footjoint are the *C footjoint* and the *B footjoint,* shown in Figure 3-5. Like the other options, choosing the footjoint is a matter of personal preference. Many beginners' flutes come with low C as standard, because it's the less expensive option (shorter tube and one less key), and because young beginners have an easier time with a lighter instrument. However, some beginners' models also feature a low B option. Most flute music doesn't go all the way down to low B, but you do run into the occasional low B. The added tubing and extra key found on the B footjoint also changes the sound of the flute slightly — most would agree that it makes the flute sound a bit darker. Some people prefer the sound that a C footjoint creates — lighter, brighter, and arguably more resonant. You'll generally find more flutes sporting C footjoints in Europe than in the United States.

If you can't decide which footjoint you prefer, some custom flutemakers offer *convertible B/C footjoints.* This removable extension enables the flutist to play with the low B or take it off at will. These convertible footjoints come in handy for those who like the sound and feel of a low C footjoint, but want to be able to play a low B when necessary.

Still another option is a *D footjoint,* which eliminates the C and B extensions altogether, but still has the D♯/E♭ key (for your right hand pinky). This one is pretty rare — some flutists like to have one in order to create a light, delicate sound for certain pieces. But you can find beginning flutes with D footjoints as well. These usually also include a curved headjoint in order to shorten and lighten the flute as much as possible for very young (and tiny) beginners.

Some custom flute builders offer custom key configurations. These specially designed keys, which are shaped and placed to the client's exact specifications, are intended to facilitate comfortable playing for the flutist and flutemakers can incorporate them just about anywhere on the instrument. Companies that offer these types of options don't always advertise them, so it pays to ask. The maker works individually with the client to achieve the desired modifications. The company may also have a demo book of custom keywork they've done before so that the maker and the buyer can work from the book or start from scratch. I have a custom key configuration on one of my footjoints, which helps my right hand pinky reach the lowest notes on the footjoint a little bit more easily. This particular option (see Figure 3-6) didn't add anything to the price of my flute.

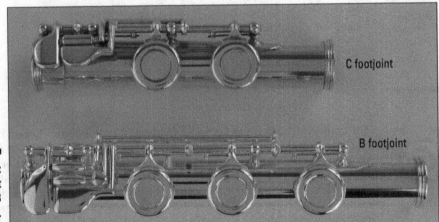

C footjoint

B footjoint

Figure 3-5:
A C footjoint
and a B
footjoint.

Figure 3-6:
A B foot-
joint with
customized
keys.

Boehm's G♯ key

Theobald Boehm's original key system included an open G♯ key. With this type of G♯ key, the player's left hand pinky was pushing down on the G sharp key to play every note except G♯ and high C, for which the finger was lifted. Most modern flutes have a closed G♯, which means that the player doesn't need to operate the G♯ key unless actually playing a G♯ or high C. Some flutists, especially those who play the old Louis Lot flutes, still adhere to Boehm's original system. After you've learned one system, switching is difficult, so just about everyone stays in their respective G♯ camp after they've learned how to play.

Choosing keys and mechanisms to make your life easier

The *mechanism* refers to the moving parts of the instrument and how they're attached to the ribs and/or tube. The mechanism includes the keys, rods, and posts as well as the smaller parts that hold it all together, such as screws and pins.

You'll encounter both *pinned* and *pinless* mechanisms when looking at flutes. In most flutes, and just about all student models, steel pins are used to attach the keys to the rods. The pins work pretty well, but stability is always an issue. The more stable the mechanism, the more consistently the pads will cover the tone holes, and the fewer funny-sounding or nonexistent notes you'll have to deal with while you're playing. Quite a few makers have figured out how to stabilize the flute mechanism by eliminating pins and using other ingenious ways to connect keys to rods and each other instead. The pinless mechanisms are more stable and therefore the pads cover the tone holes more consistently. This type of mechanism also helps partnered keys, which need to move together, to work better in tandem.

I recommend (and use) pinless mechanisms, although a pinned mechanism can work nicely if it's made well.

Innovative and experimental mechanisms pop up in various high-end flute shops from time to time. I've seen mechanisms that use ball bearings and ones that use magnets. But so far, the traditional pinned or pinless versions are still the standard.

Always check for play in the mechanism when purchasing a flute, whether it's new or used. To do so, grab one of the keys on either side and try to move it back and forth on the rod (see Figure 3-7). You should feel very little to no side-to-side movement. Handmade flutes should have no visible motion at all, while very slight movement is usually found on good machine-made models. If the mechanism feels like it has loose teeth, put it down and walk away! A lot of side-to-side motion means that the pads won't seal consistently over the tone holes because they'll be moving around randomly.

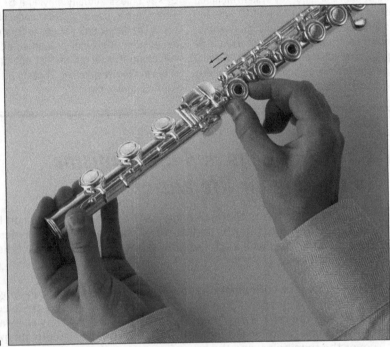

Figure 3-7: Checking for play in the mechanism.

Quite a few extras are available on flutes these days. The more expensive the flute, the more key options are usually offered. These special keys and mechanisms are designed to improve response and/or tuning on certain notes or to facilitate fingering tasks. The prices for these options vary by flutemaker, but as a general rule, they get more or less expensive relative to the price of the flute.

Here's a comprehensive list of most every extra bell and whistle you'll run into when looking at flute options:

✔ **Gizmo key:** Yes, that's really what it's called. This little lever on the footjoint, operated by the player's right hand pinky, closes the low B key by itself (see Figure 3-8). This action effectively shortens the flute tube so that some of the high notes speak more easily. Usually, the gizmo key comes standard with a B footjoint, but it's a good idea to make sure.

I don't recommend buying a B footjoint without a gizmo key because some of the high notes will be pretty difficult to play without it.

Figure 3-8:
The gizmo
key.

Gizmo key

TIP

✔ **C♯ trill key:** This key eliminates the awkward left hand B to C♯ trill, which normally is executed with the left hand index finger and thumb moving in opposite directions. (I talk about trilling in Chapter 16.) With the C♯ trill key, you can play the B to C♯ trill with the right hand index finger only. The C♯ trill key also makes a number of other handy fingerings possible. (See Appendix A for details.)

The C♯ trill key does add to the price of a flute, but if I had to pick only one option, this one would be it — it solves a number of problems in one fell swoop.

✔ **Split E mechanism:** This ingenious mechanism stabilizes the flute's high E, which can be a troublesome note. The high E on the flute has a tendency to crack or play other notes instead. You can get around this issue with clever fingerings (see Chapter 15 and Appendix A), but they're not always practical, depending on the note combinations at hand. No extra keys are involved in the split E mechanism, just a change in how the keys work as a group, and it doesn't change any of the fingerings, either. Choosing this option can add a hefty sum to the price of your flute, but it can save you from many cracked notes and a lot of frustration. A few multiphonic fingerings (see Chapter 17) don't work well if you have a split E, but these fingerings are specialized, and you won't come across them unless you're playing contemporary music with unusual sounds. Some makers also offer a split E with an on/off switch so that the player can choose whether to play with or without split E at any given moment. This switch is my option of choice, but I almost always play with the split E on, and most flutists are well served by the split E without the switch.

✔ **Lower G insert:** Also sometimes called the high E facilitator or simply the donut, this little disc is inserted into the lower G tone hole. Like the split E mechanism, it stabilizes the flute's high E, but unlike the split E, it doesn't cost a bundle. It does affect the flute's tuning, though: It lowers the note A in the first two octaves of the flute slightly.

✔ **Half-closing thumb key:** The high G♯, like the high E, tends to crack, and it's quite sharp compared to most other notes on the flute. The half-closing thumb key, also known as the high G♯ facilitator, is a lever that brings the thumb key closer to its tone hole whenever you play a high G♯ or a high C. This action stabilizes the note and adjusts the pitch. More and more flutists (myself included) are requesting this mechanism, although, like the split E, it comes with a rather steep price tag.

✔ **D♯ and C♯ rollers:** These little extras for the footjoint are strategically placed to enable the right hand pinky to slide from one place to another quickly and smoothly (see Figure 3-9). The D♯ roller is a more common option than the C♯ roller. They're a bit of a luxury, as a well-adjusted footjoint and proper finger position are enough to get the job done. (You can also try a different, much cheaper trick to allow for smooth sailing on the footjoint — see Chapter 9 for details.)

Avoiding unnecessary extras

As you find out from reading this chapter, it all comes down to personal preference. If you're just starting out and looking at student model flutes, you won't have all that many decisions to make. But the options formerly found only on high-end flutes are starting to show up on the lower-priced models, so staying up to speed on the various options is a good idea. That way, if and when you're ready to buy a step-up, conservatory, or professional model, you'll already have done your homework.

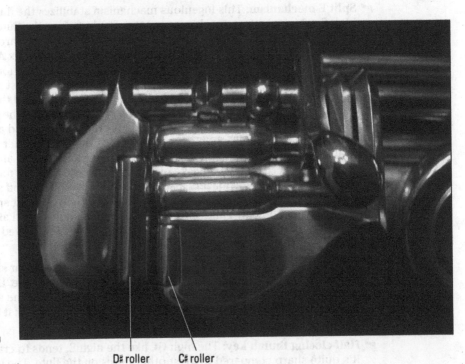

Figure 3-9:
D sharp
and C sharp
rollers.

D♯ roller   C♯ roller

You may encounter some brand-new bells and whistles while shopping for a flute — flutemakers are always experimenting and coming up with new ways to make flutists' lives easier. But make sure that you keep your head on straight and don't buy the latest and supposedly greatest thing just because it's new. It may or may not be the right thing for you. Ask questions, do your research, comparison shop, and ask a more experienced flutist (preferably someone other than the salesperson, who's trying to sell you a flute, after all) for advice.

The All-Important Headjoint: The Soul of the Flute

The headjoint is the one part of the flute most responsible for what sort of sound comes out of the instrument. Switch out your headjoint, and it can change the sound of your flute completely. The headjoint can also make a difference in the feel and response of a flute. Like fingerprints or snowflakes, no two flute headjoints are exactly alike — even headjoints that appear to have exactly the same cut and are made by the same maker using the same minute measurements will have slight variations in how they play.

Student models always come with a preselected headjoint, as do most conservatory models. But if you buy a professional model custom flute, you're usually able to choose the one you like best from several headjoints. Some companies will even let you keep switching them out over the course of a year (provided you keep them in good shape) until you find "the one." If you live in the same city as the flutemaker, you can just stop by whenever he has a new batch of headjoints available to see which one you like best. If you live far away, trial exchanges are done via the mail.

The most cost-effective way to upgrade a flute without buying an entirely new instrument is to shop around for a new headjoint. Many flutemakers sell their headjoints separately, and some make only headjoints, no flutes at all. You want a couple of years of flute-playing experience under your belt before you invest in a new headjoint so that your flute chops are in place and you can tell what the differences are.

No one else can pick a headjoint for you as well as you can, because everyone has a unique lip and mouth shape as well as a unique playing style. Selecting a headjoint is the most personal choice you'll ever make regarding your instrument. When you're ready, try out quite a few different makers before you settle on a style you like. Don't rush this process; it's a bit like shopping for fine wines. You don't want to try too many at one time, or your senses will get befuddled. You want to be able to appreciate all the subtleties and cultivate your preferences over time.

To discover headjoint makers you like, check out local shops and flute club events (see Chapter 18) or locate a flute shop or large band instrument retailer you can visit when you're traveling. You can find many flutemakers in the Boston area, but many more flutemakers and specialty flute shops are all over the country, and indeed all over the world.

The art of headjoint cutting

Headjoint makers put their own personal stamp on each headjoint, literally and figuratively. Because players switch out headjoints often, the maker engraves a logo and sometimes a serial number on the headjoint tube for easy identification. Each headjoint maker also has his own individual style of making headjoints, which evolves over time.

Headjoints come in the same materials as flute bodies. The headjoint sets itself apart from the other parts of the flute with its embouchure hole, lip plate, and riser. Flutemakers have worked with many different combinations of metals (and sometimes nonmetals) for the tube, lip plate, and riser. But the biggest difference in headjoints is in the cutting of the embouchure hole. Because your air moves across the embouchure hole to make the sound, the tiniest change can affect the sound in a big way.

On the surface, most embouchure holes look like oval or slightly square cut-outs in the lip plate. But when you take a closer look, you find many other variables. The size and shape of the hole and the shape of the lip plate are a factor. Variations in the height of the riser and lip plate are also taken into consideration. Beveling the sides over or underneath the embouchure hole in certain ways helps the player direct the airstream and helps sound production. (These techniques are known as *overcutting* and *undercutting*.)

- ✔ **Production headjoints:** The headjoints on many student model flutes have embouchure holes that a machine has punched out. Machine-cut headjoints have improved greatly over the years with advances in headjoint design, and a small amount of overcutting and undercutting is possible with a machine. The edges on these holes are still fairly rough, though —a machine can only do so much with regard to fine adjustments. Using these machined headjoints helps the manufacturer keep the prices low on student model flutes.

- ✔ **Hand-cut headjoints:** Although some undercutting and overcutting is possible via machine, it's really best done by hand. The basic shape and size of the embouchure hole is one thing, but it takes a skilled hand to get exactly the right angles and to smooth the rough edges so that the headjoint supports the flutist's playing optimally. Judicious, minute amounts of cutting, shaping, scraping, and filing are the finishing touches that no machine is able to reproduce. It takes some real finesse to make a world-class headjoint. Because handmade headjoints are labor-intensive, they're not cheap: They range from $1,400 to upwards of $7,000, depending on processes and materials used. But considering that a $1,400 headjoint can make your $2,000 flute sound like a $10,000 flute, they can be a real bargain!

✔ **Specialty headjoints:** An amazing array of specialty headjoints are on the market today. Some companies offer *wing style* headjoints with specially cut lip plates that help direct the player's air for optimal sound. Some are shaped to allow the flutist to play vertically instead of horizontally. Others are angled to make flute-playing a more ergonomic experience. Avant-garde flutist Robert Dick even invented something called a *glissando headjoint,* which enables the flutist to slide the pitch up and down on any note at will. Again, a lot of experimentation is going on, and it remains to be seen which innovations will become popular fare.

Most flute and headjoint makers recommend matching tubing thicknesses from flute to headjoint as much as possible. If your flute tubing is .014-inch thick, you can try .014 inches and thinner tubing in headjoints. A .016-inch headjoint is too large for a .014-inch flute — it won't fit into the flute barrel, so you won't even be able to try it out. Although flutemakers usually prefer to fit tubing of the same thickness together (.014 inches to .014 inches, for example), fitting a .012-inch headjoint to a .014-inch flute is possible. You can also mix metals, fitting a gold headjoint to a silver flute, for example. Headjoints are made to be loose in the flute barrel while you're trying them out to allow for slight differences in barrel sizes for different manufacturers. During the trial period, you can stick regular clear tape onto the headjoint to temporarily fit it so that it won't slide out of the barrel. (Some flutists prefer Teflon tape for this task. It's also known as plumber's tape and is available at hardware stores.)

After you choose your headjoint, you need to have a flutemaker or an experienced repair technician fit the new headjoint to your flute, which will give you a better seal than simply using tape. To fit the headjoint, the technician widens the headjoint's tenon slightly so that it fits properly into the flute's barrel without slippage. Be sure it's the one before you have it fitted, though: Most flutemakers won't accept a fitted headjoint for return, and in case you want to sell it or have it fit into a different flute later on, you may have to have it re-sized.

Headjoints uncorked

Believe it or not, the type of cork and crown assembly a headjoint uses can make a difference in your flute's sound and general ease of playing, too. Along these lines, some flutemakers carry their own special crowns or assemblies and sell them as accessories for their headjoints. These items can range from jeweled crowns to weighted solid crowns (rather than the standard hollow variety), to special assemblies made of various materials which replace the original cork assembly. Switching out the different corks and crowns, though, won't make as much of a difference as changing the whole headjoint.

Chapter 4

Understanding Music Notation

In This Chapter

▶ Identifying notes using the staff

▶ Getting to know your key signatures

▶ Tackling time signatures and rhythm

▶ Articulating with slurs, dashes, dots, and accents

▶ Observing dynamics, expression, and repeat signs

The language of music was around way before people got the idea to write it down. If you've ever hummed a tune, you speak the language. The next step is to learn the various symbols, indicators, and nomenclature that have been created over centuries to bring the magical language of music to life. These symbols are what's called *music notation*.

In this chapter, you gain knowledge of (or review) the notation used in flute music. I include only topics that relate to reading flute lines. I don't cover things that you need to know for reading piano music, such as the bass clef. When you get into playing music for flute and piano, for example, you'll want to add a bit to your notational knowledge base so that you can read the part that the pianist is playing with you.

Finding Notes on the Staff

Musical notes, those dots with various lines attached to them, are organized on a five-line classification system called the *staff*. When you see the dots rising on the staff, the *pitches*, or sounds, are also going higher. Similarly, descending notes reflect pitches going lower, all measured out in varying degrees and indicated as such by staff lines and indicators that tell you how much or to what degree the pitch is changing. At the beginning of each staff is an important indicator called the *clef* that tells you what the specific note names are within the five lines (staff) they're printed on. These notes can appear in the spaces between the lines, directly on the lines, or above and below the staff. After you start naming some notes, I talk about how they are partitioned into specific rhythms via measures and rhythmic values. It's all pretty logical, actually.

Nothing but treble: The clef

Clefs, named after the *clavis,* the Latin word for key, appear at the beginning of each line of music. As a general rule, high instruments use the *treble clef,* and low instruments use the *bass clef.* A couple of more clefs fall in between as well, such as alto clef and tenor clef. All flute music is written in just one clef, the treble clef. (Some instruments use two or three clefs, sometimes simultaneously, so flutists are pretty lucky in the scheme of things.)

The treble clef is also known as the *G clef* because the design of the clef shows the reader where the note G is located (see Figure 4-1).

Figure 4-1:
The treble clef on the staff with the note G.

The staff: Lines and spaces

The staff, as you can see, consists of five horizontal lines. Those lines are a cataloguing system for the notes. Because flutists play only one note at a time, they have only one line of staff to read — unlike pianists and harpists, who often read two lines of music with multiple notes stacked on top of one another.

On the staff, a note is centered on either a line or a space (see Figure 4-2).

Figure 4-2:
The note G (on a line) and the note A (on a space), divided into two measures.

The vertical lines you see in Figure 4-2 are called *bar lines.* They divide the notes rhythmically into *measures.* (See the upcoming section "You've Got Rhythm!" for more on bar lines and measures.)

Name that note: The musical alphabet

The first identifying factor of a note is its note name, which comes from its location on the staff. Going upward on the staff one by one, via line, space, line, space, the note names coincide with the letters of the alphabet from A to G (see Figure 4-3). After G, they start over with A again. So the notes progress upward like this:

ABCDEFGABCDEFGABCDEFG

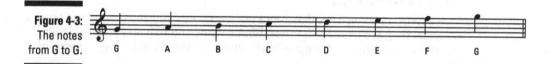

Figure 4-3:
The notes
from G to G.

Notice that if you count the number of notes from the first G you see in the progression to the next G, you get eight notes. The first G and the next G are therefore an octave apart. (Eight=Octave.) Notes that are an octave apart always have the same name.

The first note names to memorize are those of the notes directly on the staff, not above or below the staff. Dividing the staff into lines and spaces is helpful for identifying the notes on the staff and learning them quickly. The notes that are placed on the spaces only are F, A, C, and E (see Figure 4-4). Coincidentally, the notes on the spaces spell FACE so that makes them easy to remember, and in fact, you may remember this acronym from your music classes in school.

Figure 4-4:
The notes
on the
spaces spell
F-A-C-E.

The notes placed on the lines are E, G, B, D, and F (see Figure 4-5). Unfortunately, they don't spell a word, but many music teachers make the letters into an acronym to help students remember: EGBDF=Every Good Boy Does Fine.

Figure 4-5:
The notes
on the lines
are E,G,B,D,
and F (Every
Good Boy
Does Fine).

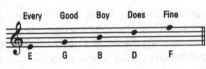

Half and whole steps

One important thing to notice about any two notes you see in music is how far apart they are from each other. Whole steps and half steps, in particular, can help you identify where any particular note stands in the big scheme of things.

- ✔ **Half step:** When two notes are a *half step* apart, no other notes exist in between them. A half step is the closest possible *interval* (distance) you can have between two different notes,

  Example of a half step: E and F: E♯ is the same as F♭.) (See the next section for more about flats and sharps.)

- ✔ **Whole step:** A *whole step* is made up of two half steps. When two notes are a *whole step* apart, you could put one other note in between them.

  Example of a whole step: G and A: G♯/A♭ is a half step higher than G and a half step lower than A. (See the next section for more about flats and sharps.)

Flats and sharps

Besides the note name, the other identifying factor in naming notes is the symbol preceding it (or lack thereof). Table 4-1 shows you these symbols and explains their functions.

Table 4-1	Flat, Sharp, and Natural Signs
Name and Symbol	*Meaning*
Flat (♭)	Half step below the main note
Sharp (♯)	Half step above the main note
Natural (or no symbol)	Main note stays as-is with no changes.

Seeing double: Double flats and double sharps

Every so often, you may come across a double flat (♭♭) or a double sharp (×). These symbols mean exactly what you would think: A *double flat* lowers the note by two half steps, and a *double sharp* raises it by two half steps. And why, you might ask, doesn't the composer just use the next note name up instead? Good question. We could get into that in a few music theory lessons. But suffice it to say that it has to do with chord structures and the given note's function within the harmony. Enough said, for now at least.

In Figure 4-6, *G flat* is played one half step lower than the note G. *G sharp* is played one half step higher than the note G. *G natural* means that the G is left as-is, just plain G.

Figure 4-6:
G flat, G sharp, and G natural (with and without natural sign).

Notes that look different but sound the same are called *enharmonic notes* (see Figure 4-7).

Figure 4-7:
G♭ is the same note as F♯.

Most of the time, a set of two natural letter name notes, such as F and G, are a whole step apart. They have one note in between them, which is a flat or sharp note (G♭ or F♯), depending on the context.

Two sets of natural letter name notes are only a half step apart — they don't have a flat/sharp note in between them. Therefore, E♯ is the same note as F, F♭ is the same note as E, B♯ is the same note as C, and C♭ is the same note as B (see Figure 4-8).

Figure 4-8:
E♯=F, F♭=E,
B♯=C, and
C♭=B.

E sharp = F natural   F flat = E natural   B sharp = C natural   C flat = B natural

Other than these notes, natural letter name notes are always a whole step apart, and thus one flat or sharp note is always in between them as in Figure 4-9.

Figure 4-9:
F♮, F♯=G♭,
and G♮.

F natural   F sharp = G flat   G natural

This may seem confusing at first, but you'll get the hang of it. Table 4-2 simplifies identifying notes with flat and sharp symbols.

Table 4-2	Notes Between Naturals: Enharmonic Equivalents		
Note Below	*Note Above*	*Number of Notes in Between (Half Step or Whole Step)*	*Enharmonic Equivalents*
E♮	F♮	0 (Half Step)	E♯ =F♮ F♭=E♮
F♮	G♮	1 (F♯/G♭) (Whole Step)	F♯ =G♭
G♮	A♮	1 (G♯/A♭) (Whole Step)	G♯ =A♭

Note Below	Note Above	Number of Notes in Between (Half Step or Whole Step)	Enharmonic Equivalents
A♮	B♮	1 (A#/B♭) (Whole Step)	A# =B♭
B♮	C♮	0 (Half Step)	B# =C♮ C♭ =B♮
C♮	D♮	1 (C#=D♭) (Whole Step)	C# =D♭
D♮	E♮	1 (D#/E♭) (Whole Step)	D# =E♭

To get familiar with all the notes on the staff, take a look at Figures 4-10 and 4-11. The first comprises all the notes in the one-octave span from G to G, including the flat and sharp notes, but not repeating any of the same (enharmonic) notes. This series of notes, which is made up exclusively of half steps, is called a *chromatic scale*. The version shown in Figure 4-10 uses sharps only, no flats.

Figure 4-10:
A one-octave ascending chromatic scale from low G to high G.

G   G sharp   A   A sharp   B   C   C sharp   D   D sharp   E   F   F sharp   G

The example in Figure 4-11 is exactly the same scale, but descending from high G to low G, and using flats instead of sharps. These notes are exactly the same as in Figure 4-10, but in reverse order.

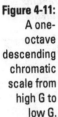

Figure 4-11:
A one-octave descending chromatic scale from high G to low G.

When a note goes from one octave to the next, its placement changes from line to space or from space to line (see Figure 4-12). (See Chapter 2 for more on octaves.)

Figure 4-12:
The notes E, F, and G, each in two different octaves.

Ledger lines: Moving into the stratosphere

The flute can play more than four octaves' worth of pitches, which adds up to a whole lot of notes. So to take advantage of the full range of the flute, you have to play notes that are lower and higher than what can be written on the staff.

Ledger lines extend the staff by putting lines in equal increments to the staff's lines above and below the staff. All you have to do to read notes with ledger lines is to pretend that the staff keeps going and keep reading note names up or down respectively. The example in Figure 4-13 shows four octaves of Cs and all the notes in between, which span a three-octave scale, with no flats or sharps.

Figure 4-13:
A three-octave C scale.

Because the flute's lowest note is usually either C or B, depending on the footjoint (I explain footjoints in Chapters 2 and 3), the ledger lines in flute music don't extend very far below the staff. But flute music does entail quite a few high notes with multiple ledger lines. They can be a little tricky to read when you're getting started, especially as more ledger lines are added in the highest octave, but you'll get used to them quickly. At first, you'll be counting every line, and after a while you'll start to recognize the notes on sight. It will become second nature, just like reading a book. You were faced with a similar task when you learned your alphabet and then started to read and look where you are now!

The 8va symbol: Higher and higher

Sometimes, the ledger lines get to be a bit much, even if you are used to reading them, as in the excerpt from *Poem* by Charles Tomlinson Griffes in Figure 4-14.

Figure 4-14: Excerpt from *Poem* by Charles Tomlinson Griffes, using ledger lines.

Using an *8va symbol* makes an otherwise ledger-line-heavy passage easier to read (and it saves ink, too). Any passage marked with an 8va symbol and a dotted line indicating the length of the passage in question is to be played one octave higher than written. Figure 4-15 contains exactly the same music as Figure 4-14, but strategic use of the 8va symbol makes the excerpt much easier to read.

After the 8va symbol, at the end of the dotted line, you often see a *loco* marking. No, this does not mean that you've lost your mind. Loco may mean "crazy" in Spanish, but it's also the Italian word for "place." It's just a reminder for you to stop playing an octave higher.

Figure 4-15:
Excerpt
from *Poem*
by Charles
Tomlinson
Griffes,
using the
8va symbol.
This is how
it's usually
printed.

All Keyed Up: Knowing Your Key Signatures

Key signatures appear at the beginning of each line of music, like clefs, and they consist of anywhere from one to seven sharp signs, or one to seven flat signs, or none of the above. The key signature indirectly tells you what key the piece of music is in. If a piece is in a certain key, that means it gravitates around a certain note as its home base. This home note is called the *tonic*. Playing a scale in a particular key means that you start on the tonic note and go up one note at a time, observing the flats or sharps in that particular key's key signature.

In order to have a key, or center around the tonic note, the piece will tend to have certain sharp or flat notes in it. Rather than marking every single flat or sharp note, the composer instead gives you a key signature (Figure 4-16). That way, you already know which sharps or flats to play before you start playing, and you can easily decipher the key, or tonic note, of the piece just by looking at the sharps and flats in the key signature indicated at the beginning of the piece.

Major keys

Major keys are the building blocks of Western classical music. Generally, pieces written in major keys tend to sound happy.

The handy chart in Figure 4-17 is called the Circle of Fifths, and it organizes all the keys into a logically laid-out circle. Every musician should have a copy of this chart.

Figure 4-16:
A musical
example
with a key
signature
containing
B♭. Every B
you see in
this example
would be
played as
a B♭.

The Circle of Fifths

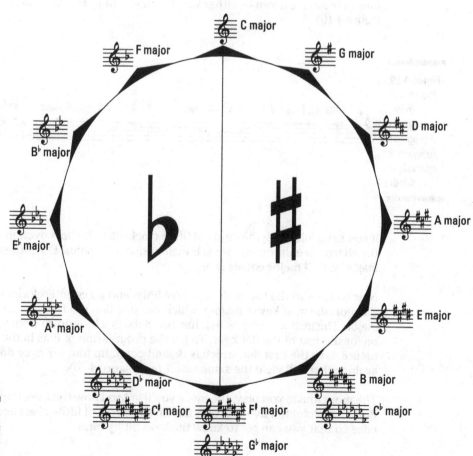

Figure 4-17:
The circle of
fifths.

To understand the circle of fifths, you first need to know what a *fifth* is. A fifth is an interval, or simply a defined distance between two notes, such as a whole step, half step, or octave. Notes that are a fifth apart are five letter name notes apart, counting the bottom and the top note (see Figure 4-18).

Figure 4-18:
Intervals of
a fifth.

Start at the top of the circle of fifths with C major, which has no flats or sharps. Notice that if you follow the circle of fifths clockwise, each key listed there is five notes apart, and that after C major, each key signature increases by one sharp. Starting from G major, which has only F♯ in its key signature, you can find each subsequent sharp by counting either five note names up or four note names down — either way it comes out to the same note name (see Figure 4-19).

Figure 4-19:
The sharps
in key
signatures
progress
upward in
intervals of
a fifth.

If you keep following the circle of fifths clockwise, the flats overlap with the sharps in enharmonic keys: B major equals C♭ major, F♯ major equals G♭ major, and C♯ major equals D♭ major.

Now go back to the top of the circle of fifths and go counterclockwise. After C major, the next key (F major), which has one flat, is a fifth down from C major. The next key (B♭), which has two flats, is a fifth down from F, and so on for the rest of the flat keys. To get the progression of flats in the key signature, take the first flat, which is B♭, and count up four notes or down five — again, either will yield the same result (see Figure 4-20).

The more music you play, the more you'll get to know the keys intuitively. But it is helpful to have the formula and the circle of fifths chart as a reference so that you can get to know the keys bit by bit.

Figure 4-20:
The flats
in key
signatures
progress
downward
in intervals
of a fifth.

If you're looking at a key signature and need to figure out what key the piece is in quickly (provided it's a major key), you can use two formulas:

- In a sharp key signature, the tonic note of the key is always one half step up from the last sharp.

- In a flat key signature, the tonic note of the key is the next-to-last flat in the key signature. (With this formula, you're out of luck with F major, though, because it only has one flat. You'll just have to memorize that one.)

Minor keys

Minor keys are also used often in Western classical music. Minor keys are pretty easy to identify when you're hearing them because they tend to sound sad. Think of the most depressing song you've ever heard, and I guarantee you it's in a minor key.

If you've got a handle on your major keys, the minor keys should not be a problem for you. Basically, minor keys have all the same key signatures as the major keys, but they center around different tonic notes.

Take the key signature of C major, with no sharps or flats. If you take that key signature but use the note A as your home base instead of the note C, you'll be in the key of A minor. If you're playing a scale in that key, you play an octave A to A with no flats or sharps (see Figure 4-21).

Figure 4-21:
A C major
scale and
an A minor
scale.

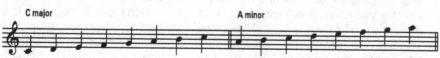

To calculate what note a minor scale starts on for any given key signature, start with the major key. Counting the first and last notes, go down four notes via half steps (not skipping any notes) from the tonic note of the major key (see Figure 4-22).

Figure 4-22:
Calculating
the minor
key's tonic
note using
the major
key.

Figure 4-23 is the circle of fifths again, this time including the minor keys. The minor keys are listed underneath the major keys that have the same key signature.

The beauty of key signatures is that the task of playing in a certain key is already done for you if you observe the flats or sharps (or lack thereof) on the left side of the staff. But knowing which note is home base is extremely helpful; it's like knowing your starting point and ending point before you go on a road trip.

Accidentals waiting to happen

Composers don't always stick to the notes in a particular key when they're writing a piece of music — sometimes they wander off into other keys or find clever decorations to add onto the main notes. (After all, some road trips don't go as planned either. Sometimes you can find very beautiful country roads right off of the highway.)

Major or minor?

When you look at a piece of music for the first time, checking the key signature will tell you what key you're playing in, but it won't tell you whether you're in the major key or the corresponding minor key with the same key signature. You can look for several different clues to see whether you're in a major or minor key. One telltale sign is the last note of the piece — more often than not, pieces of music end on the tonic note of the key. If that method of deduction doesn't work because the last note isn't the major or minor tonic for that key signature, try playing through the piece or listening to a recording of it. If it sounds happy, it's probably in a major key. If it's a sad sounding piece, you'll be singing the blues in a minor key.

The Circle of Fifths

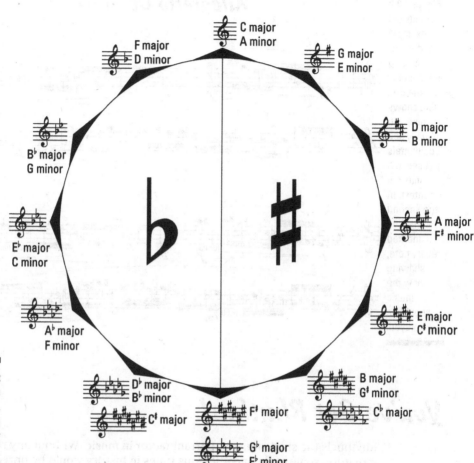

Figure 4-23:
The circle of fifths, including the minor keys.

This is where *accidentals* come in. Even though a key signature dictates which sharps or flats to play throughout the piece, a composer can add a flat, sharp, or natural sign to cancel out the key signature. An accidental isn't only valid on the note where you first see it. In addition to that, accidentals carry through to the next bar line you see (see Figure 4-24). (The next section contains more details about measures and bar lines). If you see a B, for example, and a B♭ is in the key signature, you play it as B♭ *unless* an accidental precedes it —say a natural sign, in this case. You would then play the B as a B♮, and every other B you would encounter before you get to the next bar line would also be played as a B♮.

Figure 4-24:
A musical
example
demon-
strating
accidentals.
The first
line shows
how you
usually see
accidentals
used in a
musical
context. In
the second
line, I've
marked
every note,
showing
how the
music
should be
played.

Allegretto Op. 116

By Benjamin Godard

You've Got Rhythm!

Rhythm is the single most important factor in music. Without any rhythmic structure, some of the most famous tunes in history would be unrecognizable. (Try humming Gershwin's *I Got Rhythm* with no discernible beat, and it will becomes an amorphous muddle.)

Rhythm, like pitch, has a specific system of notation, which developed out of the desire to communicate music on paper. This section outlines commonly used notation methods, so that you can recognize those beats, as well as variations on them, on paper.

Rhythmic values of notes

If you've ever tapped your foot along with a song, you already know what a *beat* is. In music, that tap is represented by what is called a *quarter note*, which is generally worth one beat. On the page, a quarter note has a solid black oval note head with a plain vertical line called a stem emerging up from the right side or down from the left side of the note head (see Figure 4-25). Whether the stem goes up or down depends on where a particular note is located on the staff — high notes have descending stems, and low notes have ascending stems. There's no reason for specific stem placement other than it helps with the legibility of the music on the page.

Figure 4-25:
Quarter
notes.

Using the quarter note as your building block, with each quarter getting one beat, you can now gauge the lengths of other rhythmic values using this single beat as your starting point.

The easiest way to learn the longer note values is to glue multiple quarter notes together to make longer notes. In order to do so, I use a symbol called a *tie,* which is just a curved line over the top of the notes whose values you'll add together.

For example, a *half note* is generally worth two beats, or two quarter notes tied together. A half note looks just like a quarter note, except that the note head is just an outline, not filled in (see Figure 4-26).

Figure 4-26:
A half note
is worth two
beats, the
same as
two quarter
notes.

one half note   =   2 quarter notes

A *whole note* (not to be confused with a whole step, which is an entirely different animal — see the "Half and whole steps" section, earlier in this chapter) is just an outlined note head and has no stem. A whole note is worth four beats, the same as four quarter notes or two half notes tied together (see Figure 4-27).

Figure 4-27:
A whole
note is
worth four
beats, the
same as
four quarter
notes or two
half notes.

one whole note   =   two half notes   =   four quarter notes

Getting into smaller note values, an eighth note is only worth 1/2 beat, or half of a quarter note. It looks like a quarter note, because it has a black note head and a stem, but it also has a flag at the end of the stem (see Figure 4-28). Sometimes eighth notes have single flags, or if more than one appears consecutively, they may be *beamed* together. A beam appears as a heavy straight line connecting multiple notes at the end of the stem. Smaller note values are usually beamed together when their collective value adds up to one full beat, which makes it easier to see where the beats are in the measure.

Figure 4-28:
An eighth
note by
itself and
beamed
together
with other
eighth
notes.
Eighth notes
are worth
1/2 beat, or
half a quar-
ter note.

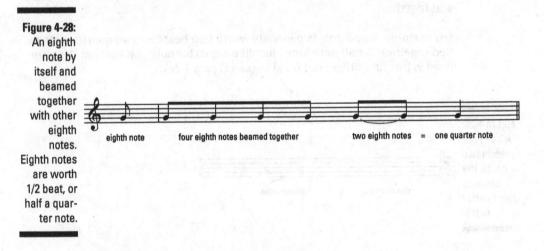

eighth note   four eighth notes beamed together   two eighth notes   =   one quarter note

From that point on, adding additional flags decreases the note value by half. Sixteenth notes are quite common — they have two flags and are worth 1/4 beat. It takes four of them to equal one quarter note (see Figure 4-29).

Even smaller note values are 32nd notes, 64th notes, and 128th notes. The latter two are fairly rare. Each additional flag or beam halves the note's rhythmic value. Anything with a note value smaller than a quarter note can be beamed together, even if the note values are different. Usually, the notes that are beamed together add up to one full beat, or one quarter note (see Figure 4-30).

Figure 4-29:
A sixteenth note by itself and beamed together with other sixteenth notes. It takes four sixteenth notes to equal one quarter note.

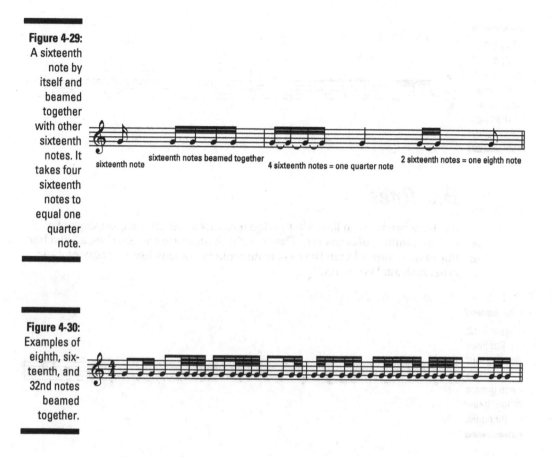

sixteenth note   sixteenth notes beamed together   4 sixteenth notes = one quarter note   2 sixteenth notes = one eighth note

Figure 4-30:
Examples of eighth, sixteenth, and 32nd notes beamed together.

Dots enable an uneven number of beats per note. Adding a dot to the end of a note increases its rhythmic value by half (see Figure 4-31). A dotted half note, for example, is worth three beats (2+1=3), the same value as if a half note and a quarter note were tied together.

dotted half note   =   half note + quarter note   =   3 quarter notes   dotted quarter note = quarter note + eighth note   =   3 eighth notes

dotted eighth note = eighth note + sixteenth note = 3 sixteenth notes   dotted sixteenth note   =   sixteenth note + 32nd note   =   3 32nd notes

Figure 4-31:
Some dotted notes and their equivalents.

Notes can also appear as *triplets,* which means that the player needs to fit three notes into a beat or part of a beat. Triplets are indicated by a bracket and/or a number 3 over a group of three notes (see Figure 4-32).

Figure 4-32:
Sixteenth
note, eighth
note, quar-
ter note, and
half note
triplets.

Bar lines

Bar lines are vertical lines that divide measures, which are groupings of a certain number of beats (see Figure 4-33). A measure can also be called a bar, not to be confused with the establishments musicians like to frequent after rehearsals and concerts.

Figure 4-33:
Bar lines
dividing four
measures
into groups
of four quar-
ter notes.

Time signatures

Time signatures appear at the beginning of a piece of music or a section of music, after the clef and before the key signature. Time signatures tell you how the beats are divided. They look like fractions, but don't be fooled: the rules are different here.

The top number in a time signature indicates how many beats there are per measure, and the bottom number tells you which type of note gets one beat. In the previous section on note values, I assume that the quarter note gets one beat. This assumption is true if the bottom number on the time signature is 4, which is very often the case. However, it is also possible to get a 2 as the bottom number, which would mean that the half note gets one beat, and an 8 would mean that the eighth note gets one beat.

Table 4-3 shows you some common time signatures. Notice that there are symbols for ¢ and ₵. These are interchangeable with the numbers. ¢ is also referred to as *common time,* and ₵ is often called *cut time.*

Table 4-3	Time Signatures Deciphered	
Time Signature	*Beats Per Measure*	*Note Value Worth One Beat*
2/4	2	♩
3/4	3	♩
4/4 or C	4	♩
2/2 or ¢	2	♩
6/8	6	♪
9/8	9	♪

Tempo is the Italian word for time. Although it's not technically part of the time signature, the *tempo indication* is an important factor in the rhythmic feel of any piece of music. The tempo indication gives you an overall *tempo,* or speed, of the beat. A tempo indication often uses Italian musical terms, such as *Adagio* (slow) or *Allegro* (fast). But the tempo may be indicated in a language other than Italian, depending on the nationality of the composer. A *metronome marking,* which consists of a note value and a number, may also be present; this marking makes interpreting the tempo less subjective than just using words to describe it.

To have the player deviate slightly from the general tempo of the piece, markings like *ritardando* (gradually slowing down) or *accelerando* (gradually speeding up) or their abbreviations, *rit.* and *accel.,* are often used.

Mozart's little tempo joke

The longest (and most amusing) tempo indication I've ever seen appears in the *Quartet in A major* for flute and strings, K.298, penned by none other than the legendary Wolfgang Amadeus Mozart (1756–1791). The tempo marking reads

Allegretto grazioso, ma non troppo presto, però non troppo adagio. Così-così-con molto garbo ed espressione.

The English translation would go something like this:

Gracefully somewhat fast, but not too quick, yet not too slow. More or less with lots of elegance and expression.

The man definitely had a sense of humor. Perhaps he was messing with his musicians and patrons just a little!

And the rests

Counting rests is just like counting note values, except that you're counting values for the silences within the music rather than the actual notes, or time that you're *not* playing. Instead of a quarter note, you have a quarter rest, instead of an eighth note, an eighth rest, and so on. It's very zen when you think about it, making the time you're *not* playing as important as the time you *are* playing — just like the negative space in a painting. After all, it's the space *inside* the jar that makes it useful, not the jar itself.

Table 4-4 lists the common types of rests and their equivalent note values. (I assume a ⅔ or ¼ time signature.)

Table 4-4	Rhythmic Values of Notes and Rests	
Note	**Corresponding Rest**	**Value**
♩	𝄽	1 beat
♩.	𝄽·	1½ beats
𝅗𝅥	▬	2 beats
𝅗𝅥.	▬·	2½ beats
𝅝	▬	4 beats
♪	𝄾	½ beat
♪.	𝄾·	¾ beat
𝅘𝅥𝅯	𝄿	¼ beat
𝅘𝅥𝅯.	𝄿·	⅜ beat

The fermata

All rhythmic bets are off when you encounter a *fermata* (⌢) placed above a note or rest. *Fermata* means "stop" in Italian. A fermata is an invitation to hold the note or rest longer than the notation indicates, without regard to rhythm.

Slur to Staccato: Articulation Markings

Articulation markings let you know which notes should be connected to each other and which should be played separately. Quite a few other markings take care of the grey areas, too, such as whether to play separated notes long, short, or in-between. (I talk about how to articulate notes on the flute in Chapter 10.)

If a particular note doesn't have any kind of articulation marking on it, the interpretation depends on the context. In the case of Baroque or Classical music, the articulation marks are often left up to the performer. If the music is any later than the classical period, the composer's intentions were probably that the note or notes be played separately, at a medium length.

Slurs and ties: Phrase markings

Like ties, slurs are like glue that join the notes together. While ties connect notes that are the same pitch, slurs connect notes that are different pitches (see Figure 4-34).

Slurring notes together means that the air flow isn't interrupted between them. The effect is much like that of a singer tying together many different notes while staying on one vowel sound.

A tie looks a lot like a slur, but a tie occurs between two notes of the same pitch, so they just end up sounding like one long note. The tie's function is to write longer notes than merely writing note values would permit. Often, a tie is used to hold a note over a bar line.

You may see the Italian word legato in music occasionally. *Legato* is the Italian word for "bound," as in "tied up." Nothing untoward here: The word legato is sometimes used to refer to a slurred passage, but can also mean notes that are separated, but so long that they are almost connected.

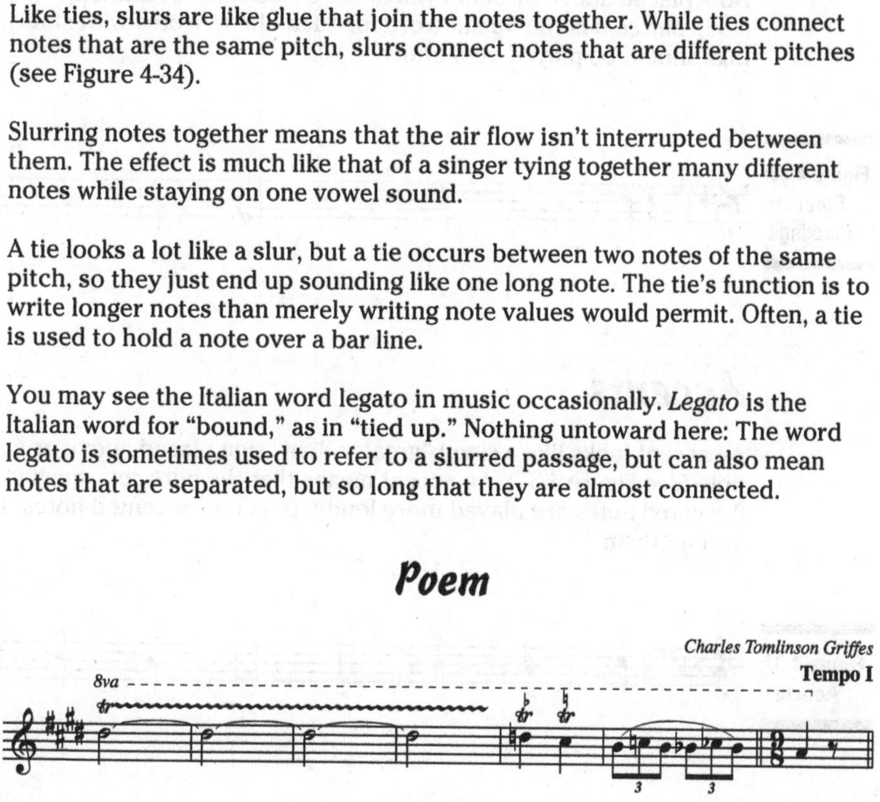

Figure 4-34:
Examples
of slurs
and ties in
an excerpt
from *Poem*
by Charles
Tomlinson
Griffes.

Poem

Charles Tomlinson Griffes
Tempo I

Dashes: Tenuto markings

Dashes placed above or below notes are called *tenuto* markings (see Figure 4-35). *Tenuto* is the Italian word for "held." Notes with tenuto markings should be held for the full value of the note, but still separated from other notes.

Figure 4-35:
Tenuto
markings.

Dots: Staccato markings

Dots placed above or below notes are called *staccato* markings (see Figure 4-36). *Staccato* is the Italian word for "detached." Notes with staccato markings should be played very short.

Figure 4-36:
Staccato
markings.

Accents

An accent looks like a small "greater than" sign placed above or below a note (see Figure 4-37). An accent means that the note gets special emphasis. Accented notes are played more loudly than non-accented notes directly around them.

Figure 4-37:
Accents.

Beyond the Notes

After you're successfully reading notes, rhythms, and articulations, you still have more markings to consider. These markings can be about interpretation, such as dynamics and expression, or they can be markings akin to road signs, telling you where to go next.

Italian is the standard language for musical terms. The terms in this chapter are enough to get you started, but if I were to print an exhaustive list in this book, I'd be talking *War and Peace* proportions. I recommend having a Dictionary of Musical Terms on hand for reference. You can either buy a book or go online; www.music-dictionary.org is a free online music dictionary.

Dynamics and expression

Dynamics are the composer's volume button. With dynamic markings in place, the performer will know when to play loudly, softly, or somewhere in between. Table 4-5 is a chart of commonly used dynamic markings, which are abbreviations for Italian words.

Table 4-5	Dynamic Markings and Their Meanings	
Dynamic Marking	*Italian term*	*Meaning*
pp	pianissimo	very soft
p	piano	soft
mp	mezzo-piano	medium soft
mf	mezzo-forte	medium loud
f	forte	loud
ff	fortissimo	very loud
cresc. or <	crescendo	gradually becoming louder
> or *dim.*	diminuendo	gradually becoming softer

Repeat signs and road maps

Music has a lot of repetition. Because it is a waste of resources to write exactly the same music over and over, composers use *repeat signs* and other clever devices to have the player go back to a certain point and start again.

Musicians call particular configurations of these sorts of markings a *road map,* for obvious reasons. A typical road map may have you repeating the first section, then going on to the next section and repeating it, then going back to the first section but playing it without repeats this time, and then skipping to the ending. I outline many terms that you find in road map situations in Table 4-6.

Table 4-6	Common Symbols Used in Road Maps		
Marking	*Term*	*Italian Translation*	*Meaning*
‖: :‖	Repeat sign	n/a	Repeat the music between the two Repeat Sign brackets. If there is no first bracket, repeat to the beginning of the piece.
D.C.	Da Capo	To the Top; To the Head	Go back to the beginning of the piece.
D.S. 𝄋	Dal Segno	To the Sign	Go back to the sign.
Coda ⊕	Coda	Tail	An ending tacked on after the main part of the piece is over. You may have to skip to the Coda from various points in the music if there is a Da Capo or a Dal Segno present.
Fine ‖	Fine (double bar)	End	The end of the piece. If a Da Capo or a Dal Segno is present, the Fine, or end, may or may not be at the bottom of the last page of music.

Part II

Playing the Flute: Just Wiggle Your Fingers and Blow!

The 5th Wave   By Rich Tennant

"Remember, you're trying to slur the note, not slander it."

In this part . . .

In this part, you develop some basic skills on the flute. First, I cover some fundamentals like breathing and posture. Then you start to make flute sounds, first on a glass bottle and then on various parts of the flute before you put it all together. After that, it's all about the notes: You discover all you need to know about the first two octaves of the flute's range. For ideas about what to do between the notes, I also address slurring and tonguing.

Chapter 5

Getting Down to Basics: Before You Begin

In This Chapter

▶ Gathering the tools you need besides your flute

▶ Breathing well

▶ Using the correct posture for flute playing

his chapter is about laying the groundwork for good flute playing. It outlines what other tools you'll want to have besides your flute, such as a music stand and metronome. It also covers a number of basic skills you'll need to master before you pick up the flute and play.

Knowing What You Need to Get Started

Before you get started playing your flute, you'll need a few essential tools. You can purchase most of these items at your local music store or from online retailers.

✔ **Music stand:** Please don't try to read music lying flat on a table or bed. This positioning will lead to very bad habits — you don't want to be slouching over your music while you're playing the flute, because you won't be able to breathe well that way. (For more on breathing, see the section "Breathing Right," later in this chapter.)

✔ **Mirror:** Your reflection can be helpful in assessing whether your lips, hands, and body are in the correct playing position. (For more on body alignment and positioning, see the section "Stand Up Tall: Posture," later in this chapter.) Just trusting that you're doing the right thing by feel can be misleading, and a quick visual check can keep you from making fundamental mistakes.

✔ **Metronome:** This gadget, which has a perfectly measured, even clicking sound that is adjustable to any speed, will help you keep your rhythm and tempos straight. You can find free metronomes online, such as the one at www.metronomeonline.com, which is a promotional tool to sell a metronome application for your cellphone. Or look for a small electronic one — accurate and portable, too — at a music store or online retailer. If you want to go all-out, you can buy a metronome that will subdivide beats for you to help you count complicated rhythms. Depending on what options you want, you can spend from $10 up to around $200 for a metronome.

Stay away from the old-fashioned mechanical wind-up metronomes, though. They tend to get uneven and inconsistent over time.

✔ **Tuner:** These useful little machines will detect which note you're playing and tell you whether you're flat, sharp, or right on the money. They're available in just about any size, from ones so tiny they'll fit on a keychain ($10 and up) to big, elaborate boxes (up to $5,000 — but those are definitely overkill) and every size in between. Tuners offer a wide array of features, but all you really need is a clear readout of the note you're playing, an indication of whether or not it's in tune, and if not, whether it's too low or too high. You can find reasonably priced electronic metronome/tuner combos now, too, which are pretty cool and very handy. The combos run anywhere between $20 to about $400, and they're a great option for beginners.

✔ **Cleaning cloth:** You'll need a soft, absorbent cleaning cloth, preferably silk, to clean the inside of the flute. (Condensation builds up during flute playing, and you need to get rid of the water, especially before you put the flute back in the case.) Using a silk cloth or swab helps preserve the pads — even soft cotton can wear them out.

✔ **Polishing cloth:** Cleaning the outside of the flute with a chamois-like polishing cloth will prevent fingerprints and tarnish. Be sure that the cloth you choose doesn't contain *jeweler's rouge,* an abrasive substance used in cleaning jewelry, as it can harm the finish. Instrument polishing cloths are fine — but they can contain jeweler's rouge, too, so be careful.

Just stay away from any cloth that looks red and feels gritty, and you should be okay.

✔ **Pad papers:** Pad papers from a music store, *end papers* (perm papers used in permanent waving) from a beauty-supply store, or cigarette papers from a tobacco shop will remove water bubbles from your keys and prevent or treat sticky pads. If you get cigarette papers, make sure that you have I.D. with you (selling to minors is prohibited by law in some states) and that you get ungummed papers. (Otherwise, you'll end up with sticky pads instead of preventing them).

✔ **Recording device:** This one is optional, but a recording device lets you hear yourself objectively and be your own teacher. It's amazing what you can miss while you're busy playing.

Virtual accompaniment

SmartMusic, a computer accompaniment program, includes a metronome, a tuner, and many accompaniment tracks for flute music. You can play exercises into a microphone, and it will evaluate your performance. You can even record your playing, alone or with the accompaniment tracks, save the file, and e-mail it to your family and friends. The only thing it won't do is wash your dishes for you while you're practicing. So if you're even marginally tech-savvy and want to make the investment, I'd recommend looking into this option at www.smartmusic.com.

Building a Good Foundation with Practice

"Practice makes perfect," the old saying goes. Well, nobody actually is perfect. How boring would that be? But practice is the most effective tool for improving your skills and can be nearly perfect if you make sure to practice well. Playing through stuff mindlessly won't get you anywhere. You've got to target your practice time and be efficient with it.

There's nothing too complicated about practicing a musical instrument. It's a lot like mastering an athletic skill, only you're training much smaller muscles than a runner or gymnast. In order to train, most athletes go to a gym or other dedicated venue where they have the necessary tools and the uninterrupted time to focus on their work. Like an athlete, you'll also need a dedicated practice area and a window of time that's relatively free of distractions.

Carving out quality time

While you're learning new skills, don't do any multitasking — you'll need to engage your brain fully to set up all your good flute playing habits and keep bad ones from starting. When you play the flute, you'll already be doing several things at once: blowing the air, moving your fingers, reading music, and listening to yourself, all at the same time. Talk about multitasking. You may as well be a circus juggling act! So find a way to keep the kids busy (if you have them), turn off the TV (unless that's how you're keeping the kids busy), leave any thoughts of work or household chores or the Big Game behind, and go to a quiet place in your house or apartment.

You'll also need to schedule a block of time for practice. Setting up a routine so that you're practicing at the same time each day is helpful. Here are a few general guidelines to get you started:

- ✔ If you're a beginner or working on the skills covered in Part II of this book, 30 to 45 minutes per day will do just fine.

- ✔ If you've progressed to the intermediate topics in Part III, count on 1 to 1½ hours of daily practice time.

- ✔ Once you're at the level covered in Part IV, the sky's the limit — depending on how much time you can devote, of course.

- ✔ If you're steadily working on your sound, technique, and classical flute pieces, you can spend 2 to 4 hours practicing each day, depending on the level of proficiency you want to achieve. At that point, you can start dividing up your practice time — it's okay to do an hour in the morning and an hour in the evening, for example.

Taking a few minutes of break time every 30 minutes or so can be very beneficial. Just make sure that you keep a dedicated practice time so that you can avoid losing your momentum by getting involved in other tasks while you're practicing.

After about 4 or 5 hours of practice, the musical version of the Law of Diminishing Returns starts kicking in. Spend more time than that practicing the flute in a day, and you may experience undue frustration as your newly honed skills start to wane. Your body and brain can just burn out — so pace yourself.

Building a practice schedule

Whether you're just starting out on the flute or you're headed off to Juilliard, you'll always need to cover three things equally in your practice sessions:

- ✔ **Work on your sound.** Whether you know only three notes or are working on elaborate sound studies and melodies, the concept is the same: Play slowly, listen to your sound, and figure out how you might continually improve upon it.

- ✔ **Work on your technique.** You may be just learning the fingerings (see Chapters 8, 9, and 11) or playing arpeggios at lightning speed (see Chapter 17), but either way, play carefully and cleanly while watching your finger position.

- ✔ **Work on making music.** Learn music that is realistically within your skill level and learn it well. Pay attention to all the details on the page and do your best to focus on the composer's intentions. Start with rhythm and notes and then address articulation, dynamics, intonation, phrasing, and musical expression as you study the piece.

You can practice all these things through repetition. When musicians visualize practicing an instrument, they think of playing a musical passage over and over. The most important thing to remember, though, is that you'll learn only if you repeat something correctly. Repeating mistakes means that you're learning mistakes.

In order to practice well, you must listen well. How will you know if you're repeating something correctly unless you're really listening to yourself? This tip may seem obvious, but you can really miss a lot if you're not paying attention.

Slowing down for rapid results

The famous burlesque star Gypsy Rose Lee once said, "If a thing is worth doing, it is worth doing slowly . . . very slowly." I agree completely. Make this advice your golden rule of practicing.

Practicing slowly is like putting things under a magnifying glass. Working on your sound slowly allows you to really feel what's going on in your body as it relates to the flute. Practicing your technical exercises at a leisurely pace affords you the luxury of noticing whether or not your fingers are working efficiently, and if your air is working well in tandem with them. You therefore avoid unnecessary tension in your embouchure, throat, torso, and hands — tension that can impede your progress with sound production and technique.

When you're studying a piece of music, start slowly and methodically so that you don't miss any details on the page as you're learning. Unlearning mistakes is so much more difficult than learning a piece correctly the first time around.

Ironically, you learn much faster by going slowly than if you hurry. This applies to getting your new skills under control as well as learning music.

Practicing for improvement

The things you don't do well should always take priority in your practice sessions. The things you've already mastered obviously don't need as much work, though you shouldn't neglect them entirely.

Before you dive into your daily practice routine, take each practice topic — sound, technique, and music — and decide what about that topic needs the most work. From there, plan out how to best target your practice.

A typical practice session for a beginner might look something like this:

- ✔ **Sound:** Hold a note as long as possible to concentrate on sound and breath support. (For more on breath support, see the section "Controlling your air with breath support," later in this chapter.) Look in the mirror to check body position.

- ✔ **Technique:** Review notes learned so far and practice various finger combinations. Check hand position in the mirror. Learn new note(s) and skills.

- ✔ **Music:** Work on easy pieces in a flute method or collection such as *Forty Little Pieces in Progressive Order for Beginner Flutists* by Louis Moyse. (See Chapter 11 for a more in-depth description of this book.) Practice the more challenging passages before playing through, work with a metronome to facilitate correct rhythms and steady tempo, and address dynamics and articulation.

An efficient practice session for someone with two to three years of experience or more may look like this:

- ✔ **Sound:** Play a few warm-up notes and then target trouble areas. (Low notes? High notes? Soft playing? Working toward getting more volume?) Check embouchure and body position in the mirror. Work from a melody book, such as *Tone Development through Interpretation* by Marcel Moyse. (For more on melody books, see Chapter 17.) Use a tuner to check pitch.

- ✔ **Technique:** Plan a challenging finger workout that focuses on a specific area, such as *Top Register Studies for Flute* by Thomas Filas. The term *top register* in this context simply means that you're working specifically on the high notes covered in Chapter 14 of this book. Start slowly and check finger position in the mirror and gradually increase speed.

- ✔ **Music:** Work on classical flute repertoire, such as one of the Sonatas by G.F. Handel or *Fantasie* by Gabriel Fauré. Practice challenging passages before playing through, work with a metronome to facilitate correct rhythms and steady tempo, and address dynamics and articulation. Use a tuner to check pitch. (You can hear the first movement of Handel's *Sonata in F Major* on the CD that accompanies this book, and I include the flute part in Chapter 12 so that you can play along with the CD accompaniment track. You can also hear an excerpt from Fauré's *Fantasie* on the CD. The Fauré excerpt appears in Chapter 10.)

As you can see, the basic premise of practicing remains the same, whether you're a novice or a budding virtuoso. Approach your practice time methodically, and your flute playing will blossom.

When you're practicing a piece of music, you don't always have to start at the beginning. If you do, you're likely going to be trying out the beginning of the piece much more often during your course of practice than the middle or the end. Switch it up by picking a spot in the piece that is giving you trouble and start there. That way, you're fresh when you're working on the most challenging section.

Should you sit or stand while practicing? The answer is both. Flutists play standing up during solo recitals and seated in ensembles, so you need to be comfortable either way. And I do recommend practicing both ways, as each will feel slightly different, especially for breathing.

Playing just for fun

You'll be tempted to play through the things that already sound great, just for fun. There is nothing wrong with this approach. As a matter of fact, I hereby give you permission to have fun playing your flute. Just enjoy your own dulcet tones with the awareness that you're playing, not practicing, and don't sacrifice practice time for play time. You want to keep improving, right?

For example, I adore playing *Madrigal*, a lovely little piece by Philippe Gaubert. It has a beautiful melodic line that is a joy to play. It has a few technical passages, but mostly it is just an absolutely gorgeous melody. Say I give in to my desires and play *Madrigal* day and night, just enjoying my pretty sound (if I do say so myself). I'm neglecting the fact that the other aspects of my playing, such as technique or endurance, may need some work. If enough time goes by without working on those things, the next time I am faced with a challenging technical passage, I'll either fall flat on my face, or I'll have to take a good long time working on my technique from scratch so that I can play the passage. It would be better for my playing (and my ego) to maintain and build on my technique regularly.

So notice the things that you would like to improve and address them in every practice session.

Breathing Right

Breathing is highly recommended whether you play an instrument or not, but if you play an instrument that relies on air to make a sound, whether it be a flute, a contrabassoon, a pennywhistle, or a kazoo, breathing is absolutely crucial. The better you breathe, the more easily things will work on the flute — it's that simple. In order to breathe efficiently for flute playing, you just need to be aware of a few things.

Breathing is important

In many ways, playing the flute is very similar to singing — the breathing and breath support processes are almost identical. (See the section "Controlling your air with breath support," later in this chapter, to find out more about breath support.) Instead of producing sound with the vocal cords, you produce notes on the flute by exhaling across the embouchure hole, with nothing for the lips to grab onto and nothing covering them up. (You can experience this sensation if you practice blowing across a bottle and making a sound with your flute's headjoint, which I address in Chapter 6.) So in both singing and flute playing, the performer isn't blowing directly into a mouthpiece or against the resistance of a reed. (See Chapter 2 for more on reeds and resistance.) Both singers and flutists have complete control over the process of breathing during both the inhalation and the exhalation, making their own resistance within their bodies by regulating the flow of air with their breathing muscles. (See the "Breathing easy" section, later in this chapter, to find out more about your breathing muscles.) Also, keep in mind that because you're blowing across the embouchure hole, not into the instrument, some of the air you expel won't be contributing directly to producing the sound. Because you're blowing some of your air out into the wild blue yonder, breathing efficiently is doubly important so that you'll have lots of air at your disposal.

At first, you'll be tempted to think only about your exhalation, because that's where the sound actually comes from. But you need to think about the whole process of breathing; how you inhale affects the quality of your exhalation and therefore the quality and quantity of your flute sound. Your body connects to the flute to make music, so when you think about it, the musical instrument you're learning how to play is really your body *plus* the flute.

So take some time right now to work on your breathing. It'll make you into a better flutist, even before you pick up the instrument!

Breathing for flute playing

The good news is that you already know how to breathe. Your body breathes for you every day of your life, and it's been doing a pretty good job so far — I mean, you're still here, aren't you? Your breathing mechanism really is an amazing piece of engineering. It does an incredible amount of work every day just to keep oxygen in your system, and you never really even notice it. Breathing for flute playing is merely an extension of this natural system, though you will be training yourself to breathe much more deeply than you normally would. But if you master this part of it, you'll be well on your way to greatly improving your playing.

TIP

When you inhale to play the flute, your gut will quite naturally get bigger as your breathing mechanism expands. Just let it go — don't hold it in! You'll get more air that way. And you'll need lots of air to play the flute.

TECHNICAL STUFF

The muscles in your breathing mechanism

Your *diaphragm* is a large dome-shaped muscle, which, in its relaxed state, sits about two-thirds of the way down your rib cage. It goes all the way around your torso, front and back. As you inhale, the diaphragm contracts and moves downward, making room for the lungs to expand and get some air. As you exhale, the diaphragm goes back up into its relaxed state (see figure).

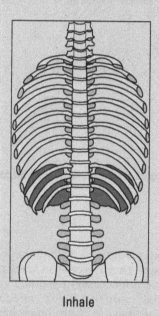 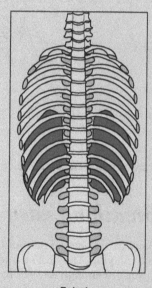

Inhale   Exhale

The *intercostals* are the muscles between your ribs. They expand as you inhale to help the ribcage move up and out, making room for the lungs. They contract as you exhale, which makes the ribs move in and down, helping the lungs push the air out. To get an idea about how your ribcage works, you can imagine the movement of an old-fashioned fireplace bellows (see figure).

If you've ever done crunches or sit-ups, I'm sure you're already familiar with your abdominal muscles. As you inhale, the abdominals expand to make room as the lungs fill with air, and as you exhale, they contract to help squeeze the air out. In order to breathe well, you need to be able to expand as well as contract your abs at will.

(continued)

(continued)

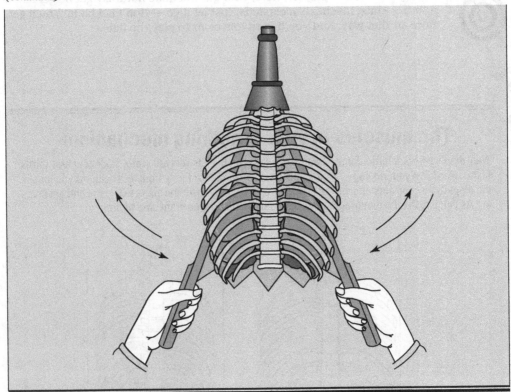

Breathing easy

Many people get all bent out of shape (literally) when they're breathing for flute playing. They tense body parts they never even knew they had trying to suck in enough air. Try to avoid unnecessary tension. Pay particular attention to your shoulders to make sure that they're not coming up as you breathe, which will only shrink the space in your upper chest and throat. You'll want to keep the air passageways as open as possible so that you can breathe efficiently.

Keep your neck and throat relaxed. Think about keeping the back of your neck long without tucking in the chin. Your head should feel like it's floating freely on top of your spine. Move your head up and down and side to side slowly and find the place where it feels like you're using the least amount of muscle power to keep your head erect.

In other words, lighten up, let your breathing mechanism do the work, and relax everything else.

Trying a simple breathing exercise

The purpose of a simple breathing exercise is to help you identify the breathing muscles and let you feel them working. The more aware you are of your breathing mechanism, the more you'll be able to isolate the muscles involved and take conscious control of them.

If you've ever watched dogs or cats breathe as they're enjoying a leisurely daytime nap, you've watched the breathing mechanism in action. Their ribs seem to just float in and out with each breath. Visualize and try to mimic this relaxed, rhythmic motion as you do the following exercise:

1. **Stand up.**

   Make sure that you're standing up straight and that you feel relaxed.

2. **Put your hands on your ribs, near the bottom of your rib cage.**

   Make sure that your hands are really sitting on your ribs so that you can feel them.

3. **Exhale slowly and completely.**

   Exhale as much as you possibly can. If you think you've gotten rid of all your air, try exhaling some more. The purpose of this step is to get all the air out of your lungs. As you're exhaling, feel the ribs moving in and down underneath your hands. After you've exhaled fully, immediately go on to the next step.

4. **Don't do anything; just let go.**

   Let your body do the inhaling for you. Your body already knows how to inhale; you just need to be the observer and notice what it's doing. As long as you relax the muscles in your torso, your rib cage will start expanding on its own.

5. **Repeat Steps 1 to 4 a couple of times.**

   Notice what's happening in your body each time. Feeling your ribs expand and contract helps you gain awareness of your breathing mechanism.

6. **With your hands still on your ribs, exhale quickly and forcefully.**

   Your ribs should rebound to inhale at about the same speed as you just exhaled.

7. **Continue to do a few more of these exhalation/inhalation sequences, alternating fast and slow.**

   On the slow ones, see just how far you can expand your ribs on the inhale; try to get as much air in as you can. You'll be amazed at how far your rib cage will expand if you keep your muscles relaxed, especially the muscles that make up your breathing mechanism. (For more on these muscles, see the sidebar "The muscles in your breathing mechanism.")

Circular breathing

Imagine playing a piece of music without ever having to take time out to breathe! *Circular breathing*, a specialized technique for woodwind instruments, enables the player to effectively inhale and exhale at the same time, creating the illusion of not breathing at all. Circular breathing is accomplished by puffing out stored air from the cheeks to make the sound while inhaling through the nose. A number of flutists have accomplished circular breathing, but learning it is a challenging and time-consuming process. A good how-to book is *Circular Breathing for Flute* by Robert Dick, published by Multiple Breath Music.

Try this exercise again when you're in line at the grocery store, at the bank, or at the movies. At the very least, you'll be entertaining people waiting in line behind you.

After you achieve an awareness of your breathing mechanism, you'll be able to practice breathing efficiently while you're playing the flute. All you've got to do is get out of the way and let your body breathe for you. You'll be consciously directing the speed and the volume of your air through the flute, but if you're using only the necessary muscles and not any misguided effort or undue tension, you'll be breathing well, and it'll make playing the flute much easier to learn.

Controlling your air with breath support

Supporting your breath has to do with managing your exhalation, the part of your breathing that actually makes the sound on the flute. Basically, you'll want to take absolute control of your air as you blow — that is, exhale slowly while engaging your breathing muscles. Using breath support may feel a little strange at first — you've been using your breathing muscles all your life, but probably not quite as intensely as will be required of you for flute playing. The bottom line is that you'll need to be proficient at controlling your exhalations so that you can use the appropriate amount of air for whatever music you're playing at the moment. Good breath support facilitates playing loudly and softly while controlling your pitch (see Chapter 15 for more on pitch and dynamics), and it contributes greatly to the consistency of your sound. Technical passages become easier as well when you have a nice, even air flow underneath your moving fingers.

To get the feel of good breath support:

1. **Spread your hands over your belly.**

    You should be able to feel both your abdominal muscles and your rib cage.

2. **Inhale as far as you can.**

3. **Exhale while saying a long, very loud "Ssssssssss."**

4. **As you're exhaling with a loud hiss, feel the breathing muscles engage.**

Because of the resistance created by the hissing, you'll be able to feel what the breathing muscles do when you're supporting your air. They should feel like they're doing something — it'll be almost a squeezing sensation in your belly. Don't get as tight as a drum, though; otherwise you won't be able to play expressively or fluidly. You want to be able to control your air, but in a flexible way. When you play the flute, you'll need to engage your muscles the same way you did in this exercise.

Stand Up Tall: Posture

Good posture is important in your daily life. Carrying yourself properly helps you avoid discomfort, pain, and even injury, and supports efficient functioning of all the body's systems. In flute playing, you'll be pushing certain parts of your body to perform at peak levels. Therefore, how you use your body while you're playing can either help you or hold you back.

When your body is in proper alignment, all the things you need to do to play the flute become easier. Standing or sitting taller makes more room in your torso, so you can breathe more efficiently. With good body alignment enabling a relaxed neck and unconstrained, open throat you automatically produce a more beautiful sound. With the absence of excess tension, your finger technique is more fluid. I have seen countless students dramatically improve their flute playing simply by correcting their body position. Give yourself the advantage of good body alignment from the very beginning, and you'll be starting off ahead of the game!

Body alignment

Good posture is really nothing more than putting your body in a position to work at its best, in effect setting yourself up physically to be able to perform at a high level for often long periods of time. Personally, I don't like using the word *posture,* because when people start thinking about their own posture, they usually start pulling their shoulders back, sticking their chests out, and sucking their bellies in. But pulling, pushing, and forcing isn't really what efficient use of your body is all about.

A pioneer of the study of body mechanics, F.M. Alexander, coined the term *mechanical advantage,* which is a more appropriate description of what most people would call good posture. Being in a position of mechanical advantage means that your head, neck, shoulders, and spine are in proper alignment, and that your torso is balanced comfortably over your hips, as you can see in Figure 5-1. Because only minimal muscular effort is required for this state of equilibrium, your body is ready for any task you might set for it — for as long as necessary — and will be ready at a moment's notice to move easily, fluidly, and rapidly in any direction.

Your body already knows how to carry itself naturally. Unfortunately, most people get in the way of their body's built-in alignment mechanism. Many people end up tilting the head and chin upward as the back of the neck shortens, which creates a chain reaction in the rest of the body to give in to gravity and pull downward as well. Effectively, other parts of the body over-compensate for the poor balance created by the shortening of the neck and the tilting back of the head. The rib cage moves back and down, obstructing the airways, the shoulders hunch upward, the hips move forward, further distorting the breathing mechanism, and the small of the back tightens. The pattern usually looks something like what you see in Figure 5-2.

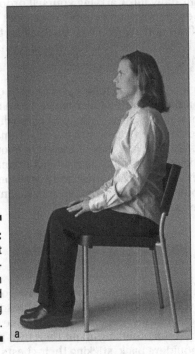 

Figure 5-1:
Correct body align-ment in sitting and standing positions.

The Alexander Technique

F.M. Alexander (1869–1955) developed *The Alexander Technique* over a number of years as a method of studying and perfecting what he called "the use of the self." A Shakespearian orator, Alexander began his studies as a direct result of losing his voice due to overuse and strain. He was certain that, through self-exploration of his own body mechanics, he could discover those physical factors — body tension under stress, lack of balance, poor body alignment, compacting of the neck, head and shoulders — that were contributing to his vocal difficulties and find ways to correct them. As a result, he not only was able to self-correct those things in his carriage that were contributing to the loss of his voice, he was also able to identify a way of training others that afforded them a "mechanical advantage" across a wide range of physical pursuits.

Athletes, musicians, dancers, stage actors — thousands have discovered ways to better prepare for their endeavors by adopting F.M. Alexander's techniques. Fans of The Alexander Technique include famous flutists Sir James Galway and William Bennett. To find out more about The Alexander Technique, go to www.alexandertechnique.com. Other helpful body alignment methods that have been influenced by The Alexander Technique include *Body Mapping* (www.bodymap.org) or check out the book *Body Mapping for Flutists* by Lea Pearson, DMA, (GIA Publications), and the *Feldenkrais Method* (www.feldenkrais.com).

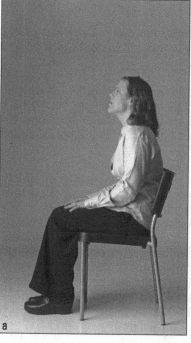

Figure 5-2: Downward pull results in poor posture, whether you are sitting or standing.

a

b

Instead of giving in to the pattern of downward pull, you can relax and lengthen the back of your neck, creating a chain reaction of good balance and thereby achieving a position of mechanical advantage.

Here are a few guidelines for achieving mechanical advantage. They apply whether you're sitting or standing.

- Relax and lengthen the back of your neck.

- Moving your head forward and backward, find the place where it feels like you're using the least amount of effort to hold it up.

- Extend the sensation of length through to your spine. Feel your back lengthening and widening.

- Move your shoulders to the front and to the back. Find a place where you're using the least amount of muscular effort. You should find it right about in the center, where your shoulders are in line with your neck.

- Relax your hip bones. Like the shoulders, you can move them front to back and find that place of balance. When they're in a good place, you won't feel tight in your low back or low abs.

- Imagine that you're a puppet dangling from a string attached at the top of your head. Allow your body to fall into place from the top.

- Check yourself in the mirror. Look at yourself in profile to see that your spine is straight, your shoulders are in line with your torso, and your neck is nice and long.

- As you move, try to come from a place of balance and ease. Don't start shortening muscles, especially those in the back of your neck and spine, to execute the task at hand.

All this being said, it's a tall order to maintain excellent body mechanics while you're learning a new skill like playing the flute. No matter how conscientious you are, you're bound to tense up or slouch from time to time. Just check in with the mirror periodically to monitor your neck, shoulder, and torso alignment.

Take a look at your favorite musicians, dancers, actors, or athletes. You'll see that the ones who are at the top of their respective fields are invariably the ones who make it look easy. This apparent ease comes about as a result of using their bodies well. They usually have great body alignment — watch for a long, relaxed neck in particular. You won't find elite performers or athletes with unnecessary tension — their energy goes right into the task at hand without any wasted effort. You can approach your flute-playing sessions exactly the same way, which will virtually guarantee good results right from the start. In fact, thinking of yourself as an athlete — visualizing it and applying the same self-awareness and self-discipline that an athlete brings to his sport — will greatly help you as a musician.

A flutist's body position

The flute brings with it a unique set of challenges. It's the only instrument in the woodwind family that is held off to the right side of the player instead of vertically. Human bodies are built more or less symmetrically, so playing a side-blown instrument like the flute can feel awkward, unwieldy, and downright uncomfortable. To manage the instrument comfortably, you have to stay relaxed and work to the best of your ability to preserve the integrity of your body alignment and overall balance while at the same time managing to hold a three-pound piece of metal to one side for long stretches of playing.

If you try sitting or standing with your body facing forward while playing the flute, you'll find that your chest, shoulders, and elbows will feel like they're crowded and cramped.

Here's a step-by-step overview to help you better manage your body position and alignment:

1. **Grab a straight-back chair and sit down in front of a mirror.**

   The chair (and you) should be facing the mirror straight-on.

2. **Put your hands up to the right side of your body at shoulder level as though you're playing the flute, with your left hand hovering not far from your right shoulder and your right hand off to your right side.**

   Notice how your chest, shoulders, and arms feel in this position — your left arm has to cross closely over your chest to get to your imaginary flute, so your upper torso will likely feel a bit constricted.

3. **Now move the chair, angling it slightly to the right.**

4. **Put your hands up into flute-playing position again, as in Step 2, with your body facing in the same direction as the chair.**

5. **Twist your torso slightly to the left so that your upper body is now facing the mirror again.**

   Start the twisting movement from the lowest part of the spine so that you're distributing the effort throughout the torso and you're not just working from the shoulders. Remember to keep the back of your neck and your spine relaxed and long. Notice that this adjustment helps open up the chest, shoulders, and arms — it should help your flute playing position feel a lot more comfortable.

6. **Get rid of the chair and repeat Steps 1 through 5 while in a standing position.**

   Without the chair, you start facing the mirror and then assume the flute-playing position. Then you angle your full body slightly off to the right, and while still pointing your toes right, you twist the upper body slightly to the left, maintaining length in your neck and spine.

This process really opens up your torso area and can help you get comfortable with playing your flute. Pretty soon, you'll arrive into your flute-playing position (see Figure 5-3) without having to think about all the steps. Just think about angling the feet slightly to the right while you move the upper body to the left, just enough to open up the chest and get the elbows slightly away from your sides.

Pay attention to your elbows. They shouldn't be scrunching in to your sides, constricting your breathing, but you don't want them held so high away from your body that it puts a strain on your shoulders.

Figure 5-3:
Correct
sitting and
standing
positions for
flute
playing.

a   b

Hold the flute in an approximately horizontal position. It doesn't need to be absolutely parallel to the ground (unless you're playing in a marching band), but you don't want it migrating downward until your head has to dip sideways to compensate, either.

When you bring the flute up to your face to play, do exactly that. Don't bring your face to the flute, or you'll end up shortening the back of your neck as you thrust your head forward. Just leave your body in its most comfortable, aligned position, with the back of your neck long and relaxed, and bring the flute up to you.

Chapter 6

Making Flute Sounds

In This Chapter

▶ Creating flute sounds without a flute

▶ Using your flute's headjoint to make flute sounds

▶ Making a playable mini-flute out of your flute's headjoint and footjoint

H ere's where the fun begins. In this chapter, you make your first flute sounds, but you don't even need a flute to get started. The flute's headjoint comes into play (literally), but you still don't need to worry about keys or fingerings. And later in the chapter, it really starts to be play time. Attaching the footjoint to the end of the headjoint adds just a few keys to the mix, to give you the capability to actually play a few notes without adding the entire complement of keys and levers to your repertoire just yet.

Making a Flute Sound — No Flute Required!

An embouchure is a fancy French word for what you do with your lips when you play the flute. It comes from *bouche,* the French word for "mouth." All woodwind and brass instruments require the use of an embouchure — without which the player would not be able make a single sound.

Making sounds by blowing across the top of a bottle is a simple, non-intimidating way to start forming an embouchure for flute playing.

You may have tried the following exercise at some point in your life. If you haven't (or even if you have), it's a quick and easy way to illustrate the basics of embouchure, affording you an opportunity to begin creating flute sounds without even getting the flute out of the case.

1. **Get a glass bottle with a narrow neck.**

   If you don't have one in the house, you can purchase a drink at your nearest grocery store, and use the bottle from that. Just make sure that it comes in an old-fashioned glass cola bottle or any other narrow-necked glass bottle — those will be the easiest kind to get a sound out of. Start with the bottle about half to two-thirds full of a drinkable liquid.

2. **Pick up the bottle and place your bottom lip on the edge of the opening.**

   Place the very top of the bottle opening right around where your bottom lip stops — that is, where the red part of your bottom lip ends and the flesh color of your chin area begins.

3. **Close your lips.**

   Don't smile or frown. You want to keep your lips in a fairly natural position as you go on to the next step.

4. **Part your lips slightly and take a full breath.**

5. **Blow some air across the top of the bottle to make a sound (see Figure 6-1).**

Figure 6-1:
Sounding off
on a bottle.

The object is to aim your air so that it hits the opposite edge of the bottle from where your bottom lip is perched. Don't actually blow *into* the bottle, but across the mouth of it. If you don't get a sound right away, don't despair. Try one or all of the following tips:

- Try moving the bottom of the bottle away from you and toward you as you blow, which will adjust the angle of the air. When/if you get a sound, keep holding the bottle in that position.

- Adjust the speed of your air. Imagine a lit candle right in front of you. Think of blowing your air toward the imaginary flame — just enough to make it flicker and move, but not enough to blow out the candle. Using the candle imagery should give you the right amount of air to make a sound.

- Move the top of the bottle ever so slightly lower on your lip. Blow some air. Then move it slightly higher and try again. Everyone has different lips, teeth, and mouth shapes, so it may take some trial and error to find the position that works for you.

- Experiment with jaw and lip position as you're blowing: Open your mouth slightly to drop your jaw and then close your mouth so that your top and bottom front teeth have only about 1/8-inch of space between them. As you move your jaw, your lips may open and close along with it, but try to control the size of the lip opening, or *aperture,* independently. Make the opening larger and smaller using your lip muscles and see what sort of difference it makes in the sound. Find the jaw and lip position that makes the clearest sound for you.

6. **Now take a few sips of your drink and repeat Steps 2 to 5.**

   Notice how the pitch of your bottle's sound has changed. You should be hearing a lower pitch now because you've just effectively made the resonating air space in the bottle bigger. Bigger instruments make lower sounds. (Think of a violin versus a string bass.) If you can't tell that the pitch is lower, take a few more sips and try again. (This step can be lots of fun, depending on your choice of beverage!)

7. **See whether you can get a higher pitch on the bottle by blowing differently.**

   Forcefully blowing a lot of air at once should make the pitch go higher. If it doesn't, try making the aperture smaller as in Step 5, which will help the air go even faster. See how many different pitches you can get out of your bottle.

Playing the Headjoint by Itself

If you're comfortable with making sounds on a bottle (see preceding section), you're ready to start playing on your flute's headjoint. The advantage of playing on the headjoint by itself at this stage is that you don't have to worry about your hand position or fingerings. You can focus on what you're doing with your lips, jaw, mouth, and air. Once you're satisfied and making some semblance of an actual flute sound, you can experiment with controlling your air. In this way, you'll set a good foundation—get your embouchure where it needs to be—before you begin to work on other things.

For your own sanity, don't try the exercises in the following sections until you're comfortable with getting a sound out of your bottle (see preceding section).

Making your first sounds

Your first sounds on the headjoint are a lot like getting your first sound out of a bottle. (See the section "Making a Flute Sound — No Flute Required!") The only real difference is that with the headjoint, you get to rest your lower lip and chin on the lip plate.

Before you begin these steps, familiarize yourself with your flute case to make sure that you always open it right side up. You don't want your flute falling out of the case when you open it.

Keep a mirror handy while you do the following steps so that you can see what you're doing rather than just feel it.

1. **Open your flute case and take out your headjoint.**

   Notice that the lip plate is larger on one side of the embouchure hole than the other.

2. **Place the larger side of the lip plate right up against your lower lip and chin.**

   The end of the headjoint will be on your right. You should feel the edge of the embouchure hole right where the red part of your lower lip meets the flesh-colored chin area. Your lip should cover approximately one-third to half of the embouchure hole, depending on what works best for you.

   Covering more than half the embouchure hole will give you a constricted sound down the road, so check yourself in the mirror.

3. **Close your lips.**

Don't smile or frown. You want to keep your lips in a fairly natural position as you go on to the next step.

4. **Part your lips slightly and take a full breath.**

5. **Blow some air across the embouchure hole to make a sound (see Figure 6-2).**

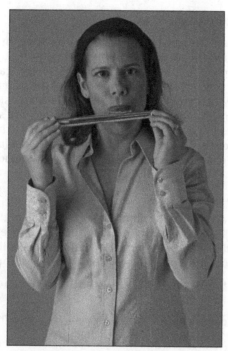

Figure 6-2:
Playing on the head-joint.

The object is to aim your air so that it hits the opposite edge of the embouchure hole from where your bottom lip is perched. Go on to the next steps whether or not you're getting a sound out of the headjoint at this point.

6. **Adjust your air speed.**

Imagine that lit candle right in front of you. To get the right air speed going, think of blowing your air toward the imaginary flame — just enough to make it flicker and move, but not enough to blow out the candle.

Now, to see how air speed affects sound, follow these two steps to experience a couple of different ways to vary your air speed.

a. Increase or decrease the amount of air coming out through your lips by blowing more or less air.

Try a few different speeds. See how the sound and pitch is affected when you blow as hard as possible as compared to when you're using hardly any air at all. Settle on a happy medium, where the sound is at its fullest, but without a lot of extraneous air noise around it.

b. Make your aperture larger or smaller.

When you decrease the size of your aperture by bringing your lips closer together, the air speed changes. Think of a garden hose: When you pinch off the opening of the hose, the water has a smaller space to travel through, so the speed of the water is faster as it comes out. When you release the pinch, the water slows down again. As you blow, try making your aperture larger and smaller by using the muscles in your lips. Notice what happens to the sound and the pitch at each stage. See whether you can find a favorite size for your aperture, where you're getting a clear sound out of the headjoint.

7. Adjust your air angle.

You can vary your air angle in a few different ways. Try all of them in the following order. Don't be afraid to experiment. Notice how every movement affects the sound in some way. Trying out all the possibilities will help you find the embouchure placements which work best for you.

a. Use your hands to roll the headjoint away from you and back toward you.

This action also causes your lips to cover and uncover the embouchure hole.

b. Move your head up and down.

Look up to angle the air up and uncover the embouchure hole and look down to angle the air down and cover the embouchure hole. Moving your head up and down will have the same effect as the rolling, but it's quicker and more efficient to maneuver this way, particularly later when you have an actual flute body attached to the headjoint.

c. Move your jaw and lips.

Movement of the jaw and lips is the most efficient and precise way of adjusting the air angle. You can try this movement without the headjoint first: Just hold your hand in front of you, palm facing you. Then blow a thin stream of air onto the middle of your palm. As you're blowing, bring your jaw back and down — this movement should make the airstream travel down to the bottom of your hand. Now bring the jaw forward and up — you should now feel the air travel up toward your fingertips. As the jaw moves, the lips follow: They go a little bit farther back as the jaw moves down, and they come forward as the jaw moves up.

Now try the same thing while blowing across the embouchure hole of the headjoint. This one takes a little practice, but it's worth it: Adjusting the air angle this way enables you to have very fine control over the airstream because the movements you're making are smaller and more exact than when you're rolling the headjoint around or moving your whole head up and down.

d. **Move the lip plate up and down on your chin in small increments.**

This action also slightly changes the angle of air in relation to the embouchure hole. By trying out different positions, you can find the placement that is the most comfortable for you and produces the best sound.

After experimenting with air speed and air angle, you should have a good idea about what works for you to produce a sound on the headjoint and what doesn't. Getting a consistent sound every time you pick up the headjoint may elude you for a while, but if you stay aware of what you're doing and keep practicing, finding your flute sound will become second nature. Don't get frustrated if you don't make a sound right away. Like anything else you do that requires muscle memory, your mind and body will help your embouchure become more consistent naturally over time.

If you have a *cupid's bow*, (sometimes also called a *teardrop*) which is a little fleshy part in the middle of your upper lip, you'll most likely have an asymmetrical embouchure. As you blow to make a flute sound, the extra flesh in the middle of your lip will move out of the way so that the air can come freely through the aperture. This off-center embouchure is okay and totally normal. Don't even try to center the aperture exactly in the middle of the lip.

Changing pitch on your headjoint

After you're relatively comfortable with making a sound on your headjoint, you can get creative and explore ways to move the pitch around, still working with the headjoint only.

In the preceding section, you can try a few different ways to adjust your air angle: rolling the flute in and out, moving your head up and down, and moving your jaw and lips forward and back. These actions help you find the best positioning to make a sound, but they also change the pitch. When your air angle goes up, the pitch gets higher as well; when the air angle moves downward, the pitch goes lower.

Try the following steps to change the pitch on the headjoint without changing your embouchure or using any of the flute's keys just yet.

In Track 1 on the CD, I demonstrate how both of these steps should sound.

1. **As you're playing a note on the headjoint, slowly slide your right index finger into the end of the headjoint and then pull it back out (see Figure 6-3).**

   As your finger moves up into the headjoint, the pitch goes up. Pulling the finger back out causes the pitch to lower again.

2. **As you're playing a note on the headjoint, place the palm of your right hand over the end of the headjoint (see Figure 6-3).**

   This action causes a sudden drop in pitch.

Go back and forth with the pitches a few times in the preceding steps so that you can get the feel of playing different pitches without moving your embouchure around.

Figure 6-3: Changing pitches on the headjoint.

Making a Mini-Flute

You can make a very short flute out of a flute's headjoint and footjoint without using the body. The footjoint has just a few keys, so a mini-flute is a great way to get the feel of making a flute sound and working some keys without having to deal with the entire instrument just yet.

To make your mini-flute:

1. **Grasp your headjoint with your left hand on the tube, between the embouchure hole and the tenon.**

2. **Grasp your footjoint with your right hand at the end, below the keys.**

3. **Fit the footjoint onto the headjoint with a gentle twist.**

   The row of keys should line up with the embouchure hole (see Figure 6-4). Don't worry about the one lonely key on the other side of the footjoint — it doesn't need to line up with anything.

   If the connection feels loose, put a small piece of adhesive tape on the headjoint tenon to tighten it so that the footjoint won't fall off.

Figure 6-4:
Fitting the
footjoint
onto the
headjoint.

This procedure works for most flutes, but every once in a while, you come across a footjoint socket that is too small to accommodate the headjoint. If your flute fits this description, you can't do much about it except to maybe borrow someone else's flute for this little exercise. Just don't try to force the footjoint on the headjoint if it doesn't easily fit. If you're not sure how it should fit, try sliding the headjoint into the flute's body at the barrel end. The degree of snugness between the headjoint and the barrel shows you how the correct fit should feel. The footjoint may feel a little bit more snug on the headjoint than the body does, but it shouldn't be too much tighter.

Discovering how the notes change

Take a look at your mini-flute. On the footjoint end, you have a couple of rectangular-looking keys. You also have one or two small cylindrical devices called *rollers*. None of these rollers have any holes under them. Their purpose is to operate the round keys that cover the holes — two or three of them on the top side (depending on whether you have a low C or low B footjoint), and one on the opposite side, off by itself. When you put the whole flute together with the body, the right-hand pinky operates the footjoint all by itself using the rectangular key and the rollers. But for now, just follow these steps:

1. **Grab the headjoint with your left hand below the lip plate, palm facing you.**

2. **Place your right-hand index finger on the first rectangular key.**

3. **Place your right-hand ring finger on the first round key.**

4. **Place your right-hand pinky on the second round key.**

   If you have a B footjoint, you will have a third round key, but you can just leave that one alone for now.

5. **Place your right-hand thumb underneath the tube to help support the footjoint.**

6. **Now put your lower lip on the lip plate and start playing notes; as you blow, operate the keys with your fingers and see what pitches you can get (see Figure 6-5).**

   Notice that covering holes with the keys effectively lengthens the tube and therefore lowers the pitch, and opening the holes effectively shortens the tube and therefore raises the pitch. Notice also that when you push on the rectangular key with your index finger, you're actually opening a hole, not closing one.

Figure 6-5:
Playing a
mini-flute.

Playing a tune on your mini-flute

After you're familiar with your mini-flute, it's time for a tune. And what better
tune to start with than "Mary Had a Little Lamb"?

Assigning numbers to the fingers that are operating the keys makes playing
this tune straightforward (see Figure 6-6):

Figure 6-6:
Diagram
of the
mini-flute
fingering
system.

✔ #0 means no fingers are active.

✔ #1 means that the right-hand index finger is down.

✔ #2 means that the right-hand ring finger is down.

✔ #3 means that the right-hand pinky is down.

So, "Mary Had a Little Lamb" (see Track 2 on the CD), in mini-flute notation, looks like

0–2–23–2–0–0–0–2–2–2–0–1–1–0–2–23–2–0–0–0–0–2–2–0–2–23

Have fun with your mini-flute and try a few simple tunes on your own. Just play with it! The more comfortable you get with this setup, the easier transitioning to the big flute will be.

Chapter 7

Putting It All Together: The Flute and You

*I*n this chapter, you really put it all together: your flute, that is! You discover how to assemble your flute properly and line it up correctly without disturbing the delicate mechanism of what is a most beautifully engineered instrument. And when you've had enough of the flute for one day, you find out how to disassemble the instrument and remove any moisture from the inside of it so that it'll be in good shape and ready to play the next time you take it out of the case. It's not as fragile as it looks, but a little care goes a long way toward keeping your flute looking — and sounding — like the world-class instrument it is.

You also explore how to hold the flute properly in order to play. Holding the flute is quite the balancing act, and not just because you hold it sideways. The rods also add weight to one side of the tube, giving it a tendency to want to roll toward you. But following the advice in the "Balancing the Flute" section of this chapter will keep you and your flute on an even keel. When you're ready to place your fingers on the keys, I show you where the *home keys* are, which is where your fingers will stay most of the time while you're playing. I address proper hand and wrist position as well so that you can avoid discomfort and overuse injury, the bane of many a musician.

Assembling Your Flute

If you're building good practice habits, you're getting your flute out of the case just about every day. So now is the time to take a close look at the best way to assemble your flute and align it properly.

When putting your flute together, always keep in mind that you want to touch the keys and rods as little as possible. Even the most well-built mechanism can go out of adjustment over time if it's grabbed and twisted improperly. All fine instruments need constant care and adjustment, but you can tell just by looking that the flute is in a class all by itself. If you're careful about where you put your hands as you assemble your flute, you'll incur far fewer unnecessary repair bills. (See Chapter 19 for more on flute repair and maintenance.)

To begin assembling your flute:

1. **Open your flute case.**

   Make sure that the case is upright when you open it so that your flute won't fall out. If your case is the molded plastic kind with visible latches, you can see that the latches close toward the top. This type of case also usually has carrying handles and the manufacturer's name printed on top of the case. If your case is French style, with no handle and hidden hinge closures, you can find the moveable parts that open the hinges on the bottom part of the case. The French style cases are usually rounded on top and flat on the bottom.

2. **Take the headjoint out of the case, grasping the tube between the lip plate and the tenon with your right hand.**

   To ensure a secure hold on the headjoint, your right hand should be in a fist position with the headjoint inside the fist.

3. **Take the body out of the case, grasping it by the barrel with your left hand, avoiding the posts, rods, and keys.**

   To ensure a secure hold on the body, your left hand should be in a fist position with the barrel inside the fist.

4. **Slide the headjoint tenon into the barrel, using a gentle twisting motion.**

   Be sure that you're feeding the headjoint into the barrel straight-on, not at an angle.

5. **Slide the headjoint all the way into the barrel until it stops and then pull the headjoint back out approximately ¼ inch.**

   Most manufacturers gauge their flutes to play best in tune when the headjoint is pulled out about ¼ inch, but the best place to put the head-joint can vary. With a new flute, seeing where that spot is can be difficult because the tenon will be new and shiny like the rest of the tube. But as you use your flute, the tenon will develop a patina, and you'll be able to see a line of demarcation between the tube and the tenon that will indicate where you should position your headjoint in relation to the tube.

After you put the headjoint on the body, be sure to always handle the flute by the barrel, not by the headjoint. If you lift the flute by grabbing the headjoint, you run the risk that the body will fall right off if the fit is even a little bit loose. And that's a chance I, for one, really don't want you to take!

6. **Go back to your case and take out the footjoint with your right hand, grasping it at the end (not the tenon), again avoiding the posts, rods, and keys.**

7. **Slide the tenon at the end of the body all the way into the footjoint socket, again using a gentle twisting motion (see Figure 7-1).**

   Be sure that you're feeding the tenon into the socket straight-on, not at an angle. (Remember, you're still handling the flute by the barrel with your left hand.)

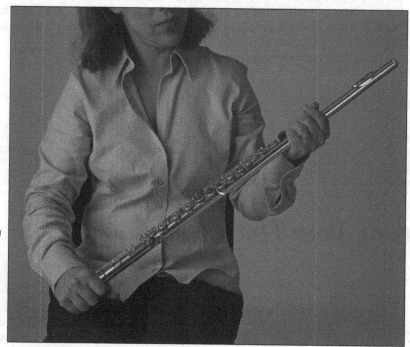

Figure 7-1:
Don't touch the keys as you're assembling your flute.

Lining Up the Keys, Posts, and Embouchure Hole

After you put your flute together, it's time to line up the keys, posts, and embouchure hole to make sure that everything is in place for you to play the flute efficiently, comfortably, and easily.

Here are the two things you need to do every time you assemble your flute:

✔ Line up the far edge of the embouchure hole (the side you don't put your lips on) with the outer edge of the first key on the flute's top line of keys — the one that's closest to and in line with the engraved company name on the barrel. I like to look down the length of the flute from the crown end to make sure that the headjoint is lined up properly. Some flutists prefer to look up from the footjoint end.

✔ Line up the rod on the footjoint with the middle of the keys on the body. Lining up the footjoint correctly is actually counterintuitive: Your first instinct will be to line up the footjoint's keys with the body's keys, because this looks more uniform. But if you line up keys with keys, your right-hand pinky has to stretch way too far to reach the D♯/E♭ key.

Your fully assembled flute should look like the flute in Figure 7-2.

Embouchure hole   First key   Footjoint rod

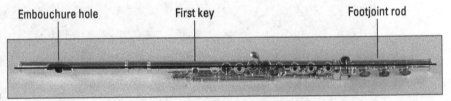

Figure 7-2: A correctly assembled flute.

Putting Your Flute Away

When you finish one of your many practice sessions, rehearsals, or performances, you'll want to be sure to put your flute away.

Don't be tempted to leave it out of the case overnight or for many hours at a time — the safest place for it is in the case. And developing the habit of cleaning it out every time you put it away will extend the time between overhauls. (See more on repair and overhauls in Chapter 19.)

As you play the flute, moisture accumulates on the inside of the instrument. If you play for a long enough duration, water even drips out the end of the flute. Contrary to popular belief, this moisture is condensation, not spit. It's the same phenomenon that occurs when sweat forms on the outside of a bottle of cold liquid on a hot day. The only difference with the flute is that the warm substance, your air, is on the inside of the tube, and the cooler air is on the outside — therefore the moisture collects on the inside. The more the temperature difference between the air outside and the air inside, the more condensation you get. So on a cold day, you're much more likely to get water dripping out the end of your flute and even sometimes forming bubbles between the pads and the tone holes.

Here's a list of reasons you don't want too much of that moisture building up on the inside of your flute:

- Moisture wears on the flute's pads, especially if they're traditional felt pads. Traditional pads absorb moisture and swell up as a result, which wreaks havoc on the seal between the pads and the tone holes, causing some funky-sounding notes.

- The new synthetic-based pads have less of a problem with absorbing moisture, but because they repel moisture, bubbles between the pads and the tone holes form more quickly. When you get such a water bubble, the flute acts as though that tone hole is covered; in other words, you may get a different pitch sounding from the flute than the one you're fingering.

- Even if it's not spit, water dripping out of the end of your instrument is just kind of gross, and if you're playing in an ensemble, you don't want to be dripping on your neighbor!

You should clean out the inside of your flute about every hour or so when you're practicing, and always before you put it away for the day.

Follow these steps to clean out your flute:

1. **Holding the barrel of the flute with the left hand and still avoiding the rods and keys, take the footjoint off of the body, using a gentle twisting motion.**

   Place the footjoint in the case for now.

2. **Still holding the flute by the barrel, take off the headjoint with a gentle twisting motion.**

   Place the headjoint and the body in the case for now.

3. **Find your cleaning rod, which should be in your flute case.**

   The cleaning rod looks like a large, very long sewing needle. Cleaning rods are made of metal, wood, or plastic. If yours is metal, consider buying a wood or plastic one — that way, you won't scratch the inside of your flute tube.

4. **Thread your cleaning cloth through the hole in the cleaning rod.**

   Put just a little bit of the cloth through the hole so that it won't bunch up as you're cleaning your flute. (For more about cleaning cloths, see Chapter 5).

5. **Pick up your footjoint and push the cleaning rod and cloth into it.**

   One pass back and forth should take care of any accumulated moisture. As you're cleaning, remember to avoid touching the rods and keys. When finished, place the footjoint back in the case.

6. **Clean out the body the same way you did the footjoint.**

   Handle the flute body by the barrel to avoid touching the rods and keys, as shown in Figure 7-3. If you have problems with the cleaning cloth bunching up and getting stuck in your flute, don't move it back and forth inside the body — just pass it straight through once and take it out from the other end. When finished, place the body back in the case.

7. **Wrap the cleaning cloth up and over the top of the cleaning rod.**

   The cloth should cover both the top and the sides of the cleaning rod.

Figure 7-3:
Cleaning out
your flute.

8. **Push the cleaning rod and cloth into the headjoint.**

   The cloth wrapped around the top end of the cleaning rod should pick up the moisture at the cork end of the headjoint. When finished, place the headjoint back in the case.

9. **Wipe off any fingerprints on the headjoint, body, and footjoint with your polishing cloth.**

   You can wipe off the keys by dabbing them gently, but be sure not to grab onto the keys as you handle the flute. (See Chapter 5 for more on polishing cloths.)

10. **As you return the headjoint, body, and footjoint into the case, check to make sure that all the parts fit snugly and securely in the case before you close it.**

    The manufacturer designed the wells in your case for the parts to fit into precisely in certain directions so that they don't get jostled when the case is carried. So be sure that you're putting the flute in the case exactly the same way each time.

Tiny bubbles: Cleaning your flute's pads

Your flute's pads don't need much in the way of daily maintenance if you clean your flute of moisture regularly and don't eat or drink a lot of sugary treats during your practice sessions. But when your pads do need a little help, pad papers, perm papers, or cigarette papers come in handy. (See more about purchasing them in Chapter 5.) These papers can help if you get a water bubble between a pad and a tone hole, or if you have a sticky pad.

It's pretty easy to tell if you have a water bubble: Suddenly, a note is coming out slightly lower than it should, or sometimes not coming out at all. If this problem occurs (and you know you've been using the correct fingering), look for the offending bubble by peering closely at your pads and tone holes. You may see a bubble or just a drop of water. Put a cigarette paper, perm paper, or a pad paper (without powder) in between the key and the tone hole and depress the key. Don't slide the paper out while the key is depressed — just lift the key and switch the paper so that a dry spot is under the pad and depress again. Keep switching out the paper until it comes out dry.

You know you have a sticky pad if your flute starts making noises that sound almost like smacking lips. Pad, perm, or cigarette papers can fix this dilemma, too. Follow the instructions for removing a water bubble. If the pad is still sticky, you can try gently pulling the paper out while the key is depressed (but don't do it too often, or you'll wear out the pads prematurely). For persistent stickiness, try powdered pad papers or a small amount of unscented talcum powder applied to the pad with a small, soft brush, such as a paintbrush or makeup brush. But use powdered pad papers or talcum powder only on isolated problem areas — don't use them to clean your pads as a matter of course. You don't want to have powder building up on your pads or in your mechanism.

Balancing the Flute

The flute is the only woodwind instrument that's held sideways, which brings with it certain balance challenges.

Take a look at your flute: The rods are on only one side of the tube, which means that when you hold the flute sideways, out to your right, gravity will pull those rods down and toward you. This gravitational pull can make the flute feel unstable and can therefore prevent your fingers from feeling free to move as needed on the keys because your hands are engaged in the ongoing battle of keeping the flute where it needs to be.

Gravitational pull on the rods also has another disadvantage. As the flute rolls toward you, the embouchure hole rolls toward your chin as well, which means that your lips start to cover the embouchure hole more and more. If the flute rolls toward you too much, it will have a negative impact on the sound you produce. (See Chapter 6 for more information on covering the embouchure hole.)

But never fear: Keeping the flute from rolling around is easier than it sounds. You just need to be aware of a few things when you pick up the flute to play. Take that, Isaac Newton!

Balancing act: The three key points

Every time you play your flute, you need to check in with the three specific points that connect you to the flute tube. These balancing points, shown in Figure 7-4, are indispensable for keeping the flute steady. Here are the three balance points:

- ✔ The place where your lips and chin make contact with the lip plate.
- ✔ The place where the base of your left-hand index finger makes contact with the flute tube, between the first two keys in the top line of keys on the flute.
- ✔ The place where your right-hand thumb makes contact with the flute tube. Your right thumb goes on the underside of the flute tube — counting up from the footjoint socket, it'll be right below the third key, or somewhere between the second and third key, whichever is more comfortable for you.

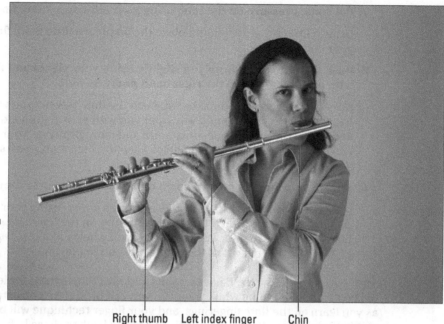

Figure 7-4:
The three
balance
points.

Right thumb   Left index finger   Chin

Follow these steps to familiarize yourself with the flute's three balance points:

1. **Assemble your flute and place it in your lap, with most of the keys facing you.**

2. **Slide your left hand underneath the flute tube, placing the top of your left-hand index finger between the first two keys you see on top of the flute (the keys lined up with the company name on the barrel).**

3. **Place the base of your index finger on the side of the tube, keeping it between those first two keys.**

   You can use your left-hand index finger to lift the flute slightly off your lap as you're completing the next steps.

4. **Count up three keys from the footjoint socket and place your right-hand thumb underneath the tube right at that point.**

5. **Now place your right-hand pinky on the D♯/E♭ key, which is the rectangular footjoint key closest to the body of the flute.**

   Let your fingers fall where they may on the flute's other keys for now, but don't grab the keys — these steps are about holding the flute using just these few balance points.

6. **With your left-hand index finger, right-hand thumb, and right-hand pinky on the flute as described in the previous steps, lift the flute and put the lip plate on your lower lip.**

7. **Put some pressure on the tube using your left-hand index finger.**

   Using a little pressure should place the lip plate a little more firmly on your chin.

8. **Push the flute away from you slightly using your right-hand thumb, with a little help from the right-hand pinky as well.**

   Notice the leverage action: As you push the flute toward you with your left-hand index finger, and away from you with your right-hand thumb and pinky, the lip plate anchors more and more firmly on your lower lip and chin. This leverage action helps keep the flute stable and secure as you play.

9. **Wiggle your fingers up and down on the keys, wherever they may fall.**

   Notice that your flute stays stable as long as you're using your balance points for leverage. Keep the gentle pressure on the left-hand index finger and right thumb. The right-hand pinky helps along as well: The D♯/E♭ key is down most of the time when you're playing.

After you get to know the balance points and how to use them for leverage to keep your flute stable while you play, you can produce a consistent sound as you learn all the flute fingerings, and your finger technique will be nice and fluid right from the beginning. Keep coming back to these balance points whenever you pick up your flute, and you'll make a lot of things easier for yourself where flute playing is concerned. Like everything else, remembering your balance points will become second nature to you as you progress through your daily practice routine.

A little help: Some gadgets to consider

You may wonder why I didn't list four balance points instead of three because your right-hand pinky helps out with balancing the flute. The reason I don't include the right-hand pinky on the D♯/E♭ key as a balance point is that sometimes your pinky is down on that key, which is most of the time, but sometimes it can be up, or it can be working the other footjoint keys. So you can't always count on that right-hand pinky to help you balance.

Unfortunately, the right-hand pinky not always being depressed creates a flaw in the flute's balancing act because using just the chin, left-hand index finger, and right thumb without the right-hand pinky can actually destabilize the flute. There is nothing all that substantial for the right-hand thumb to grab onto on the cylindrical flute tube. Try the balance points steps in the previous section without putting your right hand pinky down, and you'll find that the flute tends to roll toward you, even with the three balance points in place. Usually, when the right-hand pinky is not on any of the footjoint keys, the other fingers are depressing the other keys, so the balance shifts slightly. However, the flute's balance is still not ideal because the shifting balance can still lead to instability.

TIP

If the thumb had something to rest against to keep it from sliding around, it would release the right-hand pinky from the job of balancing the flute and would create a preferable situation for balance overall. External gadgets for the right-hand thumb provide just such a resting spot. A couple of these thumb helpers are on the market, but my personal favorite is called the Thumbport (available from music retailers — more information at www. thumbport.com). The Thumbport, shown in Figure 7-5, snaps onto the right-hand thumb area of the flute tube without scratching it and provides an adjustable lever to promote thumb stability. You can install or remove it in seconds without any damage to the instrument, so it's a commitment-free thing to try. The Thumbport can be helpful whether you're a beginner (to keep the flute from rolling) or a professional flutist (to alleviate discomfort and improve technique).

Figure 7-5:
The
Thumbport
balancing
aid.

Finding the Correct Hand and Wrist Position

When you're comfortably and securely holding the flute using your balance points (see preceding section), your fingers can float freely up and down on top of the keys without gripping them. Keeping the hands and wrists in a relatively natural position is a challenge when playing the flute. After all, your body wasn't exactly built to hold a metal tube out to your right side for hours at a time. But making your flute-playing experience as comfortable and relaxed as possible is the key to endurance and excellence in your flute playing.

As you practice holding the flute using the three balance points (see preceding section) and start placing your fingers on the flute's home keys, you need to make sure that your wrists stay in as neutral a position as possible. Try not to bend your wrists more than you have to — your hands should be roughly in line with your forearms, as shown in Figure 7-6. If you're making a sharp angle between your hands and wrists, you're setting yourself up for undue tension, discomfort, and possibly even overuse injury. So keep checking your wrists to make sure that you're not tilting them any more than necessary. (The Thumbport, which I describe in the previous section, can help to keep the right wrist neutral; it may be an option for you if your right wrist has a tendency to cave in, creating a sharp angle between your right hand and forearm.)

Don't put too much pressure on your flute's keys. A light touch should be all that's needed to get the notes to sound. If you have to push really hard to get a good, solid note, your flute may be in need of adjustment. (See Chapter 19 for more information on flute repair and maintenance.) Traditional felt pads usually require a slightly heavier touch than the newer synthetic-based pads, but should still seal over the tone holes easily without a lot of pressure.

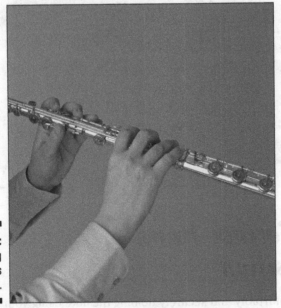

Figure 7-6:
Keeping
the wrists
neutral.

Overuse injury

If you have undue tension in your hands, wrists, or arms when you play, you're setting yourself up for fatigue and overuse injury over time. The most common localized ailments affecting flutists are

✔ **Carpal tunnel syndrome:** The *carpal tunnel* is a passageway inside your wrist that wraps around a main nerve and around the tendons that bend your fingers. If the passageway becomes inflamed, it puts pressure on the nerve and tendons and eventually causes numbness, pain, and finger weakness. Treatments include splints, anti-inflammatory or steroidal medications, or even surgery.

✔ **Tendonitis:** Flutists can experience pain and tenderness in the hand and wrist area as a result of tendon inflammation caused by overuse. Home treatments, such as ice, rest, and over-the-counter pain medications, often suffice to treat tendonitis. However, in extreme cases, corticosteroid medications, surgery, and physical therapy become necessary.

So pay attention to your hands, wrists, and body alignment (more on body alignment in Chapter 5). Practicing good habits now may save you some pain and doctor visits down the road!

Keep your fingers hovering close to the keys and don't let them fly up as you play. Fingers that are close to the keys are poised for action and ready to play any note. Beginners especially have a tendency to point the fingers that aren't engaged in depressing the keys high up into the air. Depending on which finger is flailing, you may even be inadvertently making an impolite gesture. Don't let this mistake happen to you, especially if you're playing in an ensemble with a conductor!

Keeping your fingers efficient, light, and fluid by practicing good hand and finger position as you play sets you up for good technique and many years of tension-free flute-playing enjoyment.

Home Keys: Knowing Where to Put Your Fingers

In order to start playing your flute, you need to know which keys are the home keys on the flute. If you've ever taken a typing class, you'll find that the home keys on the flute are much like those on a computer keyboard: Your fingers stay on them unless they have a good reason to move somewhere else. Unlike on the computer keyboard, though, you operate only some of the flute's many keys directly. When you pick up the flute, finding your balance points and your home keys will get to be second nature.

To find your flute's home keys, follow these steps:

1. **Assemble your flute and find your balance points as described in the "Balancing act: The three key points" section, earlier in this chapter, but don't lift the flute up to your face just yet.**

   The only balance point you're *not* finding at this point is the one on your chin.

2. **Lift the flute up to about chest level and then rest the bottom of the footjoint on your lap.**

   Your flute should now be vertical instead of horizontal, and your lap should be holding the flute right where you can see the keys as you're working with them. Make sure that the base of your left-hand index finger, as well as your right-hand thumb and pinky, are in their proper flute balancing positions.

3. **Look at the row of keys that line up with the embouchure hole and the engraved company name on the barrel; place the pad of your left-hand index finger on the second key down from the barrel.**

4. **Skip a key, and place the pad of your left-hand middle finger on the fourth key down from the barrel.**

5. **Place the pad of your left-hand ring finger on the next key, the fifth key down from the barrel.**

6. **Put your left-hand pinky on the little protruding key right next to where you just put your ring finger.**

   This key is called the G♯ key, and it's actually a lever. When you press it, it lifts a key that opens up a tone hole on the other side of the flute tube. It works the same way as the D♯/E♭ key on the footjoint.

7. **Place your left-hand thumb on the long key on the underside of the flute tube.**

   This key is called the thumb key (go figure!). The home placement on the thumb key is on the longest key only, not on the shorter key on top and to the left, which makes both thumb keys go down. Your thumb should only be depressing one key.

8. **Take a look at the footjoint and make sure that your right-hand pinky is still on the D♯/E♭ key.**

9. **On the flute body, place the pad of your right-hand ring finger on the key right next to the D♯/E♭ key.**

10. **Moving up the flute body and not skipping any keys, place the pads of your right-hand middle and index fingers on the next two keys.**

    Disregard the tiny levers between the keys, which are called *trill keys.* (I cover trills in Chapter 16.)

To help you decipher fingerings, remember the numbering system in Table 7-1 for the flute's home keys. Flute fingering charts usually use this system, and I refer to it in this book as well.

Table 7-1	Numbering System for the Flute's Home Keys
Finger	*Abbreviation*
Left-hand thumb	TH
Left-hand index finger	LH 1
Left-hand middle finger	LH 2
Left-hand ring finger	LH 3
Left-hand pinky (G♯ key)	LH 4
Right-hand index finger	RH 1
Right-hand middle finger	RH 2
Right-hand ring finger	RH 3
Right-hand pinky (D♯/E♭ key)	RH 4

Figure 7-7 summarizes everything you need to know about the flute's home keys.

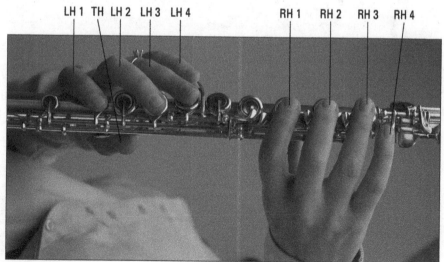

Figure 7-7: The flute's home keys.

Chapter 8

Playing Your First Notes

After you establish a good foundation with posture, breathing, and a basic embouchure (see Chapters 5 and 6), and you're comfortable holding and balancing the flute with a good hand position on the home keys (see Chapter 7), you're ready to make some music. In this chapter, I take you through your first notes on the flute. I start with relatively low notes, which are easy to produce with a beginner's embouchure. They also tend to be among the notes that feel pretty secure under your fingers, so you shouldn't have too much trouble balancing the flute at this point.

Before I get into the fingerings for those new notes, though, I talk about the embouchure so that you can steadily improve your sound as you embark on playing your first melodies.

Paying Lip Service: The Embouchure

No matter what your level of playing, you need to think about and work on your embouchure so that you can produce your very best sound on the flute. The tiny muscles in your lips adapt and strengthen as you play, so your embouchure is always evolving.

Listen to yourself carefully and be aware of how your lips are directing your air so that you support good embouchure formation. Being aware of your airstream and embouchure will ensure that you have a beautiful, consistent sound no matter what level or type of music you end up tackling from this point on. So keep your embouchure at the top of your list of things to concentrate on as you practice your first notes. (For more on the embouchure, see Chapter 6.)

Job 1: Directing the air

Just as a pianist's keys are his direct connection to his instrument, and just as the guitarist's fingertips connect the player to the strings and frets of that instrument, your lips are your first and most intimate connection to the flute. A kiss wouldn't be a kiss without your lips. Nor can you overlook the importance your lips have in your flute playing: They make the air go in the right direction to get the sound you want out of the instrument.

Playing notes on the flute is exactly like playing on the headjoint by itself or on the mini-flute (described in Chapter 6), only with a longer tube, of course. Adding length to the tube also adds the challenge of holding and balancing the flute, and using correct hand position (see Chapter 7). The steadier you hold the flute, the more precise control you will have over your embouchure, because moving around extraneously affects the direction of your airstream into the flute, and thus your sound.

Always remember that the lips' job is to direct the air where you want it to go. The air that you're exhaling is what makes the sound on the flute, not your lips. Therefore, having a lot of tension in your lips won't make the sound better: If your aperture is too small, you just end up blocking the air with your lips or pinching the air so tight that the air will be going too fast, and you'll actually lose more control than you gain.

As you work on sounding your first notes, keep experimenting with the speed and direction of your air (see the headjoint-only exercise in Chapter 6). Work on finding the embouchure position that works best for you— your sweet spot, as it were, where your sound is clear and feels easy to produce. When you find it, let that place be your embouchure's home base and work on familiarizing yourself with its feel and location in order to get the most out of your playing.

Finding the edge: Splitting the air

Your embouchure's job is to split the air across the edge of the embouchure hole. Although you can't take a real measurement on the air as it hits the edge of the embouchure hole, think of your airstream splitting in half: 50 percent of the air goes down into the embouchure hole, and 50 percent goes across the top of the hole (see Figure 8-1). Visualizing the air splitting this way is helpful when you're working on finding a home base for your embouchure. In practice, the percentage of air going into versus across the embouchure hole will vary according to how softly or loudly you're playing and indeed will differ slightly for every flutist, as determined by such factors as facial features, playing style, and preferred type of sound.

Figure 8-1:
Splitting
the air to
make a flute
sound.

After you think about splitting the air vertically, also consider what your air is doing from one side of the embouchure to the other. Your aperture should be just the right width to focus your air toward the middle of the embouchure hole. You don't want to be wasting your air by having it hit on either side of the hole, where it will just make an extraneous hissing noise instead of contributing to your flute sound.

Think of keeping your air focused toward the middle of the embouchure hole, and your lip muscles will respond by guiding the air in the right direction for you. I can't stress it enough — and if I say it once, I'll say it a thousand times — while all these details about guiding your airstream may seem like a lot of information to be absorbing, your embouchure will become second nature if you incorporate the proper elements into a regular, comprehensive, and efficient practice schedule.

Playing Your First Notes

It's time to play! Get ready for your first notes — just assemble your flute (see Chapter 7), and you're on your way.

In this section, you start with notes that you produce with a relaxed embouchure and that have easy-to-remember fingerings. These fingerings are the most logical ones on the instrument: with each successive key you depress, you get a lower note. On all the notes in this section, you have enough of the flute's keys depressed so that you shouldn't run into any major issues with keeping the instrument balanced. But make sure that you're observing the balance points I cover in Chapter 7 to hold the flute; that way, you develop good habits, and you'll cruise through the more challenging fingerings when you get to them.

It's in the B, A, G!

The fingerings for the notes B, A, and G use mainly your left hand (LH: TH, 1, 2, and 3). The only right-hand finger that needs to be down for these notes is your pinky (RH 4). Try out the fingerings in Figure 8-2.

The fingering chart diagrams in this chapter represent the home keys on the flute. When you see an outlined key, the finger that works that key should be up and hovering just over that key. Put the fingers down for the keys filled in with black. (I number each finger placement according to the numbered home keys in Chapter 7 so that you know which finger to use to depress which key.)

Just use your natural exhalation — called a *breath attack* — to play the notes. Exhale gently but firmly. It should feel like you're saying, "Ah" on each note, but instead of voicing the syllable, you blow it with your lips poised at the ready on the lip plate of your flute. You don't need to use your tongue to attack the notes yet, so you can just concentrate on the fingerings.

Feeling dizzy?

After a few verses of "Mary Had a Little Lamb," you may find that you begin getting dizzy. Don't worry; you're just hyperventilating. *Hyperventilating* means that you're breathing so fast that you're losing carbon dioxide from your blood, which causes a lightheaded sensation. It's a normal part of the process of learning how to play the flute. Just take a little break and try again. As you learn to use your air more efficiently, the dizziness will subside. (But honestly, even after playing the flute for a few decades, I'm still accused of being a bit "dizzy" from time to time!)

Use a breath attack to play "Mary Had a Little Lamb," using the music in Figure 8-3.

Track 3

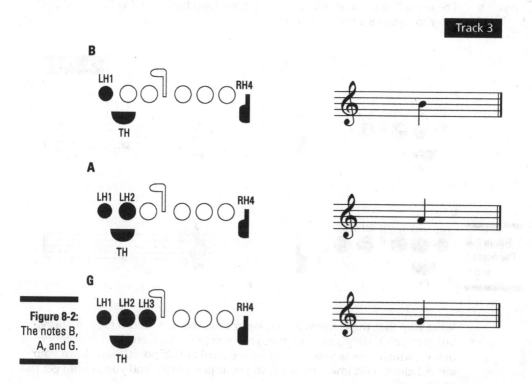

Figure 8-2: The notes B, A, and G.

Tracks 4 & 5

Mary Had a Little Lamb

Traditional
arr. Moratz/Giebler

Figure 8-3: "Mary Had a Little Lamb."

F and E

The notes F and E start incorporating your right hand, adding RH 1 and 2. Refer to Figure 8-4 for the fingerings.

Track 6

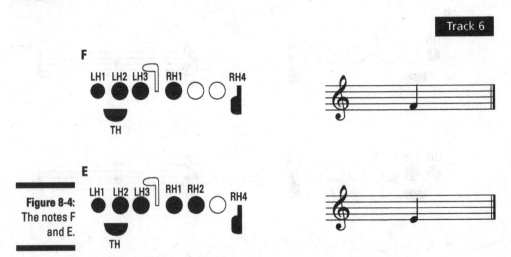

Figure 8-4:
The notes F
and E.

Make sure that these notes sound *lower* than the B, A, and G (see the previous section). If they sound higher, you're playing the F and E in the higher octave, which means you're blowing too hard at this point. Slow down your air and aim it a bit lower by dropping your jaw a little, and you should get the lower octave.

As you start depressing more keys, effectively lengthening the flute tube, you'll notice that the notes don't want to come out quite as easily — you may notice a delay between your exhalation and the note actually sounding. Meeting the challenge of these more resistant notes is a great opportunity to think about controlling your breathing. If you use smooth, even breaths, you'll get a better response as the notes get lower. This phenomenon will also improve over time as you begin to garner more and more control of your air and your flute. Remember, your body is an instrument, too, one that is played in conjunction with the flute in your hands.

Try the exercise in Figure 8-5. Use a breath attack to start the F and then slur smoothly into the E without stopping the air. There shouldn't be any sort of gap between the notes — just put down RH2 as you're playing the F, and that'll effectively slur you into the E. (For more on slurring, see Chapter 10.) In the next part of the exercise, separate the E and the F, breathing in between and using breath attacks on both.

Figure 8-5:
Trying out F
and E.

Play the melody in Figure 8-6 to start getting around all the notes you've tackled in this section. Slur where it's indicated and use breath attacks where the notes are separated.

Tracks 7 & 8

Figure 8-6:
Getting
around the
notes B, A,
G, F, and E.

Don't forget about your breathing! When concentrating on doing many things at once, such as reading a fingering chart, holding the flute, reading music, and counting out rhythms at the same time, most people have the tendency to take shallow breaths or even forget to breathe at all, which is pretty counterproductive, considering that you need your air to make the sound on your flute. Keep inhaling deeply and controlling your exhalations and also remember that your posture affects your breathing (see Chapter 5 for details). You'll get much better results that way.

Low D

The low D is the only note in this chapter that doesn't use RH4, your right-hand pinky. Although you usually need your pinky for balance (unless you're using a Thumbport as I describe in Chapter 7), the flute won't roll back toward you in this case, because most of your other fingers are down on this note and will help you keep the flute stable.

ON THE CD

Refer to the fingering chart in Figure 8-7 and try playing a D.

Track 9

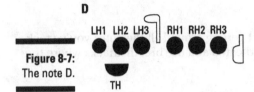

Figure 8-7:
The note D.

Because most of your fingers are down, the low D is the most resistant note you play in this chapter. If you can't get it to speak easily with a breath attack, try slurring into it gradually from the notes just above it and then try playing the D by itself again, as in Figure 8-8. Be sure that you take a big breath before you start this exercise, because you'll be slurring a few notes together without taking a breath. Use a slow, controlled air stream.

Figure 8-8:
Slurring into
the note D.

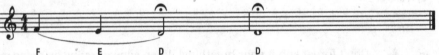

If your D sounds a lot higher than it should, you've inadvertently jumped to the next octave, which means that either your air speed is too fast, your air angle is too high, or both. Slow down and control your air so that you get an even air stream and try angling your air a little lower by dropping your jaw just a bit. Controlling your air and adjusting the air angle downward should give you the low D you're looking for.

Combining all the notes into a melody

ON THE CD

To put the B, A, G, F, E, and D together into one melody, play the example in Figure 8-9, which combines all the notes in this chapter. Don't look now, but you're playing the flute!

TIP

Practice the notes B, A, G, F, E, and D in just about any combination you can think of. Here are a few ideas to get you started:

✔ Practice playing one note over and over to perfect your embouchure. Start with the less resistant notes, such as B, A, or G, and work down from there.

✔ Slur any two notes together and repeat. Start with notes that are close together, such as B and A, and progress to notes that are farther apart, such as B and E. See how smooth you can get the transition between notes, using smooth air and efficient fingers.

✔ Slur B to A, then B to G, then B to F, B to E, and B to D. Then reverse the sequence to play D to B, E to B, and so on, always getting your best sound and the smoothest slurs possible.

✔ Try slurring D to F, then E to G, then F to A, then G to B, and then reverse the order going back down. Make sure that your fingers always move smoothly so that you don't get any gaps between notes.

✔ Make up some exercises and melodies on your own using these notes. The more you play with your first notes, the more proficient you'll be when you start adding new ones. Have fun!

Tracks 10 & 11

Figure 8-9:
Putting it all together: a melody incorporating B, A, G, F, E, and D.

arr. Giebler

Chapter 9

Higher, Lower, and in Between: More Advanced Notes

*I*n this chapter, you expand your repertoire of notes. The flat and sharp, or chromatic notes, fill in the gaps between the notes I cover in Chapter 8. The notes in this chapter also go just a bit higher and lower than those in Chapter 8, posing new challenges for your fingers as they get around new fingerings, and for your hands as they maintain the balance of your instrument. (See more about balancing the flute in Chapter 7.)

Be sure to keep the basics of posture, breathing, hand position, and embouchure in mind as you embark on the more challenging material presented here. (You can find out more about these basics in Chapters 5, 6, and 7.) The more you focus on these basic considerations, the faster you'll be able to make them second nature as your muscles and muscle memory adapt to your new skills.

Exploring the Chromatic Notes: Flats and Sharps

The *flats* and *sharps* are notes that are one-half step lower or higher than the plain note head printed on the staff. (See Chapter 4 for more details on sharps and flats.) These flat and sharp notes are called *chromatic notes*. They're basically the notes that are in between the notes I cover in Chapter 8.

In order to play the notes in this chapter, you need to become familiar with some of the keys that aren't home keys on the flute. For that reason, the fingering charts you see in this chapter incorporate all the keys on the flute, not just the home keys.

Not-so-basic B♭

Even though the phrase *basic B flat* generally means plain and uninteresting when you're talking about nonmusical things, to flute players, the B♭ is actually one of the more interesting notes you'll encounter. Why? Because it has three different fingerings from which you may choose. Of course, B♭ and A♯ are the same note, and all fingerings for B♭ therefore also work for A♯. But because you'll come across a lot more B♭s than A♯s while you're working on music, I'm just calling it B♭ here.

As you can see in Chapters 14 and 15, you can play many notes with alternate fingerings, but unlike those alternate fingerings, each of these three B♭ fingerings sounds identical to all the others. The choice of fingerings is for the flutist's benefit: All three work well in different situations, so you get to pick the one that is the most efficient (and easiest) fingering for any given context. You should learn all three of these fingerings at the same time so that you'll be adept at playing them all and can choose accordingly — and instinctively — when the time comes to use them.

You need to familiarize yourself with two new keys before trying the three B♭ fingerings:

- ✔ The **thumb B♭ key** is just above and to the left of the regular thumb key on the fingering chart. To get to the thumb B♭ key on the flute, just slide your left-hand thumb over to the left slightly. Notice that when the thumb B♭ key is down, the thumb key is also automatically depressed underneath it, and that the thumb B♭ key activates a lever that closes the third key on the top side of the flute, the key between LH 1 and 2.

- ✔ The **B♭ lever,** also known as the *side key,* is the small lever just to the left of RH 1. You use your right-hand index finger to get to the B♭ lever on the flute — just scoot your index finger over to the left slightly to depress it. If you have a C♯ trill key, it's in the same vicinity as the B♭ lever and is about the same size, but its placement is slightly to the left of the B♭ lever so that the B♭ lever is the first key you hit when moving your index finger slightly left. Notice that when you push down the B♭ lever, it activates the same lever as the thumb B♭ key, which closes the third key on the top side of the flute, the key between LH 1 and 2.

Take a look at the three B♭ fingerings in Figure 9-1. The fingering chart has a few more keys on it than the ones in Chapter 8, but the only ones you need to pay attention to now are the Thumb B♭ key and the B♭ lever.

#1: One-and-one B♭

#2: Thumb B♭

Figure 9-1:
Three
fingerings
for the
note B♭.

#3: B♭ lever

✔ Fingering #1 in Figure 9-1 is called "One-and-One B♭." This fingering is the first one you need to learn, because you can use it anywhere you have a B♭ to play.

✔ Fingering #2 in Figure 9-1 is called "Thumb B♭." This fingering makes a whole lot of B♭s a whole lot easier to play. When you're playing a piece that's in a key with B♭ in it, you'll want to use this fingering most often. The beauty of the Thumb B♭ is that you can leave your thumb down on it while you play all the other notes on the flute, with these exceptions:

  • B♮, because you want a B♮, not a B♭. (The third octave B♮ makes a really strange noise if the Thumb B♭ key is down.)

  • The third octave (high) F♯, because having that extra key down makes high F♯ sound very strange. (See more about the high notes in Chapter 14.)

- Any note on the flute for which you don't already have your left-hand thumb down (of course).

The Thumb B♭ eliminates many otherwise awkward fingering combinations, so it's a really good fingering to get to know.

✔ Fingering #3 in Figure 9-1 is called "B♭ Lever." It provides a smoother connection between B♭ and B♮ and therefore makes some technical passages easier. It's also a great way to get a nice, fast trill from B♭ to B♮. (See more about trills in Chapter 16.)

ON THE CD

Practice your three B♭ fingerings using the melody in Figure 9-2 and the following steps (*Note:* This melody includes the middle C note. Check out Figure 9-9 for more on middle C.):

Tracks 13 & 14

Ode to Joy
from Symphony No. 9, Op. 125

Ludwig van Beethoven
arr. Moratz/Giebler

Figure 9-2:
A tune to
help you
practice
your B♭
fingerings.

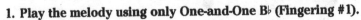

1. **Play the melody using only One-and-One B♭ (Fingering #1).**

2. **Play the melody using only Thumb B♭ (Fingering #2).**

3. **Play the melody using only the B♭ Lever (Fingering #3).**

4. **Switch it up!**

   Try using all three B♭ fingerings in the melody. See whether you can find the best place to use each one.

   Use a breath attack (see Chapter 8) to articulate the notes that are separated, but be sure not to close your throat as you do so. To avoid closing the throat, just think of saying "ah" as you blow (not literally voicing the sound but rather letting the feel of it open your throat). Slur the notes together where it's indicated. (For more on slurring, see Chapter 10.)

REMEMBER

Whenever you're playing a piece that uses a lot of B♭s, survey the surrounding material to determine which B♭ fingering(s) will be easiest to use. A little planning goes a long way toward learning music quickly and efficiently. If you're not sure which fingering to use where, try this general rule: If a B♭ is in the key signature, use the Thumb B♭. If you see a B♮ or a third octave F♯ directly around a B♭, see whether you can find a good place to take off your Thumb B♭ and then put it back on again after the B♮ or F♯ has passed.

A♭/G♯, G♭/F♯, and E♭/D♯

Unlike B♭, each of the three notes you practice in this section have only one basic fingering. The note A♭/G♯ uses LH 4, so it'll be the first note you play which uses that key (see Figure 9-3).

Figure 9-4 includes a few lines of music incorporating G♯/A♭, D♯/E♭, and F♯/G♭. The first line just introduces you to these notes via the notes directly around them. After that, you've got two melodies to play. B♭ makes an appearance here as well.

Track 15

A♭/G♯

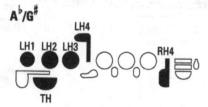

G♭/F♯

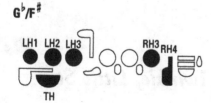

Figure 9-3: Fingerings for the notes A♭/G♯, G♭/F♯, and E♭/D♯.

E♭/D♯

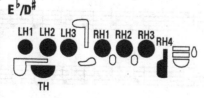

How the G♯/A♭ and D♯/E♭ keys work

The G♯/A♭ key (LH 4) and the D♯/E♭ key (RH 4) are both levers that actually open a tone hole on the other side of the flute when depressed. Consider the fingering for G (TH, LH 1, 2, and 3, plus RH 4). Not counting RH 4, which is just keeping a tone hole open anyway, the length of the flute tube now effectively extends from the headjoint down to and including LH 4 (which is closed when you're not working the G♯ key).

When you depress the G♯ key, or LH 4, the tone hole on the other side opens, effectively shortening the tube so that it now extends only from the headjoint down to and including LH 3. Shorter tube = higher pitch — thus the G becomes a G♯. The D♯/E♭ key works in a similar way when all the tone holes above it are closed: D becomes D♯ by opening the hole on the other side of the tube.

Track 16

G   G sharp   A   G   F sharp   F   D   D sharp   E

Tracks 17 & 18

arr. Giebler

Allegretto

E flat!   A flat!

Tracks 19 & 20

Twinkle, Twinkle, Little Star

Traditional
arr. Moratz/Giebler

Figure 9-4: Introduction and two melodies incorporating G♯/A♭, D♯/E♭, and F♯/G♭.

Andante

F sharp!

Getting Around on the Footjoint

This section deals with the notes that you produce by closing keys on the footjoint. The first footjoint key, the D#/E♭ key, raises the low D to a D# by opening the tone hole on the other side of the tube. The other footjoint keys are all there to close tone holes rather than open them. Longer tube = lower pitch, so depressing those keys gives you notes that are all lower than D, because as you know you're now effectively lengthening your flute tube.

The more keys you have down or closed, the more resistant the note becomes, so you may need to give the lowest notes on the flute a couple of tries before you get them to speak correctly. Use a slow, steady air stream and direct the air slightly downward by dropping the jaw a little bit.

Low C# and C

Your right-hand pinky controls the footjoint exclusively. If you take a look at your footjoint, you'll see that there is one rectangular key along with one or two rollers just to the right of your D#/E♭ key. Depressing the rectangular key closes the first round key directly to the right. Putting down the first roller closes the next key down, and if you have a B footjoint, the second roller closes the key after that.

The fingering chart in Figure 9-5 shows you the fingerings for low C# and C.

Track 21

D♭/C#

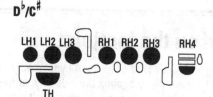

C

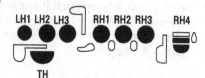

Figure 9-5: Fingerings for the notes C# and C.

As you can see from the fingering chart, the rectangular key and the first roller need to be down in order to get the low C. Luckily, the roller is built so that it automatically takes the rectangular key down with it when you push it, so you can concentrate on just getting that roller down and the rectangular key will take care of itself.

Even though you're focusing on your right-hand pinky when you're practicing the footjoint notes, keep an eye on the other right-hand fingers in the mirror, too. (You're incorporating a mirror in your daily practice routine, right?) Make sure that those fingers aren't starting to skew toward the right, which may affect how those tone holes are sealing.

Figure 9-6 is a melody containing both low C♯/D♭ and low C. Go through it a few times so that your right-hand pinky can get accustomed to working the footjoint.

Tracks 22 & 23

My Country 'Tis of Thee/God Save the Queen

Traditional
arr. Moratz/Giebler

Figure 9-6:
A melody incorporating low C♯/D♭ and low C.

Sliding around on the footjoint

Sometimes flutists are faced with challenging low register passages involving E♭, C♯, C, and B in varying combinations. Passages that have the pinky sliding from the D♯/E♭ key directly to the other footjoint keys are particularly troublesome because it's difficult to get a smooth connection with those note combinations. Some flutists buy flutes with custom D♯ and C♯ rollers, which are designed to make these transitions smoother for the right-hand pinky. (See Chapter 3 for information on C♯ and D♯ rollers.) However, most flutists use a trick of the trade that is far cheaper than custom flute gadgets, although it sounds kind of gross. All you need to do is rub your pinky against the side of your nose or on your forehead to pick up a small amount of oil from your skin. Your pinky will then magically and effortlessly glide over the footjoint keys, and the connections between these notes will suddenly become much smoother. Try slurring a low E♭ to a low D♭ with and without using this trick — you'll be amazed! (I sometimes mark the word "nose" in my part in pencil to remind myself when to get that oil if a tricky footjoint passage is coming up.)

Low B

If you don't have a low B footjoint, skip this section. With a C footjoint, the lowest note you can play is a C. (For more about C versus B footjoints, see Chapter 3.)

If you have a B footjoint, you have a second roller just above the one that produces the low C. This roller is connected to the very last key on the foot-joint, which produces a low B. In order to get the low B, you need to be pushing on both footjoint rollers, but again, the rectangular C♯ key at the bottom will take care of itself as long as you have that first roller down securely.

Play a low B using the fingering in Figure 9-7.

Because so many tone holes need to be sealed in order to get a low B, you need to concentrate even more than usual on good hand and finger position. Putting just the right amount of finger pressure in the center of each pad should give you a good, tight seal on each tone hole, which in turn should give you a nice, clear low B.

Track 24

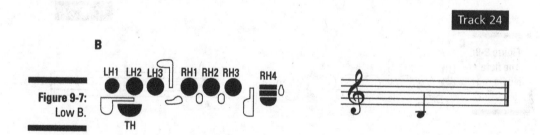

Figure 9-7:
Low B.

Try playing the exotic little melody in Figure 9-8 using the low B. This one is quite challenging because it moves back and forth between low C♯ and low B several times. Don't expect perfection right away, but think of it as an intense exercise to get your pinky moving all over the footjoint. (Pinky pushups, anyone?) Make sure that you take a break if your pinky is feeling tired or starts to cramp up. This exercise is a lot of work for that little finger.

Tracks 25 & 26

Figure 9-8:
Adding
the low
B to your
footjoint
repertoire.

Traditional
arr. Moratz/Giebler

Tackling the Tricky Balancing Notes

In the last couple of sections, you play lower and lower notes by closing more and more tone holes with each successive key. The notes in this section take you higher than middle B, which is the first note I discuss in Chapter 8. From the B (TH, LH 1, RH 4), you start taking away keys to produce the flute's middle register C and C♯. Because you're depressing so few keys on the flute, balance can become an issue. While you're trying out these new fingerings, you need to make sure that you're using your balance points, which I describe in Chapter 7, to keep your flute from rolling toward you.

The flute's middle C

Playing the flute's middle register C is just like playing middle B, but without the thumb. So overall you have two fingers down (see fingering chart in Figure 9-9.)

Track 27

Figure 9-9: The flute's middle register C.

Remember to use your balance points! The side of your left-hand index finger pushes the flute tube toward you, and your right-hand thumb acts as a lever, pushing that side of the flute away from you to bring the headjoint and upper part of the flute body more firmly toward your lower lip and chin. Your right-hand pinky can help the thumb along because it's down on the D♯/E♭ key. (More on balance points in Chapter 7.)

Play through the melody in Figure 9-10 a few times to get used to the feel of lifting your left-hand thumb for middle C.

Tracks 28 & 29

Frère Jacques

Traditional
arr. Moratz/Giebler

Figure 9-10:
Middle C in
a melody.

Middle C♯

The middle C♯ is probably the trickiest note on the flute for balance because the only key that's down on this C♯ is the D♯/E♭ key (RH 4). Play a C♯ using the fingering in Figure 9-11.

As long as you're using your balance points correctly and pushing firmly on them to keep the flute stable, you should be fine playing the C♯. This would also be a great time to try a right thumb balancing aid, such as a Thumbport (see Chapter 7.) The middle C♯ fingering shows you exactly how these little gadgets can be helpful.

D♭/C♯

Figure 9-11:
Middle C♯.

To get used to the feel of this C♯, play the excerpt in Figure 9-12. It's the beginning of the flute solo in Claude Debussy's *Prelude to the Afternoon of a Faun.* It's one of the most beautiful flute solos in the orchestral literature. (See Chapter 2 for more on the flute's role in orchestral music.) And if you commit this one to memory, you'll always have something to impress your mom or your grandfather or your significant other when you're asked to "play something" or "show what you're learning!" Every musician needs a trusted piece to show off with. This excerpt is one of the best!

Don't worry too much about the rhythm in this excerpt right now — just concentrate on getting a comfortable balance, a nice sound, and smooth connections between the notes.

To get an idea of what sort of sound you're shooting for and to put this excerpt into context, listen to a recording of Debussy's *Prelude to the Afternoon of a Faun*. The flutist plays this solo at the beginning of the piece and repeats it throughout the work with the rest of the orchestra playing wonderfully lush harmonies underneath. If you don't own a recording of it, borrow one at your local library, download an mp3, or listen to a clip of the beginning at an online CD store. You can also find many performances of this work on YouTube (www.youtube.com).

Because you close so few tone holes on the middle C♯, the note has very little resistance and therefore tends to sound a bit hollow. You can improve the C♯'s sound quality by opening the back of your mouth as you play, which will make the note sound more full.

Just think about the feeling you get when you're suppressing a yawn — that's about the right placement to get a nice-sounding C♯.

Figure 9-12:
The opening of *Prelude to the Afternoon of a Faun* by Claude Debussy (1862-1918).

Prelude to the Afternoon of a Faun

Claude Debussy

Moving Up

When you play the middle C♯, you're effectively playing on an open tube. To get notes higher than the middle C♯, the fingerings need to change drastically because you can't shorten the tube any further. From this point on, you get into fingerings that are based on the lower notes — essentially, you're taking the lower notes up an octave and then starting the process of lifting one key at a time to go higher, note by note.

Middle D

You may have inadvertently produced a middle D while you were practicing the low D: Blow a little too hard on the low D fingering, and the low D jumps up an octave. Follow these steps to gradually arrive at a middle D by starting on a low D:

1. **Play a low D (fingering chart in Chapter 8).**

2. **Lift LH 1.**

   Lifting the left-hand index finger should automatically give you a middle D.

   That's it!

To get your best sound on the middle D, you may need to lift the airstream slightly by bringing your jaw forward and/or increasing the speed of your air just a little.

The chart in Figure 9-13 gives you the middle D fingering.

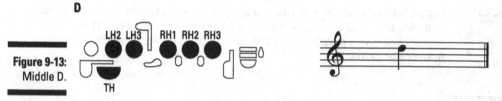

Figure 9-13:
Middle D.

ON THE CD

Play "On Top of Old Smokey" in Figure 9-14 to practice the fingering for middle D.

Tracks 30 & 31

On Top of Old Smokey

Traditional
arr. Moratz/Giebler

Figure 9-14:
"On Top
of Old
Smokey."

TIP

Make sure that you always lift LH 1 when you play middle D. The note is easier to produce that way and it also sounds better. If you try the note with LH 1 down, you'll notice that it sounds a bit muffled. The exception to this rule: If you're playing a very fast technical passage, you may want to leave LH 1 down on middle D to facilitate efficient finger movement. At the faster speed required by many up-tempo technical passages, the difference in the sound would be lost to the listener anyway.

A finger twister: Middle C, C♯, and D

Because the middle register C and C♯ fingerings are so different from the fingering for middle D, they create a technical challenge for the fingers when you play them in close succession.

Try playing a middle register C and then slurring it right into a middle D. As you switch from C to D, LH 1 and RH 4 come up, and all the other fingers, including the thumb, go down: All your fingers switch from down to up or up to down at the same time. This type of switching action is called *contrary motion*. Contrary motion tends to be a lot more challenging than simply lifting up or putting down fingers: Here, you're lifting and putting down keys at the same time.

Figure 9-15 is what I like to call a *finger twister* — a challenging passage that you play over and over to work on a certain area of difficulty. This finger twister helps you practice the contrary motion between middle D and the notes right below it.

Figure 9-15:
A finger
twister to
help you
practice
contrary
motion
between
middle D
and the
notes
directly
below it.

Track 32

Vivace

mf

Notice the repeat brackets: After you get going on this exercise, play it at least four times in a row. Your fingers will thank you later.

Practice each two-note finger combination slowly before you put the whole finger twister together. Make sure that your fingers are hovering close to the keys when they're not depressing keys. Listen closely to hear whether any little blips or bumps are happening between notes. If there are, it means that your keys are not all going up and down exactly together.

Chapter 10

Between the Notes: Slurring and Tonguing

In This Chapter

▶ Slurring notes together

▶ Tonguing to clearly articulate notes

T his chapter is all about basic articulation techniques. *Articulation* refers to how you start and end notes in music. (See Chapter 4 for more on articulation.) You need to articulate on the flute to express musical ideas clearly. Just as you use vowels and consonants to articulate distinctly when you're speaking, the language of music has its own method of clearly shaping musical ideas. (However, in music, unlike in speech, slurring notes together is sometimes desirable!)

In this chapter, I explore various ways of playing notes together as a group with slurring and tying. I also tell you how to use your tongue to separate notes, experimenting with different note lengths — long, short, and in-between.

Slurring: Tying Things Together

Music is a universal language, and you find vowels and consonants in all language. Think of your flute sound, created by your steady airstream and traveling smoothly through slurs and ties, as the vowel sound. The musical examples in Chapters 8 and 9 have you slurring notes together. But in this section, I give you a few tips on the finer points of slurring. I also explore how to execute slurs versus ties — the musical notation for them looks the same (see Chapter 4), but in practice, they turn out to be quite different.

Taking the air through the phrase

When you slur two or more notes together, the object is usually to connect them smoothly, unless you see some other type of symbol under the slur, such as accents, dots, or lines. (See the "Differentiating between slurs and ties" and "Long" sections, later in this chapter.) To get the smoothest connection possible, you need to strive for an even airstream that moves independently of your fingers. In other words, when you change fingerings during a slur, your airstream should remain constant and unwavering.

Maintaining an even airstream through note changes can be trickier than it sounds — it's a coordination challenge, kind of like patting your head and rubbing your belly at the same time. The first instinct is usually to back off on the air as the fingering changes. Listening to yourself closely, and perhaps recording yourself, can be extremely helpful in finding "gaps" in your slurs.

If you have a flute-playing friend, you can split up the job of flute playing by having her work the fingerings for you as you simply make the sound on the headjoint, hands-free. This trick is actually very useful; if you don't know exactly when the fingerings are changing, you don't have the opportunity to react by diminishing your airstream, so you're automatically blowing all the way through the slur without interruptions.

Use the exercise in Figure 10-1 to practice slurring smoothly between notes. Proceed through the sections of the exercises in numerical order, playing the easiest-to-balance and least resistant notes first. Follow these steps for the best results:

`Track 33`

Figure 10-1:
Practicing
smooth
slurs.

1. **Play section #1 and work on getting a super-smooth airstream.**

   Keep the air going between the notes. You may even want to think of increasing the air right when you're changing fingerings so that you make sure not to drop the airstream. Repeat each three-measure section as indicated. That way, you have a chance to make it even smoother the second time around.

2. **Work on section #2 the same way you did #1.**

Watch the C♯/D♭ — make sure that you're balancing the flute well. Try to match the sound quality of the C♯/D♭ to that of the other notes. (See Chapter 9 for more on middle C♯/D♭.)

3. **Add section #1 to section #2. Play from #2 all the way through #1, still observing all repeats.**

4. **Work on section #3 the same way you did #1 and #2.**

Pay particular attention to the connection between the middle D, C♯, and C. Make sure that your fingers are moving smoothly (see Chapter 9) and try to match the sound quality on all three notes.

5. **Play sections #3, 2, and 1 in succession, observing all repeats.**

6. **Now work on section #4.**

The notes will have more and more resistance as you add more and more keys. Again, keep your airstream and your sound quality consistent.

7. **Play sections #3, 2, 1, and 4 in succession, again observing all repeats.**

After you use the preceding steps to work through this slurring exercise, your smooth-slurring skills will definitely have improved, and you'll have better control of your airstream. The extra bonus is that you're working on your sound and embouchure at the same time. Return to this exercise often to really hone your new-found skills.

Differentiating between slurs and ties

Ties look exactly like slurs, but while slurs connect notes of different pitches, ties connect notes that are the same pitch. (See Chapter 4 for more about the notation of slurs and ties.) Composers have varying reasons for writing ties. Sometimes they want to write a rhythmic value that isn't practical to write with just one note head — rhythmic values often need to be tied over a bar line. Other times, a composer may have an expressive reason for writing a tie. For example, say that the composer wants you to hold out a note for three beats, but put an accent on the third beat without actually separating that note: Instead of a dotted half note, he could write a half note tied to a quarter note and place an accent symbol over the quarter note. (For more about accents and music notation, see Chapter 4.) Usually, when you see the same note repeated two or more times under a slur, those repeated notes should be tongued lightly. But if a tie appears over the repeated notes placed under the big slur, it means that those repeated notes should be tied together — that is, played as one long note.

Figure 10-2, an excerpt from the *Fantasie* for flute and piano by Gabriel Fauré (1825–1924), illustrates one of the most common uses of ties: extending rhythmic note values over bar lines. (Fauré's *Fantasie* is one of the many pieces included in the sheet music collection *Flute Music by French Composers*, which I tell you about in Chapter 17.)

Tracks 34 & 35

Fantasie
Op. 79

Gabriel Fauré

Figure 10-2:
An excerpt
from Gabriel
Fauré's
Fantasie.

As you play this beautiful excerpt, count very carefully across the bar lines. Make sure that you're slurring smoothly.

When you move from the C to the E in the first two notes of this excerpt, be sure that you're moving your right-hand pinky from the C roller back up to the D♯/E♭ key. Without the D♯/E♭ key down, the E sounds quite flat, so you should make sure that the pinky is down for the E whenever possible. However, when you go from the E back down to the C, you don't need to slide your pinky to the C roller: The pinky slide in this case is a tricky maneuver. If you take your pinky off for the last split second of the E, you can then just place it down on the C roller without sliding. If you perform this maneuver quickly, no one will be the wiser.

Tonguing: Putting Some Space Between the Notes

On the flute, you *articulate*, or separate notes, using the tongue, which is (aptly) called *tonguing*. So think of tonguing on the flute as your consonants in the language of music.

In Chapters 8 and 9, I advise you to use a breath attack to start notes. This type of attack uses your air only. But on the flute, to get a quick, precise attack on a particular note or succession of notes, you need to use your tongue as well as the air.

Your air is what produces the body of the note, the vowel sound, as it were. But tonguing shapes the beginning of the note and allows you to play separate notes in quick succession.

To tongue a note on the flute, follow these steps:

1. **Place the very tip of your tongue on the roof of your mouth, just behind your front teeth.**

2. **As you begin playing a note, lower your tongue back down to its natural resting position.**

That's really all there is to it. Basically, you'll be completing both of the preceding steps whenever you single tongue a note. Double tonguing, which I address in Chapter 16, is a technique used for faster tonguing, but you should start with just the single tonguing here and progress to double tonguing later.

The preceding steps tell you what to do to execute single tonguing, but what they don't tell you is that just about infinite variations on exactly *how* to use your air and tongue exist within that context. For example, you could lower your tongue a split second before you blow the air so that you're getting just a tiny bit more definition at the beginning of a note than with a breath attack. Or you could let the air pressure build up behind your tongue while it's lifted and release it with a strong popping noise. All sorts of possibilities exist in between those two scenarios, and all of them are legitimate approaches for different kinds of music. The longer you play the flute, the more you'll discover the various subtleties of different types of tonguing. Right now, though, you can start finding your best spot for tonguing: the place that gives you a reliable, clean beginning for your notes without a lot of extraneous noise.

Thinking of saying "duh" at the beginning of a note works best for clear articulation, but don't actually say "duh." First of all, you don't want to give anyone the wrong impression about flute players. But seriously, you don't want to actually voice the syllable. Just think about saying "duh" as you play to get your mouth and tongue in the right place to articulate. Using this syllable gives you the same action as the preceding steps, but it also gives you a more specific placement for your tongue.

You may have previously learned a syllable beginning with T, which a lot of teachers use, but I find that using the D consonant prevents a lot of extraneous, uncontrolled air. Without playing the flute, but replicating your embouchure, try saying D and T to yourself a few times. Notice that when you say the T, you can feel the air moving rapidly behind your lips, like a little explosion of air. This air is pressurized from having been built up behind your tongue before you speak, so it rushes out in an uncontrolled way when you release it. The D, on the other hand, lets you manage the air entirely with your breath support. The result is better control over your air so that you can continue to aim it exactly where it needs to go and articulate clearly without losing extra air out the sides of your embouchure.

To practice your tonguing, listen to Track 36 on the CD and try the following:

1. **Pick a note.**

   A note without a lot of resistance is good to start. C, B, or A, or any of the surrounding notes will do — or try a few different ones.

2. **Articulate the beginning of the note using a "duh" syllable.**

   Just articulate the note and then hold it for a beat or two to make sure that your sound is stable. Look in the mirror to make sure that you aren't moving your lips around a lot as you're tonguing. Your movement should be efficient: Just do as much as is necessary to make the note speak clearly. Don't open and close your mouth as you articulate — leave everything in one place as much as possible and just let the tongue help the air along a little bit, working as described behind your proper and well-formed embouchure.

3. **Repeat Step 2, but instead of holding out the note, tongue it a few times as you're holding it out.**

   Your tongue is simply dividing the long note into several shorter notes. Again, be efficient with your tonguing — no large movements are needed. If the sound goes away right after you articulate, your motions are probably too big, or you're building up that pressurized air behind your tongue too much before releasing it. Control your air and use small movements with your lips, mouth, and tongue, and you'll have good, clear articulation. Again, the more you repeat these steps during your practice sessions, the easier and more natural tonguing will become for you over time.

Short

When the composer wants a note played quite short, he puts a staccato dot over it. (For more on music notation, see Chapter 4.) Playing staccato (short) notes doesn't necessarily mean that you need to tongue harder; it just means that you put more space between the notes within the indicated rhythmic time frame.

The version of "Row, Row, Row Your Boat" in Figure 10-3 is marked with staccato dots. I've written a possible equivalent in shorter note values. However, you may or may not actually choose to play them the exact lengths that I indicate here. Whenever you encounter staccato dots, you can choose exactly how short you'd like to play the notes — just kind of short, or very short, or extremely short, for example.

French tonguing

French tonguing, contrary to what its name would have you believe, is not just done in France. (Kind of like French kissing, I suppose.) This type of tonguing is similar to the traditional, tongue-behind-the-teeth tonguing, but instead of placing the tip of the tongue on the roof of the mouth, it's placed on the inside of the top lip and then drawn back into the mouth and down as the note is played. Don't try this one at home — well, okay, you can try it at home, but make sure that you're comfortable with traditional tonguing first. French tonguing is a wonderfully subtle technique, and it's great to use for certain situations and styles of music, but it's a little trickier to master than traditional tonguing.

Tracks 37 & 38

Row, Row, Row Your Boat

Traditional
arr. Moratz/Giebler

Figure 10-3: "Row, Row, Row Your Boat" with staccato dots and possible rhythmic equivalent.

rhythmic equivalent

As you play shorter notes, don't let the tongue take over completely — your air is still the driving force behind your flute sound. Remember to keep your airstream even and controlled, even when you're playing short. Try going back and forth between breath attacks and tongued attacks to make sure that you're using the air properly.

Your tongue doesn't need to stop the air at the end of the note. Let the note end when your airstream stops. This way, the note will have a ring to it at the end and won't sound muffled.

Long

Long note values come in a few different varieties, but the most common ones are

- **Staccato dots underneath a slur.** This notation means that you play the notes *almost* slurred — that is, the air continues as if you were slurring, but you tongue each note lightly without stopping the air in between notes.

- **Tenuto dashes above or below the note heads.** This notation means that you hold out the notes at their full rhythmic value, with a slight emphasis on each note. (The air does stop for a split second between tenuto notes.)

Figure 10-4 is a version of "Row, Row, Row Your Boat," with long note values. Try to differentiate the notes with the dots under the slur from the ones with the dashes.

Tracks 39 & 40

Row, Row, Row Your Boat

Figure 10-4: "Row, Row, Row Your Boat" with different types of notations for long notes.

Traditional
arr. Moratz/Giebler

In-between

Whenever you see a bare note head, with no slur, staccato dot, tenuto dash, or any other type of marking, it's usually safe to assume that you should play it at medium length — not too short, not too long. Just right, in other words.

When you're playing a piece by a Baroque or Classical era composer, such as Handel, Bach, or Mozart, bare note heads usually mean that you can add your own slurs and decide on note lengths yourself. Music before 1825 left more interpretive areas open to the performer than later music, such as that of the Romantic and Impressionist periods.

The musical example in Figure 10-5, from an etude by Ernesto Köhler (1849–1907), neatly combines all the articulations covered in this chapter. See whether you vary the types of articulation so that they're clearly different to someone who is listening. This etude would be a great one to record yourself on so that you can check your work.

Figure 10-5:
Part of an etude from *20 Easy Melodic Progressive Exercises,* op. 93, Book I, by Ernesto Köhler, with varied articulation styles.

Chapter 11

Getting Up to the Second Octave

- -

- -

After you get to middle C and C♯, the flute tube effectively gets about as short as it can get, so you've exhausted the possibilities of shortening the flute further to produce higher notes. For your next trick, you need to work with your air in a way that allows the fingerings you're already using for the low register to produce notes that are one octave higher. With some notes, you make slight adjustments to the fingerings to produce the next octave up, but for most of the notes in the next register, the fingerings will be the same as they were in the low octave, with getting to the higher note entirely depending on what you do with your airstream.

In this chapter, you find out what to do (and what not to do) to expand your range to the next octave on your instrument. Once again, one has to marvel at the engineering magic that allows for the flute to achieve such range and so many different tones, moods, and colors! In this chapter, you also get a chance to put your newfound knowledge to work with practice drills and melodies that really challenge you and demonstrate the flute's capabilities. Because you're expanding your range, the melodies and excerpts you play incorporate more notes and start to get a lot more challenging and enjoyable.

Overblowing: Why I Hate That Word

After you're getting around the flute's low to middle register — that is, from low C (or B, depending on your footjoint) to about middle D with relative ease (or at least some sense of accomplishment) — it's time to start getting up to the next octave. Many flutists and flute teachers refer to getting up to the next octave as *overblowing*. While it's true that increasing the air speed accomplishes the task of getting that next octave, I view overblowing as a negative term, because the word conjures up imagery of gale-force winds.

Directing the air to produce the octave higher involves so much more than overblowing: You have to get just the right amount of controlled air, funnel it through the aperture adjusting the air speed further, and then move the embouchure so that the air angle is in the right place to get a clear, focused, unforced, nice-sounding note in the next octave. I don't think they've come up with a word or phrase to adequately describe what you're really attempting to accomplish, so I suppose that the word overblowing is a necessary evil, until someone comes up with a better one. In the meantime, I use the word as little as possible in this chapter, just to keep you from blowing your brains out. But I describe the process as accurately and in as much detail as possible so that you can easily and successfully expand your range by about an octave within a relatively short time.

Keep in mind that as you go up the octave, although you may change the air speed somewhat using your embouchure, you want to keep the air speed on par with what you were doing in the lower octave.

Your first instinct may be to get from the lower octave to the higher one by suddenly increasing your air flow, pushing the air out all at once with great force. You can produce the high octave this way, but it won't be pretty! It'll sound shrill and forced and will tend to go sharp on you.

Instead, finesse that flute. Be patient with it, be gentle with your airstream, and adjust your embouchure in small increments to find out what works. Make use of the tools of air speed and air angle simultaneously and judiciously, and you'll get a beautiful sound in every register. You'll stand at least half a chance of playing in tune, as well, and with some of the more challenging pieces in the repertoire, a 50-50 chance is sometimes the best you can hope for!

Mastering Middle D and E♭: The Only Notes with an Octave Key

Some of the other woodwinds have octave keys or register keys that facilitate the octave jump (or other interval jump), but on the flute, most of the octave jumps from the low to middle register depend entirely on the player and her air and embouchure. However, middle D and E♭ are the two exceptions — LH 1 essentially works as an octave key to take those notes up by exactly an octave. (So I guess you could say that the flute does have an octave key for those two notes. Lucky us.)

In Chapter 9, I tell you how to produce a D by lifting LH 1 while you're playing the low D. In Figure 11-1, you find the E♭/D♯ the same way. Give it a try. And, voilà, you've played two octaves already without even lifting a finger. No, wait a minute, you did lift a finger. Never mind — the point is, you didn't have to work very hard to get there.

Track 42

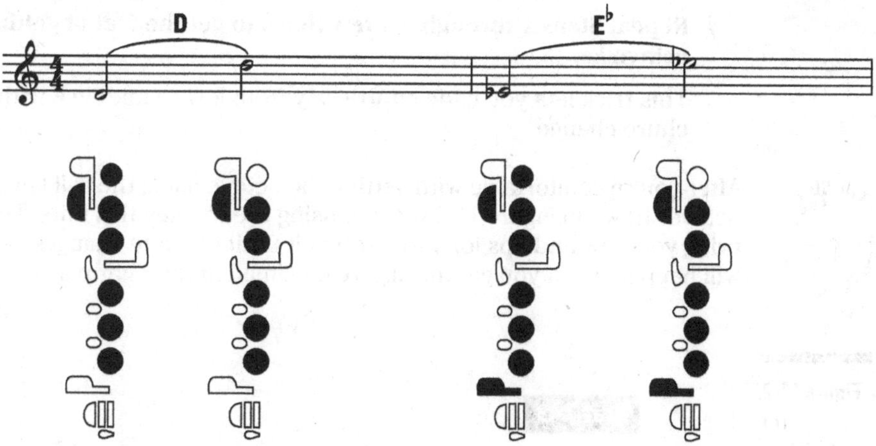

Figure 11-1:
Getting to
the next
octave from
low D
and E♭.

D   E♭

Even though lifting LH 1 gets you to middle D and E♭ automatically, you may need to lift your airstream by adjusting your embouchure forward slightly in order to get your very best sound on the middle D and E♭ once you're there.

Arriving at Middle E: Tapping the Trill Key as a Training Wheel for the Upper Octave

The next note up from the low D and E♭ is E♮. You don't get an automatic octave key for this one, but you can use a trick to get the feel of taking the note up the octave. To try it, follow these steps:

1. **Find the second trill key on your flute.**

   It's directly to the left of RH 3 (in between RH 2 and 3).

   Starting out with your fingers on the home keys, depress the second trill key with your right-hand ring finger (RH 3 finger). Notice that this key opens a small key on the underside (thumb side) of the flute — the one that is closest to the barrel.

2. **Play a low E.**

   See fingering in Chapter 8.

3. **While you're playing the low E, partially push down the second trill key, just enough to create a tiny opening in the key near the barrel of the flute, but not enough to open that key the whole way.**

Opening this key only part of the way gives you a middle E that is in tune. If you open it the whole way, the middle E will be sharp.

4. **Repeat Steps 1 through 3 a few times to get the feel of getting the octave Es.**

   This trick lets you glide effortlessly from low to middle E with no embouchure change.

After you're comfortable with getting the octave using the trill key, play the octave shown in Figure 11-2 without using the trill key this time. To do so, bring your jaw and lips forward bit by bit until the note changes — the octave will happen when you get the airstream aimed in the right place.

Figure 11-2:
The
E-octave
(low and
middle E).

As you can see, you can often find more than one way to skin a cat when it comes to your flute playing. The real trick is to make sure that you don't sound like that's exactly what you're doing. Note: No animals were harmed in the writing of this book.

Here are a few more things to keep in mind as you work on the E-octave.

✔ To find the right embouchure placement for that middle E, you need to move your jaw and lips forward very slowly while keeping your airstream constant. Feel every little increment of movement and really try to feel where your air is going. That way, when the E jumps up to the next octave, you'll know the placement so that you can reproduce it again and again with little or no effort or concentration.

✔ Your aperture may become a little bit smaller as your jaw and lips move forward. The smaller aperture increases the air speed slightly, which also helps the octave note to sound. But try not to increase the air speed too much by blowing harder — keep supporting your air evenly (see Chapter 5 for more on breath support) and don't bring your lips so close together that they start to choke off the sound.

✔ Spend some time getting the middle E to jump from the low E on command. Getting that E-octave is a crucial step toward expanding your range on the flute. If you can get this octave to work using subtle embouchure movements, the rest of the flute's range will follow suit fairly easily for you.

Delving into Harmonics

Playing harmonics is a really useful way to work on your sound and focus on the changes that happen in your embouchure as you play higher notes on the flute. Because the flute's fingerings in third octave are based on harmonics, playing harmonics now will also help you understand the fingerings better as you get to the flute's third octave later on.

Basically, when you play an octave, you're using the flute's harmonic series. The higher octave you're playing is, in fact, a harmonic of the lower note, which is also referred to as the *fundamental*. (For more on the harmonic series, see Chapter 2.) You can go through a whole series of harmonics based on one fundamental note by fingering the fundamental and directing the air upward, as you did to get the octave from low E to middle E. The farther up you direct the air, the higher the harmonic you get.

The abbreviated harmonic series in Figure 11-3 prepares your embouchure to keep moving up through the flute's registers. The small circles that appear above some of the notes indicate harmonics. The fundamental notes have no circle. Play the fundamental note and then go up to the next two notes (harmonics) using only your embouchure but not changing your fingers. (The note heads represent the pitches where the harmonics *sound*, not the fingering you're using to get them.) Then repeat the top harmonic and come back down to the fundamental.

Take a look at the tempo marking at the upper left-hand corner of Figure 11-3. Hint: *Adagio* is Italian for "slowly!"

Figure 11-3: Harmonics.

Playing the harmonic series gives you a chance to isolate what's going on in your embouchure without having to think about changing fingerings. It also lets you physically experience the workings of the instrument. The harmonic series is what makes the flute work: When you grasp this concept, you immediately understand that there is definitely more to playing the flute than working the keys.

It may take some time to really master this harmonic series, especially if you're doing it right — that is, playing slowly and deliberately considering your every move while you proceed by feel. The idea is to get your embouchure moving smoothly and efficiently through the registers while keeping your air flow constant. Because your embouchure is made up of lots of tiny muscles, it may take some time for them to coordinate and develop the necessary muscle memory. That's why you need to incorporate these harmonics into your daily practice routine. I still use harmonics as a daily warmup myself. Just ask all the barking, distressed dogs in my neighborhood.

At first, you may need to practice the ascending and descending passages separately. That way, you're starting out with the embouchure only having to move in one direction at a time. Then put it all together as written so that you're moving up and down.

As you're moving your jaw and lips forward in very small increments, do your best to keep a yawning feeling in the back of your mouth so that you keep your throat open. (Good posture will help you maintain an open throat, as well — see Chapter 5 for more on how posture affects your flute playing.)

Playing Some Real Octaves

When you've gotten to the point where you're cruising through the harmonic series in Figure 11-3, you're ready to play some real octaves. (For more on the harmonic series, see the preceding section.)

Playing octaves is, of course, a whole lot like playing harmonics. They use the same technique from an embouchure standpoint, but the resistance and feel may be a little different, depending on what note you're playing: The higher harmonics are generally more resistant than the "normal" fingerings for those notes. Produce the octaves the same way you did the harmonics in the previous section, moving the jaw and lips forward bit by bit until you get the sounding octave. Again, your aperture may get little bit smaller, but don't squeeze your lips together: You still want the air to be able to move freely as you're directing it.

Play the octaves in Figure 11-4. Remember, for the first two sets of octaves, you lift LH 1 to produce the higher note. You produce all the other octaves in this example by using the embouchure only: Play the lower note and then move jaw and lips forward to go up — don't change the fingers. (For fingering charts, refer to the fingerings for the lower notes in Chapters 8 and 9 or just look up the fingerings for these notes in Appendix A.)

Track 45

Figure 11-4:
Octaves.

Keep the back of your mouth and your throat open as you play the top notes — don't close the mouth as you're coming forward to aim the air up. Think of keeping some space between your back teeth as you go up the octave. That way, you'll keep an open, resonant sound in the higher notes.

You may be tempted to play the middle D and E♭ without lifting LH 1, but those notes sound a bit muffled with LH 1 down and tend to be a bit flat when fingered that way, as well. So lift LH 1 whenever you play middle D and E♭, unless they're in a challenging technical passage where speed is paramount, and you're playing too fast for such subtleties to be heard anyway.

Speeding Up Your Air

Getting harmonics and octaves to speak on the flute requires a combination of actions: Changing the velocity as well as the angle of the air coming out of your embouchure. In this section, I address the two different ways you can speed up your airstream to facilitate getting up to the next harmonic or octave.

Blowing faster

If you just blow like crazy and leave everything else alone, you can get the flute to go up much of the harmonic series. Try it now; just get it out of your system. Start on a low register note and just keep blowing more and more air. Blow the house down, if you must. As you can see (hear, actually), the flute doesn't take too kindly to this kind of treatment. By blowing that hard, you get a shrill, strident sound that keeps going sharper the higher you play.

Sometimes you need to use an incredible amount of air to play the flute. But the more volume of air you use, the more open your embouchure needs to be to compensate for the fast air, effectively slowing it down on the way out. And even if you're using a lot of air, you still need to be able to control the air evenly as it exits the embouchure.

The few notes in the fourth octave of the instrument (above the high C), which you can find in the basic fingering chart in Appendix A, do sometimes need very fast air in order to speak properly. These notes, which you some-times find in Contemporary music (see Chapter 17), are an exception to the general rule. (If you feel like blowing your brains out, just work on those notes for a while.)

So, in other words, for most notes on the flute, I don't recommend blowing a lot of fast air to get to the next octave.

Narrowing the air column

Making the aperture smaller is another way to speed up the air, and this option lets you keep blowing a constant airstream.

As you form your embouchure, you develop a *home base* for the low register that you come back to again and again. To find that home base, just play a middle B with your best medium-loud sound. Because B is an "easy" note with little resistance, you're probably pretty comfortable there by now. From that B, you make tiny embouchure adjustments to play the notes directly above and below it, and you make bigger adjustments to find notes that are a bit farther away, higher or lower.

From your home base (your nice sound on the B), try making the aperture smaller by increasing pressure from the bottom and top lip toward the middle of your aperture simultaneously. Once your aperture is small enough, the note will go up the octave to the higher B, the B above the staff.

Making the aperture smaller is a useful tool for making the flute's pitches go higher, but use it in moderation and don't rely on it exclusively (See the next section, "Adjusting Your Air Angle"). Don't squeeze the life out of your sound; narrowing the air column too much will make you sound tinny and your pitch sharp. Also, try not to bite down too much on the top lip — feel the pressure in your bottom and your top lip evenly. As with every technique, consistent and efficient practice are the keys to internalizing these skills, making them second nature.

Adjusting Your Air Angle

The direction of your air is key in just about everything you do on the flute. For going up octaves and harmonic series, varying your air angle is an absolutely essential tool. In the various stages of forming your embouchure, you experiment with air angle to find your best sound. As you progress to jumping octaves, practicing harmonics, and playing larger intervals, you need to make numerous embouchure adjustments as you go, always listening to yourself closely and always searching for your best possible sound.

In Chapter 6, I talk about changing the angle of the air with regards to forming a beginning flute embouchure. But in this section, my comments and advice are more about making minute adjustments as you play, especially when you're dealing with octaves and other large intervals.

Jaw and lip movement

To get up the octave, your jaw comes forward and up slightly, which directs your air upward. As you bring the jaw forward, try to keep an open feeling in the back of the mouth and throat.

The jaw decides the general direction of the air, and the muscles lining the lips guide the air gently yet precisely to its final destination. The lips follow the jaw as it comes forward.

Think of your lips as two soft cushions so that you don't start using more muscle tension than is necessary to get where you're going. Keep a tiny bit of space between the inside of your upper lip and your teeth — this will also alleviate excess lip tension.

Think about using the *inside* of your lips, the moist part, to guide the airstream — focusing on the inside of the lips will prevent you from tightening the outside of the lips, and will enhance your flexibility as you make the fine adjustments to your embouchure.

Other methods

The position of your tongue in your mouth determines air direction to some extent. Most of the time, your tongue should stay down on the bottom of your mouth, to stay out of the way as the air travels through. One exception, of course, occurs when you're tonguing, and your tongue briefly touches the roof of your mouth. But if you're aiming to keep your pitch up while playing softly (see Chapter 15) or trying to create a more closed-sounding tone color (see Chapter 12), the tongue can rise in your mouth slightly to create a smaller opening for the air to pass through. For now, though, just be aware of where you're placing your tongue as you play to get your best sound so that you have a frame of reference when you start experimenting with it later.

All the techniques I mention in this section are great for making small to very minute adjustments to the angle of your airstream, which, under normal playing conditions, are all you need to get around the flute's range and adjust the pitch here and there. But sometimes, usually when you're playing in an ensemble, you need to make extreme pitch adjustments quickly. In the formative stages of your embouchure (see Chapter 6), a beginning player can move his head up and down and roll the headjoint in and out to roughly find the correct air angle and embouchure hole coverage to produce his first sounds on the flute.

You can also apply these same methods for extreme pitch control: Say that you're playing in an ensemble, and you suddenly notice that your high G is out-the-roof sharp. You need to adjust the pitch pronto or experience the wrath of your colleagues or, worse yet, the conductor. So you do one of two things:

✔ You move your head and chin down in order to cover more of the embouchure hole. This method takes you way out of your embouchure's home base and therefore away from your best sound quality, but it does lower the pitch instantly and dramatically. Conversely, if you wanted to raise the pitch, you'd raise your head and chin.

✔ Using your hands, you roll the flute toward you, which essentially accomplishes the same thing as moving your head down: Your lips cover more of the embouchure hole, and the pitch goes lower. However, using your hands to roll the flute does upset the delicate balance you create to hold the instrument properly in the first place, and it takes some time and effort to get the flute back to where it needs to be after you've completed the maneuver. Of course, using this same method, if you want to raise the pitch, you can simply use your hands to roll the flute away from you.

Neither of these methods work very well for adjusting your air angle continuously while you're playing. Although both do change the direction of the air considerably, they don't allow you to move through a phrase with continuity, musicality, and finesse. Your playing will have more smoothness and sophistication if you relegate these two maneuvers to pitch emergencies. (For more on controlling your pitch, see Chapter 15.)

Check out the musical examples by Christoph Willibald Gluck (1714–1787) in Figure 11-5. They all make use of the newest part of your range. As you go up to the notes of the second octave, lift the airstream by moving your lips and jaw forward without speeding up the air too much. Your aperture may get a little bit smaller for the upper notes, but try not to put too much pressure on the airstream. If the lower note comes out when you want the higher octave, take a little time and lift the air slowly to find the placement for the higher note again.

Most importantly, have fun! You've got some lovely tunes to play here — enjoy them and enjoy playing your flute.

To work on melodies within the playing range covered in Part I of this book, get a copy of *Forty Little Pieces in Progressive Order for Beginner Flutists* by Louis Moyse (ed. Schirmer). (See Chapter 17 for information on where to buy sheet music.) The piano accompaniments are all available in the SmartMusic computer accompaniment program, so you can even perform them with a virtual pianist if you're so inclined. (See more about Smart Music in Chapter 5.)

Tracks 46 & 47

Aria
from *Orphée*

Gluck

Poco lento ♩ = 76

Tracks 48 & 49

Ballet

from *Armide*

Gluck

Tracks 50 & 51

Air de la Naïade

from *Armide*

Gluck

Andante ♩ = 80

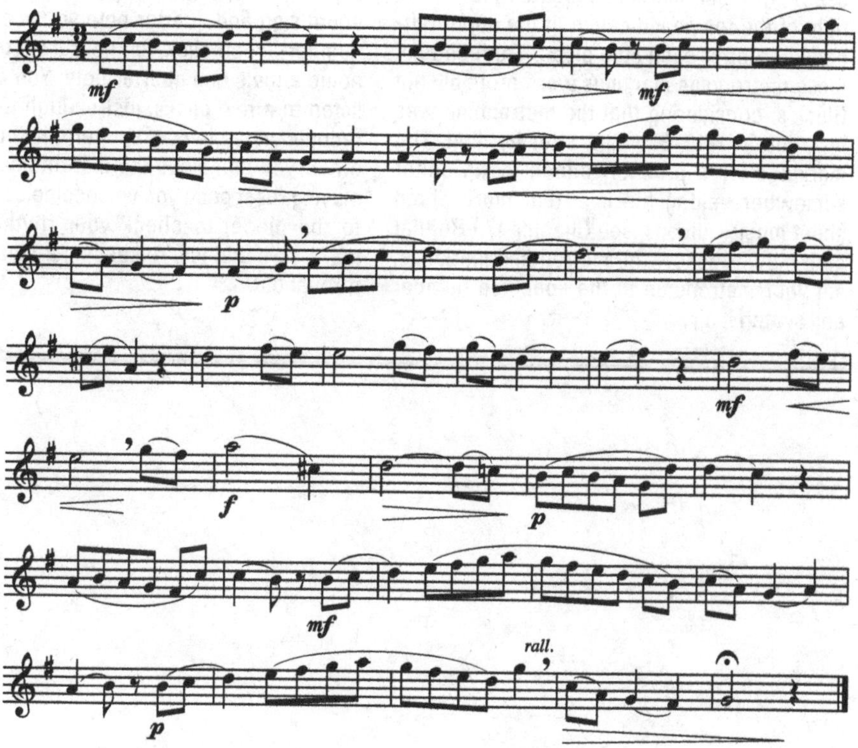

Figure 11-5: Three melodies by Christoph Willibald Gluck (1714–1787).

Setting your metronome

The three melodies by Gluck in Figure 11-5 use metronome markings, located just to the right of the tempo indication at the upper left-hand corner of each little piece. Truth be told, these metronome markings were probably not Gluck's, considering that the metronome was invented in 1812, 39 years after he died. The markings were probably added by an editor somewhere along the line. (For more about sheet music editions, see Chapter 17.) Be that as it may, to follow the metronome markings, set your metronome to the specified number and switch it on.

Because each metronome marking listed in Figure 11-5 specifies a quarter note beat (via equal sign and quarter note you see after the number), each click you hear from the metronome equals one quarter note. You can either listen to a few clicks, just enough to hear the recommended tempo, and turn the metronome off, or you can leave the metronome on while playing (best once you've become accustomed to the piece) to check your rhythm and to make sure that you're keeping a steady tempo throughout.

Part III

Above and Beyond: Essential Intermediate Techniques

The 5th Wave   By Rich Tennant

Okay, this time try not to take such a deep breath.

In this part . . .

In this part, you start to refine your flute playing. I go into the finer points of embouchure and resonance so that you can produce your best flute sound. You then add vibrato to your sound, after which you go on to start playing the high register notes in the third octave of the instrument. Refining your technique and sound and expanding your playing range give you broader access to most of the flute's vast repertoire, which you can now start exploring with confidence. To perfect your pitch, you work with your tuner and (even more importantly) your ears. Then it's time to add double, triple, and flutter tonguing so that your articulation can keep up with your budding finger technique. Apropos technique: At the end of this part, trills and tremolos really get your fingers moving. You're already sounding like a pro!

Chapter 12

Making That Elusive Big, Beautiful Sound

*I*f you've been listening to your favorite flutist(s) on recordings or at live concerts (see Chapter 21 for some suggestions on flutists to listen to), you may be wondering exactly how it is that they can produce such a beautiful, rich, seemingly effortless sound across the whole range of the instrument. Maybe you're noticing that different flutists sometimes have vastly different types of sounds — you might describe one player's sound as lush, silky, or velvety, while another player may sound more brilliant and brassy, and still another may come across as reserved, elegant, and refined. The amazing thing about the flute is that you can also describe any of these sounds as beautiful. You may have also noticed that a flutist during a single performance can evoke a number of very real and visceral emotions by transforming her sound at will to interpret the various musical passages at hand.

Lips: Relax, Please!

Whatever type of sound you're going for, you need to keep your lips as relaxed as possible. As you develop your embouchure and start to build your range, you'll naturally start to feel tempted to exercise control over the flute by tightening the muscles of the lips. Intuitively, it seems like you get the most control the more muscle power you use. But actually, if you use too much tension in your lips, you end up getting a thinner sound overall, and your notes are more likely to unexpectedly crack upward to the next harmonic. Your lips do have a job to do in directing the air, but they need to gently guide it without putting too much pressure on your airstream.

Because everyone's lips are different, only you can figure out exactly how you'll use your own lips to play your best. Following are some guidelines for you to consider as you work on getting the best possible sound out of your instrument. (Remember, your instrument is comprised of you *and* your flute!)

✔ Use only as much muscle tension in your lips as is absolutely necessary for the task at hand. Why work harder than you have to? As a rule, you end up getting the best results with the least possible amount of muscle tension. That doesn't mean your lips have no muscle tone at all — what it does mean is that you need to think about what is necessary for the task, as anything unnecessary you're doing may be the very thing that's standing in between you and your most beautiful sound.

✔ You don't want to have the feeling that your lips are stretched tightly over your teeth as you play. Bring your lips forward and just slightly off of the teeth, and they'll relax automatically. (But don't go so far as to pucker your lips, or you'll lose too much control.)

✔ Although no two embouchures look quite the same, if yours looks like a smile, you can bet that you've got too much tension in your lips. Relax the corners of your mouth and bring the lips forward just a smidge, and your sound will improve instantaneously. If you're already used to a smile-y embouchure, training yourself away from it may take time, but you can do it: Just keep checking in with your friend, the mirror. You'll be amazed at how big and resonant your sound can become after you switch to a more relaxed embouchure.

✔ If you're getting a lot of extraneous noise in your sound, release the pressure on your airstream by opening up the aperture just a little bit. Even though it feels like you're relinquishing control, this action often has the opposite effect: Slowing down the air just a bit by opening your aperture actually gives you a clearer, more focused sound. Opening up your aperture, thereby releasing the pressure on your airstream, is especially helpful if you've been squeezing the airstream a bit too hard — the result being extraneous air going in random directions. If you squeeze off the opening of a garden hose with your thumb, it increases the speed of the water coming out of the hose. But if you pinch off the opening severely, the stream of water not only speeds up, but may even change direction, splitting off randomly and becoming difficult to control. The same is true of your airstream: If you want to speed it up, you can make your aperture smaller. But if it becomes too pinched, it sends air off into random directions, creating extraneous noise in your sound.

✔ Instead of focusing your attention on the outside of your lips, think about what the inside part of your lips is doing. The moist part of your lip is actually what directs your airstream. Imagine your airstream being a long, narrow tube, like a straw, with the inside part of the lip guiding the airstream toward the edge of the embouchure hole. Focusing on the inside of the lip releases the outside of the lip from trying to control things too much, which makes letting go of any unwanted tension easier.

✔ If you experiment with relaxing your lips, your sound will likely improve. You may feel, eerily, as though you're not doing anything, yet suddenly your sound is fuller and more focused. This sensation means you're on the right track — you're starting to use your playing muscles in a more targeted and efficient way.

Placing the Notes

As you keep expanding your range on the flute, you need to be thinking about where you're placing the embouchure in order to play each note with a good sound, as well as in tune. (For more on playing in tune, see Chapter 15.) Embouchure placement isn't always the same on any particular note — it can depend on many factors, including which notes are directly around it, whether you're slurring or tonguing, how loudly or softly you're playing, and, if you're playing in an ensemble with another instrument, what note you're aiming to match or play with in harmony.

In addressing harmonics and octaves in Chapter 11, I talk about directing the airstream to get a certain note to sound. But instead of just getting the right note, you can start getting a more beautiful, open-sounding note by making small embouchure adjustments as you play. The key is to be constantly aware of your playing. With experience, you can develop a kind of sixth sense that allows you to become the best player you can possibly be.

Use the melody by Benedetto Marcello (1686–1739) in Figure 12-1 to practice placing the embouchure carefully with each note. Pay particular attention to your embouchure when you're going from a lower note to a higher one, especially if it's a wide leap. As you go up, your jaw and lips should come slightly forward. The aperture may get a little smaller, but don't squeeze the air too hard. Keep a continuous airstream throughout.

The harmonic series, which I talk about in Chapters 2 and 11, is a useful tool in many respects. In Chapter 11, it makes a great practice study for embouchure placement on octaves and other intervals. You can also use harmonics as a practice tool within a melody to help you place notes.

Say, for example, that you're having trouble getting the B above the staff to speak easily. In order to find the correct embouchure placement, you can try playing an E harmonic. Start from the low E, guide the air upward until you get the next octave (middle E), and finally angle the air up again to get the harmonic above that, which is a sounding B (even though you're still fingering the E). Hang out on that top harmonic for a while and adjust your embouchure until you're getting your best sound.

Tracks 52 & 53

Largo in D Minor

Marcello

Figure 12-1:
Largo in D Minor by Benedetto Marcello (1686–1739).

Next, approach the melody by Marcello in Figure 12-2 as follows:

1. **Play through the first eight measures of the melody, fingering the notes normally, to familiarize yourself with the music.**

2. **Play the first eight measures again, but this time, whenever you see a B above the staff on the page, finger an E instead and play the harmonic that sounds like B.**

   The Bs that you should play as harmonics are notated with little circles over them. Small Es are also marked underneath, to remind you which fingering to use.

   You still get notes that sound like B, only they're actually harmonics of E. The sound quality will be a little different; it may even sound a bit muffled. You may need to angle the air a little higher than with the real B because it's more resistant (more fingers down).

3. **Repeat Step 2 to see whether you can really nail it this time.**

   You've had one time through already to get used to the placements.

4. **Go back to Step 1 and play the first eight measures through with normal fingerings, without thinking too much about what you're doing with your embouchure.**

   The embouchure placements up to the Bs will seem a lot easier this time around!

5. **Play through the entire melody, enjoying how effortless your jumps up to B have become.**

Tracks 54 & 55

Cantabile

Marcello

Andante sostenuto ♩ = 89

Figure 12-2:
Cantabile by
Benedetto
Marcello
(1686–1739).

riten.

Playing the harmonic Bs creates more resistance than you have for the real B's. Working with the harmonic in the melody instead of the regular fingering is a little bit like walking with weights on your ankles — it feels so easy and light after you take them off. That's why the real B seems so easy after you've worked through the melody using the harmonic fingering.

Colors of Sound: Expanding Your Interpretive Palette

Dynamics and tone color are pretty much inseparable on the flute. That being said, here's a clear definition of both terms so that you can see that they are two distinct and separate concepts, yet symbiotically tied together:

- ✔ *Dynamics:* How loudly or softly you're playing at any given point in the piece. Dynamics come in many different degrees. (See Chapter 4 for dynamics in musical notation.) *Dynamic contrast* means making a dramatic difference between your loud and soft playing and/or using a lot of variety in dynamics throughout a particular piece of music.

- ✔ *Tone color:* What a particular note sounds like. Describing tone colors often involves evocative words, such as rich, full, thin, bright, light, dark, brassy, wispy, woody, tinny, edgy, metallic, warm, cool, silky, and velvety. Some musicians even like to describe tone colors with actual colors, calling a soft, wispy sound a "white" sound, for example, or a dense, edgy sound a "black" sound.

When you vary your dynamics, you use more or less air to create more or less sound. When you vary the speed of your airstream, the pitch of the note you're playing changes: If you're giving more air, it goes higher (sharper), and if you're giving less air, it goes lower (flatter). So in order to keep the pitch consistent — that is, play in tune — you need to adjust your embouchure to direct the air up if you're playing softer so that you won't go flat, or to direct the air down if you're playing louder so you won't go sharp. The size of the aperture can change to varying degrees as well: smaller for softer playing, or larger for louder playing. (For more on playing in tune, see Chapter 15.)

Dynamics and tone color are inextricably linked: When you adjust your embouchure placement for various dynamics, the tone color automatically changes. How much it changes depends on exactly how you're changing the shape of your mouth. Of course, no two players' mouths are quite the same, so you can make an infinite number of flute sounds. And that's really the beauty of it: Along with the process of learning about air and embouchure adjustment, you're finding your own voice on the flute. No one else can sound exactly like you.

You can also change your tone color while staying at the same dynamic level. By experimenting with different placements for your embouchure, you're changing your tone color. The trick is to find desirable embouchure placements — ones that promote interesting and beautiful sounds — that are in a different place from the home base you've found for your embouchure.

Talking about tone colors is subjective, and for that reason, it can get pretty nebulous. The changes in sound and embouchure are subtle, and, of course, everyone's preferences are a little bit different. I recommend doing a lot of listening — to the flute and other instruments, as well. Listening to other woodwinds, string instruments, or singers can give you a lot of ideas and inspiration for creating your own tone colors on the flute.

Vowel sounds and tone color

One way to change tone colors on command is to vary the shape of the inside of your mouth. You can achieve different mouth shapes easily by imagining different vowel sounds and forming your mouth to match them as you play. Try the following exercise for switching tone colors quickly:

1. **Play your best middle B on the staff.**

   Don't overblow to the next octave. Make sure you find a nice home base for your embouchure.

2. **Take the flute away from your face, but don't change your embouchure.**

3. **Engage your vocal cords to see what vowel sound you make when you're playing your best B.**

   It'll probably be an "ah" or an "eh" or something in between.

4. **Form and say, "Ooh."**

   Try to move your lips only minimally as you form the "ooh" vowel. The change is more about what you're doing on the inside of your mouth, versus engaging the outside of the lips in the process.

5. **Put the flute back up to your lips and play the same B, but this time keep the "ooh" vowel shape in your mouth as you play.**

   Notice that you get a slightly different sound with the "ooh" than with the first vowel sound you used. You've just changed your tone color!

You can go through all the vowel sounds you can think of this way, to see just how many tone colors you can get. Don't limit it just to one language, either — if you're familiar with vowels from any other languages, such as French or German, try those, too. From the French language, the "eu," as in the word "bleu" works well, for example.

To develop ideas about where you'd like to go with your musical palette of tone colors, listen to recordings of the flutists I mention in this book, particularly those listed in Chapter 21. Notice the variety of sound, vibrato, and tone color among all the flutists you hear. Listening to other instrumentalists and singers can also be helpful in stimulating your musical imagination and expanding your ideas about tone color.

Lifting the soft palate

The *soft palate* is the soft tissue located at the point where your mouth ends and your throat begins. Lifting your soft palate while you're playing the flute helps you produce a full, resonant sound. The most common everyday activity that automatically lifts your soft palate is yawning. Because your lips are pretty close together while you play the flute, lifting the soft palate while you're playing feels like you're suppressing a yawn. See whether you can "yawn" on command while playing the flute — try it with a single note first and then sustain the lifted soft palate as you play a few notes together and then a melody.

If you're having trouble with the yawning thing, read up on music notation in Chapter 4. Actually, though, imagining an upside-down U shape that travels from the front to the back along the roof of your mouth is even more helpful. It should feel as though you're saying, "Aww." (Having puppies or small children around also helps to hone this syllable.)

Notice that when you suppress a yawn or make the roof of your mouth into an upside down U shape, your jaw automatically drops a little bit. This action creates space in the back of the mouth, which slows down the air that you're exhaling into the flute and creates a resonating chamber in the back of your mouth.

Try to incorporate lifting the soft palate into your practice routine. It's a tough thing to check in the mirror because you can't see the inside of your mouth as you're playing, but you can feel it and hear the difference in your sound when you're doing it. Remind yourself often enough, and lifting the soft palate to create a big, full sound will become second nature.

Using harmonics to create colors in your sound

The harmonic series can also help you achieve some amazing resonance in your flute sound. (For more information, see the section "Placing the Notes," earlier in this chapter.)

To begin working on your resonance using harmonics, follow these steps, which I demonstrate on Track 56 of the CD:

1. **Play a low C and play the next two harmonics (sounding the octave C and the next G), slurring all the notes together.**

   You can hear this step as Track 56 on the CD. See Chapter 11 for more about harmonics and to see them in music notation form.

2. **When you get to the sounding G (still fingering C), hold it out and lift your soft palate.**

   Get as much sound from the harmonic G as possible, without forcing or squeezing your airstream. Make as much room as you can in your mouth, and think of that upside-down U shape. Feel the throat as being very open. When you've opened up your mouth and throat and the soft palate is lifted, add just a little bit more air to liven up the note even more.

   Keep holding the note and opening the sound up more and more, breathing whenever necessary and starting up again where you left off.

   Keep the back of your neck long so that the throat stays free and open.

3. **After the harmonic G sounds very big and open, lift the fingers of your right hand, except for the pinky (RH 4).**

   You should now be fingering a real G, having gotten there seamlessly from the G harmonic, which you fingered as low C. Notice how easy the G feels to play now and how resonant it is. You could probably swear that your neighbor down the block can hear it by now.

4. With this very resonant G, begin playing the melody in Figure 12-3.

In the scene of the opera where this melody occurs, Don Giovanni (Don Juan) is trying to woo an innocent young lady. She is hesitant at first, but he is so gallant and disarming that he finally wins her over — he is singing "Give me your hand!" This melody needs to sound like you're singing it straight from the heart (even though the audience knows very well that he is putting on a grand show to sway his damsel into submission). Use a big, resonant sound, so seductive that it could lure sweet young damsels (or squires) up to your own castle.

Tracks 57 & 58

Figure 12-3:
The melody "Là ci darem la mano" from the opera *Don Giovanni* by Wolfgang Amadeus Mozart (1756–1791).

Là ci darem la mano
from *Don Giovanni*

W.A. Mozart
arr. Moratz

When you get a harmonic to resonate and have a beautiful, open sound by lifting the soft palate, you're doing all that against the resistance of the extra fingers you have down. When you lift the extra fingers to get the real fingering, you remove the resistance, and the note suddenly feels light, easy, and free.

If you feel that your sound is waning as you're playing this melody, try throwing in a harmonic fingering somewhere in the middle — playing the C above the staff as an F fingering, for example. Hold that harmonic, lift the soft palate, get it to sing like nobody's business, and then transition back to the real C again. Take that big sound and carry it through to the rest of the notes as well.

For yet another challenge, try playing the same melody again softly, as though you're whispering a secret to your special someone (Track 58 on the CD). Keep the soft palate lifted, but bring the embouchure forward. Try different vowel sounds that make the inside of your mouth a bit smaller. Experiment with the C harmonic up to G, as you did in the preceding steps, but softly, to get the right color for your whispering sound.

Resonance: Producing More Sound with Less Air

Lifting the soft palate and using harmonics for resonance shows you that you can get a lot of sound out of the flute using relatively little air. The more space you create in your mouth and throat, the more your sound will resonate. You can even think of your whole face, from your forehead to your chin, as feeling almost like it's being stretched vertically — creating all that space will increase your resonating power even further. (But I wouldn't recommend stretching yourself out on a rack — that would probably be going a little bit too far.)

The more notes you have under your belt and the more proficient you are at putting them together to play melodies and pieces, the more important your breath support becomes. (See more about breath support in Chapter 5.) You need to have total control over how quickly or slowly your air is going — at all times.

If you're not controlling your air from your breathing mechanism (see Chapter 5), it will exit your lungs with an uncontrolled *whoosh*. At that point, the rest of your body will work to control the air that's going too fast. Without even thinking about it, your throat, lips, tongue, and mouth will tense up, trying to control and slow down the air. You can avoid all this tension by simply controlling the air from its point of origin, freeing up all of the embouchure's components to relax, open up, and resonate.

One thing you can do to instantly activate your breath support is to push your belly area out while playing. If you've got a waistband or a belt to push against, even better. Practice playing a few notes or a short melody while actively pushing the middle of your body outward. It feels a bit odd at first, but this action keeps your breathing mechanism from collapsing and inadvertently pushing all the air out at once. When you've played this way for a little while, stop actively pushing out quite so hard and just play. You'll find that your breathing muscles will work better to control your airstream.

Play the music in Figure 12-4 using everything you know about note placement, resonance, and tone color. Play the first piece, movement 1 of the *Sonata in F Major* by George Frideric Handel (1685–1759), with a warm, full, happy sound. The second piece, movement 2 of the *Sonata in E♭ Major, BWV 1031* by Johann Sebastian Bach (1685–1750), is in a minor key, so it sounds a bit sad, but has its sunnier moments. Play it with a sweeter, more tender feeling and use a sound that's a bit softer around the edges. Notice how projecting your own emotion into a piece helps it achieve its desired effect!

I include my suggested metronome markings for both of the pieces in Figure 12-4. I also include my suggestions for slurs/articulations and a few dynamics. However, these markings are by no means set in stone. At the time Handel and Bach were composing, the metronome wasn't invented yet, so only tempo indications were used. In the Baroque era (1685–1750), dynamics and articulations were often left up to the performer. (Read about editions of sheet music in Chapter 17.) So if you have an idea of your own that you think may work, give it a try. You're making music!

In the fourth measure and the next-to-last measure of the Bach, play the smaller notes and the normal-looking notes right after them according to the rhythms marked right above the staff. (For more on these little notes and other types of ornamentation in music, see Chapter 16.)

Tracks 59 & 60

Sonata in F Major

movement 1

G. F. Handel

Larghetto. M.M. ♩ = 80

Figure 12-4: *Sonata in F Major*, 1st movement, by George Frideric Handel, and *Sonata in E♭ Major*, 2nd movement, by Johann Sebastian Bach.

Chapter 13

Adding Vibrato: You Want Fries with That Shake?

In This Chapter

▶ Figuring out what vibrato is

▶ Producing vibrato for the first time

▶ Controlling your vibrato so that it doesn't take over your sound

The purpose of vibrato is to beautify your sound, to add a shimmer on top, sort of like putting a sparkly necklace on an already very pretty lady. In this chapter, I guide you through the basics of vibrato. I tell you where vibrato comes from and what to do to produce it. I also tell you what to avoid doing so that you can keep your vibrato from becoming too obvious and taking over your sound. You also get step-by-step instructions, enabling you to acquire the tools to use vibrato expressively and elegantly.

Discovering What Vibrato Is

The musical term *vibrato* comes from the Italian verb *vibrare*, which means to shake, vibrate, or quiver. That definition pretty much tells you what vibrato is: a fluctuation of the sound and/or pitch of a note. You can hear musicians using vibrato in just about any type of music. Singers also employ vibrato to varying degrees, from pop artists who use very little to opera singers who can apply it to the point that it sounds almost unpleasant. (My husband says they sound like enraged turkeys.) Listen to singers as well as instrumentalists, and you'll quickly be able to identify the rapidly vacillating tone to which I'm referring.

Vibrato styles have changed over the years, and the way it's produced varies by style and according to the instrument being played. You can actually see the vibrato on a violin or other string instrument because the player's left hand moves rapidly back and forth on the strings to create it. This motion on the string makes the pitch rise and fall quickly and in very small increments.

Players of woodwind instruments produce these quick variances in pitch with fluctuations in their airstream, which aren't visible like they are on the violin, but they certainly are audible.

Members of the same family of instruments sometimes use varying amounts and styles of vibrato. For example, the clarinet very rarely uses vibrato at all in classical music, but in jazz, it wails away and wobbles to its player's heart's content. The bassoon, oboe, and flute, though, do use vibrato most of the time.

In the Baroque and Classical periods of music (around 1685–1830), vibrato was used very sparingly overall. Musicians of the day would vibrate on an occasional note here and there, usually for emphasis — vibrato was used as an ornament. Sometimes they even made *vibrato* (they called it *flattement*) by moving the fingers over the tone holes instead of manipulating the airstream — keep in mind that the flutes in those days only had between one and four keys, so most of the flute was made up of open tone holes. (For more on historical flutes, see Chapter 22.)

Today, on the other hand, the prevailing style is to make the vibrato by moving the airstream in gentle waves — it becomes a part of the sound and the player uses it continuously, varying it according to the style and mood of the music at hand.

Developing Vibrato

One of the most obvious ways to tell an intermediate flutist from a beginning flutist (besides the intermediate one just sounding better) is the use of vibrato. Because the fluctuating airstream required to produce vibrato can really wreak havoc on a fledgling embouchure, a beginning flutist really needs to play with a *straight* tone — that is, without vibrato — while the embouchure is in its formative stages. (For more on the embouchure, see Chapters 6, 8, and 12.) After sound production becomes more automatic, you can concentrate on things other than just getting a sound in the first place, and you can start manipulating the airstream in more sophisticated ways. At that point, you can start thinking about producing vibrato.

Sometimes vibrato kicks in instinctively as your sound and your facility with your instrument keep getting better. My first flute teacher taught me what vibrato was by singing "Twinkle, Twinkle, Little Star" with and without it. She then went on to say that judges for contests (where school kids got graded on their performances) would give higher scores to young performers who used vibrato. Well, that thought was quite an incentive. I came back for my lesson the following week using vibrato on everything. I didn't think about it again until my musical studies in college, when I realized that I needed to be more conscious about where my vibrato was coming from. I also found that I could vary the speed of it, which opened up a whole new world of expression in my playing at the time.

Whether your vibrato just comes naturally or you have to work at it a little bit, the following sections cover a few essential facts and guidelines that will have you sounding like a more accomplished flutist in no time.

Figuring out where vibrato comes from

Because the mechanics of vibrato production involve controlled movement of your airstream, the breathing mechanism comes into play. (For more on breathing, see Chapter 5.) Everything I tell you about exhaling smoothly in the previous chapters still applies when you're using vibrato. It's just that your exhalation now undulates to vary the pitch slightly. If you give more air speed, your pitch rises, and if you back off on the air speed, your pitch drops. Producing vibrato is just this phenomenon, but executed in miniature so that you get tiny, quick waves of pitch variance throughout your playing.

The pitch waves in vibrato come from various parts of your breathing and playing mechanisms, including but not limited to your abdominal muscles, your throat, and the muscles that control your rib cage (intercostals).

Basically, any part of you that helps with the breathing process, or anything that the air passes through on its way out to the embouchure hole, can play a part in making vibrato. But if you aren't playing with vibrato yet and want to kick-start the process, you can get the right motion going by moving your belly in and out as you play a long note.

A note regarding vibrato on the CD

Because I normally play with vibrato, I recorded most of the examples on this book's CD using vibrato. However, I play the single-note demos that introduce you to each new note with a straight tone in order to make it easier for you to match my pitch. Up to this point in the book, I assume that you've been playing with a straight tone, which may or may not be the case: Your vibrato may have started already quite naturally on its own, and that's fine. It's just another way in which you are making your sound your own. Feel free to play the musical examples up to this point with or without vibrato, whichever way is the most comfortable and natural for you.

If you're already playing with vibrato instinctively, good for you! But you may want to try the following steps to familiarize yourself with the muscles involved and make sure that your vibrato is developing properly. Try vibrato using the following steps:

1. **Pick up your flute and play a B on the staff (middle B) with a straight tone (no vibrato).**

   Play it at a volume level of *mf* (medium loud).

2. **Play the B again and as you play, contract your abdominal muscles, sucking your belly in as far as possible.**

   (Just pretend you're trying to fit into last year's jeans.) Notice how the pitch rises as your belly moves inward, pushing the air out faster.

3. **Keep playing as you release your abdominal muscles.**

   Notice how the pitch drops as your belly moves outward, slowing down the air.

4. **Now play yet another B; while you're playing, alternately contract and release your abdominal muscles as in Steps 2 and 3.**

   Your pitch should be alternately rising and falling, corresponding with your physical motion. Voilà, vibrato!

5. **Play around with your newfound vibrato, varying the speed and the intensity.**

   Speed it up, slow it down, and see whether you can make waves that are sharper or more intense, as well as ones that are more smooth and subtle. You may find that the physical sensation will alter as you vary the vibrato — the abdominal muscles may not be the only muscles involved. That's exactly what you want. As you experiment, use different parts of your body to do the job of making your vibrato. The motions of vibrato are a bit nebulous because you can't see them and because a lot of subtlety is involved, but you should feel the vibrato traveling upward. Vibrato is actually easier to control when it's occurring higher in the body, so you ultimately want to encourage it to travel up through your chest and even into your throat area.

Be careful not to close your throat while you're producing vibrato. You'll know when you're closing your throat because the sound momentarily stops if you do. Keep your throat open by thinking of yawning, which lifts your soft palate. (For more on the soft palate, see Chapter 12.) That way, you won't unwittingly stop your air flow — it should stay constant, even when you're vibrating.

Making your vibrato work

After you've gotten your vibrato moving, you can start controlling it so that you can use it while you're playing a tune. Practice the following steps regularly to master vibrato control (I demonstrate using a few different vibrato speeds on Track 63 of the CD):

1. **Set your metronome at 60.**

2. **Play a middle B with a straight tone.**

   As you play, listen to the metronome beats.

3. **Start vibrating very slowly, matching the waves of your vibrato to the metronome beats.**

   The upward pulses, which you produce in the previous set of steps by contracting your abdominal muscles, should correspond to the metronome click. Release the abdominal muscles as the click stops.

   Don't stop the air flow — just make smooth, even waves of rising and falling pitch without closing your throat.

4. **Set the metronome at 80 and again match your vibrato to the metronome beats as in Step 3.**

   As you increase the speed, be sure to keep your vibrato even and smooth. If your vibrato is difficult to control and/or sounds jagged and uneven, go back to practicing it at the slower speed for a while and increase gradually. Be sure to feel the undulations traveling up through your chest and throat area as your vibrato gets faster. (Speeding up your vibrato while simultaneously keeping it even and smooth may take a few minutes, or a few days, or possibly even a few weeks — be patient!)

5. **Repeat Step 4, increasing the metronome speed to 100 and then 120.**

   Now you're well on your way to producing even, controlled vibrato.

After you complete the preceding steps, try incorporating vibrato into a melody. I suggest using any of the musical examples in Chapter 12. Using your measured vibrato, count two waves per quarter note beat. Measure your vibrato for a while and then just stop thinking about it: Let it go and see where you end up. At some point, your vibrato will take on a life of its own and just become a part of your sound. Keep experimenting with speed and intensity and have some fun with enhancing your sound with vibrato.

Keeping Your Vibrato Natural

The purpose of vibrato is to enhance your sound and your expression on the instrument. It's a lot like subtly and tastefully putting makeup on an already beautiful woman. You want to notice the beauty of the woman, not the makeup. Under everyday circumstances, a comment like "Nice lipstick!" or "I love the way those false eyelashes flutter when you blink!" would not be taken by her as a compliment. In the same way, you want the listener to notice what a gorgeous sound you have and how expressively you play, and not directly the vibrato, which should be enhancing the music and helping you shape musical phrases, not wobbling out of control.

That's not to say there won't be the occasional piece of music or phrase that will be the equivalent of a costume party, in which case the vibrato — or makeup — is allowed to be the main attraction. Most music in which extreme vibrato is not only okay, but desired, involves music written in the 20th century or later. (For more on effects in contemporary music, see Chapter 17.)

The best way to find your own style of vibrato is to listen to other performers. And not just flutists — other wind players, as well as string players and singers, can give you examples of many different styles of vibrato, provided that you're listening closely. I recommend listening to classical music rather than jazz or pop for this purpose, because classical musicians use vibrato with the most consistency. Listening to classical music performed on historical instruments won't tell you how to use vibrato on your modern Boehm flute, but it will give you some perspective on how vibrato styles have changed over the years.

How you end up using vibrato is your own personal choice, guided by the conventions of today and inspired by your favorite performers. In the following sections, you find out what the vibrato variables are, and how to use them to your best advantage.

The dreaded nanny goat vibrato

The style of vibrato that every flute teacher will warn you against is the *nanny goat vibrato*, which is represented on the sixth line of the vibrato diagram in Figure 13-1. It's very fast and quite shallow, although the bottom of the wave is jagged instead of smooth. It really does sound like a goat bleating, and it happens if you have so much tension in your throat that it closes

when you back off of the air. Sometimes you can even hear the throat closing with a very soft grunting noise. It's not pretty — don't let it happen to you! To avoid the nanny goat effect, keep your airstream flowing smoothly and constantly and maintain an open feeling in your throat by lifting your soft palate. (More on lifting the soft palate in Chapter 12.)

Width

Figure 13-1 is a visual diagram of what vibrato sounds like. Here you can see the vibrato pitch waves, which you make when you alternately push and back off of the airstream. The first, straight horizontal line represents a straight tone. The next line represents what I call a natural, everyday vibrato, the vibrato equivalent of subtle daytime makeup: a smooth, even wave that travels at a medium speed, somewhere around 250 to 275 waves per minute (that's a speed of 250 to 275 on the metronome). The third line would correspond to a faster-than-normal, but still even, vibrato.

So the width of the waves in Figure 13-1 represent the speed, or width, of your vibrato. With the last set of steps in the previous section, you increase your vibrato speed, or width, to 120 waves per minute. Usually, a natural vibrato speed kicks in without your having to practice every speed in between 120 and 275. Just keep thinking about your vibrato width as you play and see whether you can vary it — the counting exercises in the "Exercises" section at the end of this chapter can help you accomplish varying vibrato widths.

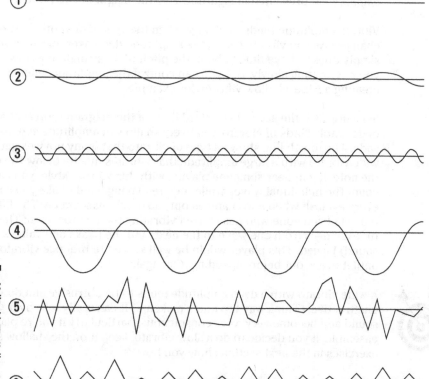

Figure 13-1:
Diagram of
a straight
tone and
various
types of
vibrato.

Vibrato in ensemble playing

When playing in ensembles with other musicians, whether it's an orchestra of 90 or a flute duet, you need to be especially sensitive with your vibrato. You don't want to use a wide, obtrusive vibrato when you're playing together with someone else. Remember that vibrato involves moving your pitch around in small increments — a deep, wide vibrato just makes it that much more difficult for you to play in tune and for your colleagues to easily match your pitch, which is essential in ensemble work. You should use a similar style of vibrato to your fellow musicians in the group. Matching vibrato styles makes it easier to blend so that you sound like a group rather than a collection of individuals playing by themselves in the same room. (For more on ensemble playing, see Chapter 18.)

Amplitude

The other variable in vibrato is how high or low your pitch goes during your vibrato waves. The amount by which your pitch rises and falls is *vibrato amplitude,* represented in Figure 13-1 by the height of each wave.

Vibrato amplitude tends to change when the speed, or width, of the vibrato changes: As you vibrate faster, the amplitude decreases, because your body simply doesn't have time to bend the pitch quite as high or as low as when you're vibrating slowly. But you can control the amplitude independently, creating a wide, shallow vibrato, for example.

In Figure 13-1, the second and third lines of the diagram represent a couple of desirable kinds of vibrato: relatively shallow in amplitude and not too wide. The fourth line shows a type of vibrato that many novices get into: a wide vibrato with a large amplitude that vibrates mostly below the pitch of the note. If you hear someone playing with this vibrato style, you can usually count the individual waves while they're playing, kind of like you can count every eyelash when a woman has put too much mascara on. The fifth line is typical of someone who has started vibrating too fast too soon: The amplitude changes from one wave to the next, and the peaks and valleys look (and sound) jagged. This player would be well served to practice vibrato slowly until it evens out before speeding it up again.

A wide vibrato with a deep amplitude tends to be obtrusive and downright unattractive. (Think way too much makeup.) It can really take over your sound and become very, very conspicuous, particularly if you're playing in an ensemble. If you decide to do a slow vibrato, keep it on the shallow side. The exercises in the next section show you how.

Exercises

The exercises in Figure 13-2 are all rhythmic vibrato exercises. Play the pitches indicated on the staff, while vibrating according to the rhythms below the staff. Notice how your vibrato feels as you speed it up: It should feel like it's traveling a little bit higher in your body than when you first started with your abdominal muscles earlier in this chapter. Don't try to pinpoint exactly where it's coming from: That's pretty tough to do anyway because you can't see it. Just feel what's going on in your body as best you can and keep your throat open throughout the exercise. By the time you're done working with these exercises, your vibrato will be on its way to becoming a part of your sound, at which point you can forget about counting it and just let it naturally flow into your music.

After you complete this set of vibrato drills, play some of the musical examples in Chapter 12 with a shallow, subtle vibrato. Now you're really making some beautiful music!

Figure 13-2: Some rhythmic vibrato exercises.

Chapter 14

High Flutin': Making the Top Notes Sing

In this chapter, you find out how to play in the flute's high register. I tell you how to play the high notes not only with the correct fingerings, but with efficient embouchure placement and a singing, open tone. After gaining confidence and control in the high register, you can start exploring the flute's vast classical repertoire — I give you some suggestions to get you started.

Third Octave Fingerings

The third octave on the flute, from the C above the staff on up, is referred to as the *high register*. The C♯ directly above this C is the highest note on the flute that has the same fingering as that of the note an octave below it. Starting with the D above the staff, the fingerings start to get pretty interesting. Some bear a slight resemblance to their counterparts an octave below, and some are completely different.

Even though the third register fingerings may seem a bit bizarre to you at first, try not to succumb to physical tension. Keep your fingers hovering right over the keys as you start playing all these new notes — don't be tempted to be even a little lax in your newfound discipline just because you're exploring new territory. Try to keep your posture relaxed, too, and especially remember to keep the back of your neck long and free, which helps keep your throat open. Check in with your torso to ensure that your ribs are moving freely and that you're not trying to hold your tummy in when you inhale. If you don't tense up, the high notes will come much more easily to you. (See Chapter 5 for more on posture and body alignment.)

The third octave fingerings and why they're different

To play a third octave D, follow these steps, which I demonstrate on Track 64 of the CD:

1. **Play low G and then go up to the two harmonics above it.**

   The two harmonic notes should be a sounding G the octave higher and then a sounding D above that. (See Chapter 11 for more on harmonics.)

2. **Play the high harmonic (sounding D) by itself and hold it out.**

   Go for your biggest, most resonant sound on this harmonic. (For more on resonance, see Chapter 12.)

3. **As you're still playing the harmonic in Step 2, lift LH 1.**

   That's your third octave D! The fingering for third octave D is TH, LH 2, LH 3, and RH 4.

You may ask (and rightfully so) why I didn't just give you the fingering for the third octave D right away, instead of making you play through a G harmonic series first. "Is she just crazy about harmonics? Or is she just mean?" you may ask. Yep, I love those harmonics: After all, they're the building blocks of music. But it also happens that they're the building blocks of the flute's high register, as well. And I seem mean only at times with some of these exercises — I'm really a very nice person. (Just ask any one of my students. . . .)

The fingerings for the flute's high register are based on harmonics from the lower notes, and not always just on the octave: In the case of the D, the basis is a fifth, so it comes from the G. That's why the fingering for the third octave D is so close to that of the G below it.

I don't tell you the harmonic that each and every high note is based on at this point: After all, you want to play the flute, not write a dissertation on the acoustical aspects of it. But you want to keep this basic fact about the high register in mind: The harmonic series helps you understand not only the fingerings for the third register, but also how some of those high notes behave when you play them.

For now, just play through the octaves in Figure 14-1 to familiarize yourself with the high note fingerings from the third octave D through the third octave B. I also throw in the fourth octave C at the end; this note is just beyond the third octave, but the high C comes up a lot more often than any of the other fourth octave notes, so it's best that you get to know it sooner than later. Here, you're slurring from the lower notes to the octave higher so that you can compare the fingerings as you play them.

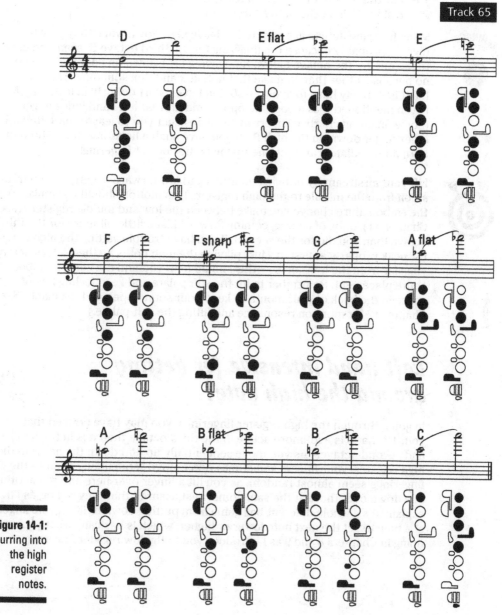

Figure 14-1: Slurring into the high register notes.

You need to use your flute's trill keys in the right hand to play high B♭ and high B. To do so:

✔ For the high B♭, move RH 2 slightly over to the left to depress the first trill key (also called the *D trill key*).

✔ For the high B, move RH 3 slightly over to the left to depress the second trill key (also called the *D♯ trill key*).

Many fledgling flutists are tempted to leave LH 1 down when they play the high B♭, probably because the fingering for the third octave B♭ seems so close to the one for the octave below. But leaving LH 1 down on your high B♭ serves no purpose, other than to make that note flat and dull-sounding. This bad habit isn't really hard to avoid — so don't even start doing it! In fact, forget I even mentioned it as a possible option and lift that left-hand index finger. (Some fingering charts even erroneously instruct you to leave your left-hand index finger down on the high B♭. If you have such a fingering chart, shred or burn it immediately and get one that lists the correct fingering!)

Lift your airstream by bringing your lips and jaw forward slightly as you transition from the middle to the high register. This motion should be similar to the embouchure change you make between the low and middle registers (see Chapter 11), only, of course, coming forward just a little bit more for the third octave than you did for the second. If you have trouble getting the high notes to speak properly at first, try just playing the high notes by themselves before you slur from the low notes — this should help you find the correct embouchure placement. Remember to lift the soft palate and keep feeling lots of space in the back of your mouth to keep your sound open and resonant. (See Chapter 12 for more on resonance and lifting the soft palate.)

Left-hand intensive for getting around the high notes

In going through the high register fingerings, you may have noticed that your left hand is a lot more active in the third octave than it is in the first and second octaves. As you move sequentially up and down the notes in the high register, your fingers sometimes don't move sequentially at all — the fingerings seem almost random, as you lift a finger over here and put another one down over there at the same time. Rest assured that they're not, as I'll explain. It's a whole different ball game from putting down or lifting one finger at a time to get the next note lower or higher, which is basically what you're doing in Chapters 8 and 9 as I introduce you to the low register fingerings.

The reason for these (at first) seemingly complicated fingerings is again related to the harmonic series. To produce good high notes, you can't just play the harmonic of the lower note with the same fingering as the low note and expect it to work: The high note fingerings are tweaked versions of the harmonic.

Try the set of steps that you use to find the fingering for the 3rd octave D in the "The third octave fingerings and why they're different" section, earlier in this chapter: The harmonic of G that sounds like D just isn't quite right — it's kind of muffled sounding and quite flat, but it's *almost* a real D. You have to lift LH 1 in order to have a true, clear sounding D that's in tune. All the high register notes come from these tweaked harmonics. Sometimes you *vent*, or uncover one or more tone holes, to get the right sound for the high register note; often, the venting happens in the left hand, which explains all the left hand activity in the high register. Sometimes you also put some extra fingers down for a high note to sound properly. One example is the fingering for high E, which is based on an A harmonic. You have to put two fingers down in the right hand in order to bring the E up to the correct pitch.

After you realize that these high note fingerings aren't as random as they seem at first, you also know that the flute isn't out to confound you: These high note fingerings are really the only way to get those high notes out and have them sound good. And you will get used to them — it's just a matter of daily practice, always starting slowly, and always remaining patient. (For more about how to practice, see Chapter 5.)

Here are a few drills to get you accustomed to playing in the flute's high register. Start playing these finger twisters slowly, using your metronome, at whatever tempo you can play them cleanly and evenly, taking a beat or two to breathe wherever necessary. Then dial up the tempo one increment at a time. You'll be cruising along in the third octave before you know it!

After you master the drills in Figure 14-2, you need to keep practicing high register finger combinations on a daily basis so that you keep developing your facility in the third octave. The book *Top Register Studies for Flute (90 Melodious Studies)* by Thomas J. Filas (Carl Fischer) is a great way to practice high register finger combinations efficiently. The studies themselves are short, only three or four lines each, so they won't take you all day to get through, no matter how slowly you start out. They're chock-full of the most awkward high note finger combinations so that you practice the third octave in an intense, yet efficient way.

Figure 14-2:
Left-hand intensive drills for facility in the high register.

Alternate fingerings for tricky high note passages

Every once in a while, no matter how diligently you practice your high register, you may come across a passage that seems unplayable at the performance tempo the composer indicates, especially if you happen to be playing advanced solo repertoire or orchestral music. Here's another instance where the harmonic series comes in handy: creative fingerings built on harmonics to facilitate difficult technical passages.

Consider the example in Figure 14-3 from *Fantasie Pastorale Hongroise, Op. 26* for flute and piano by Albert Franz Doppler (1821–1883). (Recordings of this brilliantly virtuosic piece are widely available, and highly listenable!)

To execute the harmonics in this passage (marked with a small circle over the notes), you simply finger the low notes, which are printed very small, and overblow them so that they sound like the printed high notes above them. In order to get the correct pitches to speak, you need to bring your embouchure forward quite a bit to lift the air and decrease the size of your aperture so that your airstream moves faster. (For more on overblowing and harmonics, see Chapter 11.)

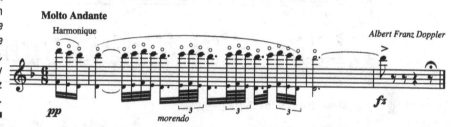

Figure 14-3:
Excerpt from *Fantasie Pastorale Hongroise, Op. 26,* by Albert Franz Doppler.

Fantasie Pastorale Hongroise, Op. 26

Molto Andante

Harmonique

Albert Franz Doppler

pp

morendo

fz

In this case, the composer (who was a flutist, by the way) wrote the harmonics right into the flute part. He was definitely going for an effect here — the harmonics have a closed, rather eerie sound, in contrast to the "normal" fingerings. Notice that the last D, marked with an accent and an *fz*, takes you suddenly and forcefully back to the clear, open sound of the real D fingering.

Even though Doppler wrote this passage as a sound effect (not to be confused with the scientific phenomenon, the Doppler Effect), you can use it as an example of why unaltered harmonic fingerings are sometimes easier to negotiate in technical passages. Try playing the passage using the harmonic fingerings that Doppler suggests and then try it using the real fingerings for the D, E, and F instead of the harmonics. The latter is vastly more labor-intensive for your left hand!

Now take a look at the famously difficult passage that Sergei Prokofiev (1891–1953) wrote for the flute in his orchestral piece, *Classical Symphony,* shown in Figure 14-4.

If you use the regular high register fingerings in the fifth through the eighth measures of this excerpt, the passage is really awkward and difficult to play, especially considering that Prokofiev asks for a tempo of 152 to the half note. However, if you use the suggestions for harmonic fingerings that I indicate in the example below the original excerpt in Figure 14-4, the passage becomes easier to manage. In the seventh measure, as I indicate in the example, you can even leave LH 1 down on the high A so that LH 1 can stay down all the way through the most challenging part of the passage. It's still tricky, but a lot more playable this way — many flutists use harmonic fingerings when they're faced with this passage, including me. (I demonstrate it with the harmonic fingerings on the CD included with this book.)

Figure 14-4:
Excerpt from *Classical Symphony* by Sergei Prokofiev.

The *Classical Symphony* excerpt, one of the most challenging pieces in the orchestral repertoire, is just one example of possible uses of harmonic fingerings to facilitate technical passages in the high register. There are really no hard-and-fast rules about how to use them. The more you experiment with harmonics, the more you'll be inclined to use them when you come across a difficult passage involving a lot of high notes. The one thing to keep in mind about these harmonic fingerings is that you want to reserve them for very fast passages, because the faster the notes are going by, the less chance the listener has to notice that the harmonic pitches sound kind of muffled and not as well in tune as the real notes would be. As a general rule, try to execute the passage the normal way first; that way, you can determine how challenging the passage is in the first place, and you give your fingers a good workout. If you overuse the easier harmonic fingerings in the high register, you won't be giving your fingers a chance to get around the real third octave fingerings, and then you may not be able to execute them when you really need them. That being said, using the harmonics can save you a lot of trouble, so it pays to experiment with them early on in your development.

Another handy (finger-y?) trick you need to know about involves the third octave Bb. In fast passages, you can leave off the first trill key (D trill key) in the right hand when you're playing the high Bb. This fingering is definitely not for use in slow passages, because it's quite flat, but it can be a lifesaver when you're playing a passage such as the one in the last movement of *Piano Concerto No. 1, Op. 23* by Pyotr Il'yich Tchaikovsky (1840–1893), shown in Figure 14-5.

Play this passage using the normal fingering for the high Bb — that is, with the first trill key. Then try the same passage without using the first trill key on the high Bb. Because RH 2 doesn't have to slide from the first trill key to get back to the big key to play the E, the passage ends up being much simpler to play. Of course, that's not saying much, considering that this passage usually goes lightning fast — about 152 to the quarter note, which means that streamlining your fingerings as much as possible is doubly important.

Figure 14-5:
Excerpt
from the
third
movement
of *Piano
Concerto
No. 1, Op. 23*
by Pyotr
Il'yich
Tchaikovsky.

Track 68

Piano Concerto No. 1

Op. 23, last movement

Tchaikovsky

Allegro con fuoco

mf

So, learn all the proper fingerings first, but when it comes to making especially tricky passages work, get creative using the ideas in this section — or come up with your own. (I've often stumbled across useful fingerings quite by accident!)

Climbing into the stratosphere: fourth octave C♯ and D

Sooner or later in your music-making, you're bound to come across a fourth octave note. The flute's highest C is technically in the fourth octave, but that note occurs so frequently that it's sort of become an honorary member of the third octave. The fourth octave, or *altissimo* (Italian for "very high") C♯ and D don't come up all that much, but when they do, they're usually pretty exposed — they either come out or they don't, and if they don't, the result won't be pretty. See Figure 14-6 for the fingerings for these two notes and have fun trying them out. (But not before you get your dog out of earshot!)

Track 69

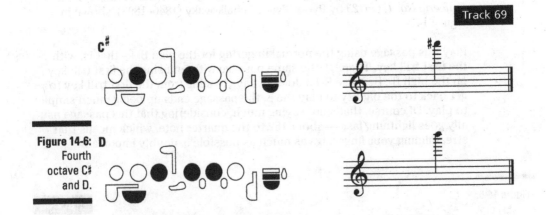

Figure 14-6: Fourth octave C♯ and D.

You've got to use a lot of air speed to get these notes to come out. That means not only blowing harder, but making your aperture smaller: For these notes, you may need to even squeeze the aperture to get enough air speed. As always, it's also a question of air angle — aim the air high by bringing your jaw forward. Be sure to play these notes from time to time so that you can remember the fingerings on command, but don't spend a lot of time on them until you're comfortable and consistent with your embouchure in the third octave. Otherwise, you can develop too much tension from practicing those altissimo notes over and over.

Prokofiev seems to have been very fond of writing fourth octave C♯s and Ds in his flute parts. His fondness for the altissimo range of the flute is very apparent in at least two of his works: his *Sonata in D Major, op. 94* has multiple high Ds in the first movement, and his *Classical Symphony* features repeated scales up to the high D in the last movement. The effect is remarkable in both of these pieces. Give them a listen!

The notes above the fourth octave C♯ and D are mainly used in contemporary music. (See more about contemporary music and extended techniques in the sidebar in Chapter 17.) I include fingering charts for notes up to a fourth octave G in Appendix A.

Finding Resonance in the Top Notes

Playing a high note on the flute is not all that much of a challenge, but playing the high register with a full, beautiful sound can take some doing. One reason is that everyone tends to associate higher pitches with more tension. Too much tension leads to narrowing of the passageways (throat, mouth, and aperture) and therefore constriction of the airstream. If the narrowing airstream starts going too fast, the result is a sharp, forced, downright unpleasant, and screechy-sounding high register.

It's true that you often need to move the embouchure more than in the low and middle registers to get up high, but don't make the mistake of overcompensating by tightening up your embouchure or, worse yet, your whole body completely.

In the following sections, I give you tools to release all that unnecessary tension or avoid it altogether, creating a full, open sound in the high register.

Using harmonics to find note placement

A lot of what causes tension when you play in the high register is the fear that the sound might crack down to the harmonic below at any moment. This fear just means that you haven't gauged the embouchure placement for the high register yet: You need to know exactly where to put it. That way, you eliminate the need for tension and excessive air speed.

Following these steps can help you know exactly where to place your embouchure as you move into the high register. One key to making a good sound in the high register is to be confident when you're playing up there. Visualize yourself playing beautifully and simply go for it, enjoying your journey to these rarified heights.

1. **From Figure 14-7, play the first note you see next to the big letter A, which is a third register E♭.**

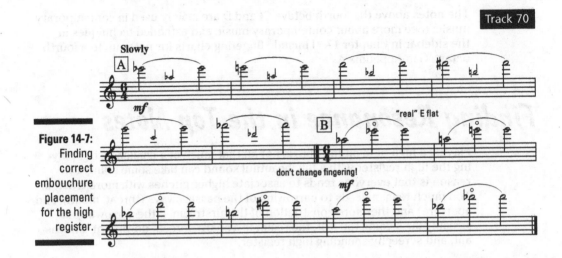

Figure 14-7:
Finding correct embouchure placement for the high register.

2. **While you're playing the E♭, slowly start aiming your airstream lower by dropping your jaw and moving your embouchure downward, bit by bit.**

   Reduce your air speed a little as you do so. Move very slowly so that you feel every increment of what's happening in your embouchure.

3. **When the note cracks down so that it's no longer an E♭, but more of a funky-sounding (extremely flat) A♭, hold out that strange-sounding lower note for a little while.**

   Make friends with this note — this is the one you're so scared of when playing the high E♭, the source of your tension. So face your fear! Hang out with it for a little while and feel where your embouchure is when you're playing it. (It's somewhere between an A♭ and a G, so don't even try to play it in tune — just hover here.) The object is to feel where you're going with your embouchure, not to sound pretty right now. But you'll definitely sound pretty in the high register later if you stick with these steps.

4. **From the weird-sounding lower note, bring your embouchure back up very, very slowly, aiming the air higher as you go, until the note switches back to the high E♭ that you play in Step 1.**

   Stay open in the back of your mouth and throat as you bring the jaw and lips forward. Move only as much as you need to in order to produce that high E♭ and then stop and hold that note. You probably won't need to move as far as you think to get to the E♭ — in other words, you've been working too hard!

Throat noises

If you play with excessive tension in your throat, which has a tendency of happening in the high register, you may end up with extraneous throat noises in your playing. Hearing your own throat noises while you're playing is difficult, so it may take a friend or a recording device for you to discover if you have them — yet another reason to record yourself while you're practicing. The noises, which sound a lot like someone grunting or starting to cough, are caused by the throat closing momentarily and opening back up just as quickly. If you find that your playing is contaminated by throat noises, you can exterminate the bothersome pests by doing lots of slow playing without vibrato in the low register before you slowly work your way back up to the high notes and then begin vibrating again. (For more on vibrato, see Chapter 13.)

5. **Repeat Steps 1 through 4 on the next five measures of Figure 14-7.**

   In Figure 14-7, the music notation shows smaller notes to represent the notes that you're cracking down to and back up from, without using the real fingering for those notes. Your last high note in this step should be the A♭ right before the big letter B at the double bar. Make sure that you're moving slowly and in small increments so that you can feel everything you're doing.

6. **Starting on the next section of Figure 14-7, after the double bar at letter B, play the first note, which is a second octave A♭.**

7. **Without changing your fingering from the second octave A♭, move your jaw and lips forward until you get a sounding E♭.**

   The E♭ harmonic that you get from here sounds slightly flat, but just try to get your best possible sound on it without worrying too much about the pitch for now. Move your embouchure forward only as much as absolutely necessary to get that E♭ and don't squeeze your aperture. Keep your sound as open as possible.

8. **Switch your fingering to the real E♭ fingering by adding RH 1, 2, and 3.**

   You're now playing a high E♭ with a nice, open sound, and with very little tension.

9. **Repeat Steps 6 through 8, applying them to the next five measures of music in Figure 14-7.**

   By moving between the middle and high registers a couple of different ways without changing fingerings, you isolate your embouchure and train it to know where it's going. Your embouchure is now primed and ready to tackle anything the high register might bring with poise and elegance, a beautiful, open sound, and no unnecessary tension.

Just say "aaahh!"

Everything you know about making a beautiful sound on the flute in the low and middle registers (see Chapter 12) applies to the high register as well. As a matter of fact, your high register embouchure shouldn't be too different from what you're doing in the lower registers — your airstream should just be aiming slightly higher, the exact direction depending on which note you're playing. If things look and/or feel a lot different in the high register, check in to see whether you might be working too hard, using the steps in the previous section. And most importantly, make sure that you still have an open feeling in the back of your mouth and throat. Think of yawning, which lifts your soft palate (see Chapter 12) and think of saying "ah" as you play, to create as much space as possible.

Melodies That Incorporate the Flute's High Register

You can use the melodies in Figure 14-8 to take your high register notes out for a spin. These melodies are excerpts from the *Petite Symphonie* for nine woodwind instruments by Charles Gounod (1818–1893), and from the *Romance* for flute and piano by Camille Saint-Saëns (1835–1921). These two melodies require a full, expressive sound all over the flute's range, including the third octave. Both excerpts start out in the low register and then repeat the same melody incorporating more of the flute's high notes. Be sure to lift your airstream to slur from the low or middle to the high register, maintaining an open, singing sound. Enjoy!

Andante Cantabile

Charles Gounod

Andante (quasi Adagio)

Tracks 72 & 73

Figure 14-8:
Two melodies incorporating the flute's third register.

Knowing your music: Periods and styles

If you play flute music in the classical genre, you'll mostly be playing within four periods of music. First of all, the word *classical* can be a little confusing because it refers to the whole genre of art music as opposed to, say, folk or pop music. But *Classical* also refers to a period of music within the classical genre, the time period between 1750 and 1825 — a style and period of music represented by Mozart and his contemporaries.

Defining periods of music and identifying their styles is not a black-and-white proposition, much like trying to exactly define what the decades of the 1950s, '60s, and '70s represented — it's just a way to try to organize a vast time span and keep track of the general characteristics of music over that period.

Here's a thumbnail sketch:

✔ **Baroque:** 1685–1750. *Composers:* Handel, Bach, Telemann, Vivaldi. Baroque music has a strong harmonic and rhythmic structure dictated by the bass line, with the flute featured in the melodic line, often with ornaments added by the player.

✔ **Classical:** 1750–1825. *Composers:* Haydn, Mozart, Salieri, Stamitz. Classical music is organized into neat four-measure phrases and sounds more incisive than Baroque or Romantic music. Its simplicity is deceptive, though; sometimes the thought and emotion that's going on underneath the brightness and clarity of Classical music can be incredibly profound.

✔ **Romantic:** 1825–1915. *Composers:* Chopin, Reinecke, Schubert, Saint-Saëns. (There's some controversy about whether Beethoven was a Classical or Romantic composer, as his music had qualities of both. As I mention earlier, the classifications aren't always as obvious as you may think.) Many composers of the Romantic period told specific stories with their music that they sometimes even indicated in the score. The Romantic aesthetic involved a lot of emotion, often with unrequited love in the picture, and the music was often quite virtuosic, and less structured than in either Baroque or Classical periods.

✔ **20th Century/Contemporary:** 1915–present. *Composers:* Prokofiev, Roussel, Poulenc, Hindemith, Copland. This period encompasses a particularly wide time span, mostly because it's difficult to define a single common style among much of the music written after 1915. The Impressionists, like Debussy, are borderline between Romantic and 20th Century, and are identifiable by their watercolor-like harmonies (the sonic equivalent of a Monet painting). Beyond that, though, the styles are so diverse that they really need to be subcategorized into styles such as Neo-Classicism, Nationalism, Avant-Garde, and the like. (See the sidebar in Chapter 17 for more on Avant-Garde flute music and techniques.)

Music That Makes Your Flute Sing: Repertoire Suggestions

Here's a list of recommended pieces that incorporate the range and techniques I cover in Chapters 8 through 14 of this book. The list includes classic intermediate-to-advanced level collections and pieces that encourage you to play with a full, singing sound. Have fun playing the flute!

✔ Collections:

- *24 Short Concert Pieces* — revised by Robert Cavally; ed. Southern

  This collection includes the complete version of Bizet's *Minuet de l'Arlésienne*. You can find an excerpt from this piece on Track 74 of the CD, and you can find the flute part in Chapter 15 so that you can play along with the CD accompaniment track (Track 75).

- *Solos for Flute* — Don Peck (Carl Fischer)

- *Sonatas* — G.F. Handel; (Bärenreiter)

  You can hear the first movement of Handel's *Sonata in F Major* on Track 59 of the CD, and you can find the flute part in Chapter 12 so that you can play along with the CD accompaniment track (Track 60).

- *Sonatas* — W.A. Mozart; (Bärenreiter or Schirmer)

- *Four Sonatas* — G.P. Telemann; (Schirmer)

✔ Pieces:

- *Variations on a Theme by Rossini* — Frederic Chopin

- *Morceau de Concours* — Gabriel Fauré

- *Madrigal* — Philippe Gaubert

- *The Swiss Shepherd* — Francesco Pietro Morlacchi

- *Joueurs de Flute* — Albert Roussel

- *Romance* — Camille Saint-Saëns

You can hear an excerpt from Saint-Saëns' *Romance* on Track 72 of the CD, and you can find the flute part in Figure 14-8 earlier in this chapter, so that you can play along with the CD accompaniment track (Track 73).

Chapter 15

Controlling Pitch: Do You Need a Tuneup?

In This Chapter

▶ Determining pitch with your tuner and your ears

▶ Knowing when your flute is likely to be sharp or flat

▶ Playing in tune

Your flute, although a miracle of modern engineering, nonetheless has built-in compromises in its design. Endless research has gone into tone hole size and placement to create an instrument with optimal intonation, but you still have to be constantly aware of pitch and make adjustments as you play if you want to have good intonation.

In this chapter, you make sure that your instrument is set up to play at standardized pitch (A=440) by comparing your tuning A to another instrument's or by using an electronic tuner. And because, as my very first band director said, "The instrument isn't tuned at the factory," you have to find out which notes on your own instrument tend to sound sharp or flat. I also cover those notes on the scale that typically want to go out of tune on any flute, and what idiosyncrasies to watch out for pitch-wise when you play louder or softer. Finally, I offer you common-sense advice and easy solutions for surmounting the flute's pitch challenges so that you can play in tune in no time . . . *not* flat!

Tuning Up

When you talk about a *pitch,* you're talking about the quality and accuracy of a single note played on your instrument. Yet within that one seemingly simple note is also a whole world of possibilities:

▶ The note may sound *sharp* — that is, pitched a little too high.

▶ The note may be played *flat* — pitched slightly too low.

▶ The note may be perfectly *in tune* — (A=440Hz) according to today's standardized pitch in the United States.

The word *intonation* in music refers to a player's ability (or lack of it) to play the notes of the scale in tune relative to each other. If you play one note a bit sharp and the next one quite flat, for example, your intonation is poor. If you can play all the way up and down the range of the instrument with all the notes in tune, you have good intonation.

You always need to be listening and adjusting to fix inadvertent pitch fluctuations or to prevent them from happening in the first place. Whether or not you're playing with other musicians, keeping your general pitch centered around A=440 is a good idea. That way, when you do end up getting together to play with a pianist, another flutist, or even your local band, you'll already be in the ballpark (speaking of pitches).

In order to keep your pitch consistent overall, you need to first check the general pitch of your instrument: If your flute is set up to play optimally at A=440, you stand a much better chance of being able to play in tune throughout the full range of the instrument.

The traditional way to check an instrument's general pitch is to check one or more tuning notes against a tuner or another instrument's tuning note(s). If you've ever attended an orchestra or band concert, you've probably noticed that the oboe gives a designated series of tuning notes before the concert begins — this way, the musicians can check the pitch of their instruments right before they start playing. The oboe gets the job of giving the tuning note (or *giving the A*) because it has the most penetrating sound and stable pitch of all the orchestral instruments. The oboist usually has an electronic tuner on hand to ensure that the oboe's pitch is correct as the A is given.

You need to check pitch regularly — before rehearsals and concerts and during practice sessions. Temperature can greatly affect intonation: Heat makes the pitch rise, and cold makes it fall. The temperature on a particular day or in a certain room can make your flute sound significantly sharper or flatter. When you take your flute out of the case, it's relatively cool, but as you play, the warmth of your breath actually heats up the instrument and raises its pitch. So you need to keep checking your tuning notes at regular intervals as you practice and play — at the beginning of every practice session, and about every hour or so after that. Make checking your pitch a habit, like brushing your teeth. Your ears — and your musical colleagues — will thank you.

Using your tuner

Tuning your instrument using an electronic tuner is easier than tuning to another instrument — it does some of the work for you. (For more information on acquiring a tuner, see Chapter 5.) To tune up, follow these steps:

1. **Turn your tuner on and make sure that it's calibrated to A=440.**

Follow the manufacturer's instructions. If your tuner doesn't have a calibration feature, then you can assume that it's set at A=440, unless you bought it in a country outside of the United States where A=440 is not the standard pitch.

2. **Set the tuner on your music stand.**

3. **Play a low A (the lowest A on the flute) and watch the tuner's needle or LED moving, noticing where it lands.**

   Use very little or no vibrato on your tuning note so that you can get a true reading on your pitch.

   If the needle lands directly on 0, stop here — you're done!

4. **If the needle is to the right or left of 0, pull out or push in your head-joint slightly to get your flute closer to the correct pitch.**

   The needle tells you how sharp or flat you are so that you can gauge how much you pull out or push in accordingly.

   • If the needle lands to the right of 0, you're sharp. Pull the head-joint out. Because your pitch is too high, you need to pull out your headjoint to make your flute a bit longer, which brings the pitch lower.

   • If the needle lands to the left of 0, you're flat. Push the headjoint in. Because your pitch is too low, you need to push in your headjoint to make your flute a bit shorter, which brings the pitch higher.

5. **To check your work, repeat Steps 3 and 4 until the needle lands and stays on 0.**

   Now your instrument is ready to play optimally at standard pitch.

Using your ears

Because so many variables affect pitch on different instruments, musicians in ensembles tune to each other. Whether 2 or 200 musicians are in the ensemble, the process is the same: One person gives the tuning note, and the other(s) play their tuning note(s) along with it, comparing the pitches and adjusting as necessary.

Why not always just use an electronic tuner, and have all instruments in the ensemble tune to it? In some ensembles, this method may be practical, but some instruments in an ensemble may not be able to adjust on the spot — for example, a piano. A piano tuner adjusts the pitch of all the piano's strings periodically, but if the temperature in the room has caused the strings to move slightly, the pianist can't stop everything to re-tune. So when an ensemble includes a piano, often the players will tune to it. In an orchestra or band, typically the oboe tunes to the piano and then gives the A for the rest of the ensemble.

Tuning by ear can be an intimidating process. You definitely feel a sense of ritual when you hear an orchestra tune, and many people are mystified by it. And, of course, when you tune to other instruments, you have people watching and listening as you tune, which can be unnerving. It's a simple process, but you have to listen carefully and be ready to try again if you don't get it quite right the first time. Don't sacrifice good pitch in order to get the tuning process over with quickly — adjust carefully and if you're having trouble comparing your pitch to the tuning note, don't be afraid to ask someone else whose ears you trust. Every musician knows that tuning can sometimes be tricky.

To practice tuning your instrument to a tuning A, follow these steps:

1. **Find the feature on your tuner that plays a tuning A for you.**

   If you can't find the feature on your tuner, try your metronome. One or the other or both should be able to play an electronic A for you. Your device will keep playing this A for you until you're done tuning, or until the batteries run out, whichever comes first.

2. **While the electronic note is sounding, play your low A, at a medium-loud volume and with your best sound, but without vibrato and then compare your pitch to the electronic pitch.**

   Don't adjust your embouchure to match the electronic pitch. Just listen carefully and see whether you can tell how your pitch compares. (Hint: If you're hearing extraneous buzzy, oscilliating sounds, or beats, when the two notes play together, you're either sharp or flat, but you're not in tune.)

3. **If you can't tell whether your pitch is high or low to the tuning note, roll the headjoint toward you and away from you very slowly.**

   If the buzzing and oscillating goes away at any point and you get more of a straight tone sounding when you're playing with the tuning note, that means you've adjusted your pitch to match the tuning note. Determine whether you were rolling the flute toward you or away from you to match the tuning note.

   • If you rolled the flute toward you to match the tuning note, then you started out sharp and made the pitch flatter in order to play in tune. To tune your flute, pull the headjoint out slightly to lower the pitch of your instrument.

   • If you rolled the flute away from you to match the tuning note, then you started out flat and made the pitch sharper in order to play in tune. To tune your flute, push the headjoint in slightly to raise the pitch of your instrument.

4. **To check your work, repeat Steps 2 and 3 until you're satisfied that your A matches the tuning note.**

The tuning A is traditional — the first string that violinists tune is the A string. So, of course, you do need to be able to tune to an A. But you can play more than one note around a tuning A, which helps your ear to put it in context and therefore get a more accurate reading. To see how the tuning process works with playing more than one note, try these steps:

1. **Have your tuner (or metronome) play a tuning A for you.**

2. **While the tuning A is sounding, play your low A, again with your best *mf* sound, but without vibrato.**

   Notice whether or not you hear any beats, or oscillations, to indicate that you may be sharp or flat. If so, see whether you can tell whether your pitch is lower or higher than the tuning note. Don't adjust anything yet.

3. **Now play another A an octave higher.**

   Listen and compare again.

4. **Now play a middle D — the one in between the two A's you just played.**

   Keep listening and comparing.

5. **After you have a better idea of where you stand pitch-wise, go back to the previous set of steps and tune up your flute from the low A by listening and adjusting.**

   To check your work, you can come back to trying the octave A's and the D against the tuning note again.

Playing the A an octave higher as well as the middle D may give you a better idea of how your pitch compares to the tuning note than just playing the low A by itself. Because the octave A's can sometimes differ in pitch — the high one tends to be a bit sharper than the low one — it gives you a chance to see how your intonation is faring over a little more of the range of the instrument. If your two A's don't give you the answer you're looking for, the middle D probably will. Middle D is one of the most stable notes on the flute, in part because of the resistance created by having so many tone holes closed. Your pitch may slide around a bit more on the A's, but it'll be rock-solid on the D. It's also pretty easy to hear whether or not a D is in tune when you play it with an A — again, you can listen for the beats in the sound. When the A and D are in tune with each other, they'll both sound crystal-clear, with no buzzing noises or oscillations.

Most ensembles tune to an A, but sometimes bands and wind ensembles, which are groups made up of mostly wind instruments, tune to a B♭. The tuning procedure will be essentially the same — except, of course, that you'll play a B♭ instead of an A. (Trust me, you'll have a hard time making an A sound in tune when you play it against a B♭!) For your three tuning notes to compare with the B♭, you could play the B♭ in two octaves, and a middle E♭, as well.

Although you're shooting for a perfect number (440) when you play your tuning A, intonation is never an absolute. Environmental factors, such as temperature and humidity, affect every instrument differently, so you never know exactly what pitch you're going to have to match. And even if the tuner's needle is right on zero when you check a particular note, the harmony that accompanies that note in the music may require that you budge the pitch up or down a bit to get it perfectly in tune. (Yes, harmony — and a note's function within that harmony — can change the exact pitch required for a chord to be in tune!) The tuner gives you a frame of reference, but it's up to you (and your ears) to do the fine-tuning after that.

Dealing with the Flute's Pitch Tendencies

In order to be able to play in tune with other musicians, you must be able to play in tune with yourself first. Playing in tune with yourself and others means developing good intonation all the way up and down the range of the flute.

Today's flutes have a more accurate scale than those of years past (see Chapter 3), but they still require the player to make adjustments while playing to achieve good intonation.

Checking your flute's cork placement

The cork that sits inside the headjoint near the top, right underneath the crown, has a specific placement that ensures the flute's best possible intonation, and the maker meticulously checks this placement before every new flute leaves the shop. But because the cork can gradually move over time, especially as it shrinks with age, you should check its placement from time to time. To easily and quickly check your cork placement using your cleaning rod, follow these steps:

1. **Find the cork placement line (also called a *register mark*), which is a straight line about ¾ inch from the bottom of your cleaning rod.**

2. **Insert the bottom end of your cleaning rod into your headjoint.**

The embouchure hole should be facing you. Make sure that the cleaning rod is parallel to the sides of the wall of the headjoint, and that the bottom end of the cleaning rod is resting right up against the cork assembly at the top of the headjoint.

3. **Check your cork placement by seeing whether the register mark looks like it's right in the middle of your embouchure hole.**

If it's not exactly centered, take your flute in to your repair technician and have him adjust the cork for you. (Read more about repair technicians in Chapter 19.) If the cork has shrunk to the point where it's loose inside the headjoint, it may also be time to replace the cork.

Pitch tendencies vary from one flute to another, and because every flutist's embouchure is slightly different, they can vary from player to player as well. This section tells you what you need to know about the idiosyncrasies of the flute's scale in order to fine-tune your intonation. You also find out how the flute behaves pitch-wise when you change your dynamic level or vary your articulation.

Up and down the scale: Discovering your flute's pitch tendencies

Because pitch tendencies can vary on different brands of flutes, the only way you can really determine what yours are is by checking all your flute's notes with your tuner. You can check your flute's scale by following these steps:

1. **Power up your tuner and place it on your music stand so that you can see the display as you play.**

2. **Use the tuner to check your tuning notes.**

   You want to tune your flute to A=440 before proceeding to the next steps. (To tune, use the previous two sets of steps in this chapter.)

3. **Play a B on the staff and hold it out at about a *mf*.**

   Play all the following steps at *mf* as well.

   In case there's any confusion, the B you should be playing is the first note you play in Chapter 8. The term *on the staff* just refers to the B that's notated right on the third line of the staff, not above or below it.

4. **Check in with the tuner to determine whether your B is sharp, flat, or in tune.**

   Your B should be giving you pretty much the same readout on the tuner as your A. If it doesn't, go back to Step 2 and try tuning again and be sure to keep your embouchure consistent — don't move it around too much!

5. **Slur from the B down to a B♭; keep checking with the tuner to see whether or not your B♭ is sharp, flat, or in tune.**

   Don't make any adjustments to your flute or embouchure. Just notice where the pitch is and continue.

6. **Now repeat the B♭, tonguing the beginning of the note, while watching the tuner.**

   Notice whether you hear any difference in pitch with tonguing versus slurring.

7. **Slur from the B♭ to the A below it and then tonguing the A, always checking in with the tuner. (You're repeating Steps 5 and 6 a half step lower.)**

8. **Repeat this pattern, going chromatically downward, not skipping any notes, all the way down to the lowest note on your flute (C or B, depending on the footjoint).**

   Notice what happens to the pitch readout on your tuner as you descend.

What you discover in the preceding steps is that the intonation tends to drop with each successive note as you descend from the low B — the lower the note, the lower the pitch. It's a pretty uniform dropping of pitch on the way down the scale.

In the next set of steps, you take the same sequence upward, to see whether the same applies to the middle and top registers:

1. **Play a B on the staff (at about *mf*) and hold it out, checking with the tuner to make sure that your flute is still at about the same pitch level it was when you were executing the previous set of steps.**

   Play all the following steps at about a *mf* as well.

2. **Slur the B into the C just above it, watching the tuner for any changes.**

3. **Repeat the C, tonguing the beginning of the note; watching the tuner, notice any pitch changes between the slurred C and the tongued C.**

4. **Slur the C into the C♯, repeat the C♯, tonguing it, and keep watching the tuner.**

5. **Repeat this pattern, going chromatically upward, not skipping any notes, all the way up to the fourth octave C (high C).**

   Watch your tuner carefully as you ascend.

Checking the pitch of each note all the way to the top of your range reveals some unexpected insights: The pitch does go higher as the notes go higher, with the top C being the sharpest note, but what happens in between your first B and the top C isn't quite as uniform as you would think. The middle register has only one real problem note: the C♯, which is vastly higher in pitch compared to its relatively trouble-free neighbors, C and D. As you get into the high register, however, instead of going progressively sharper, you seem to have a mishmash of pitch possibilities. Some notes tend to be sharper than others, while still others want to be on the flat side.

In Figure 15-1, I list the problem notes between the B on the staff and high C — that is, the notes that don't just uniformly rise in pitch on the way up the scale. Below each staff, I also tell you what the general pitch tendencies of these notes are for most flutes. (Remember, though, that every flute is a little different — that's why you went through the last two sets of steps to figure out your own instrument's particular pitch characteristics.)

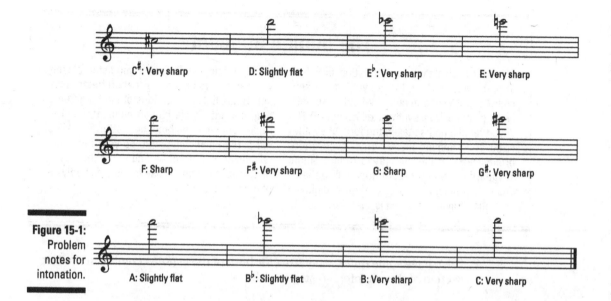

C#: Very sharp   D: Slightly flat   E♭: Very sharp   E: Very sharp

F: Sharp   F#: Very sharp   G: Sharp   G#: Very sharp

Figure 15-1:
Problem
notes for
intonation.

A: Slightly flat   B♭: Slightly flat   B: Very sharp   C: Very sharp

Those pesky difficult notes: High E and F♯

If you've been playing in the high register for a while, you may have already developed those dreaded diseases, E-itis and F♯-itis. I'm not making up these ailments; many flute teachers refer to these conditions (or are they syndromes?) when their students develop problems with sound production and intonation on the high E and/or the high F♯. Not only do these notes tend to be quite sharp, but they're also not very stable: They both want to crack down to the next lower harmonic counterpart. The fingering for high E is based on the note A, so if you bring your air angle lower to try to keep the note from being sharp, you'll likely crack down to a note that sounds like an A, unless your flute has a split E mechanism or a lower G insert, in which case you'll experience fewer problems with cracking on the E. (See Chapter 3 for details on these extras.) The fingering for F♯ is based on the note B, and it tends to crack downward as well. Unlike the E, though, the F♯ doesn't have an extra mechanism available to help you cope (unless you count the *brossa F♯ lever,* which is indeed a mechanism designed to facilitate the flute's high F♯, but you hardly ever see it, as most manufacturers don't offer this feature).

In order to keep the high E or F♯ from cracking downward, many flutists end up using a lot of tension to squeeze the embouchure and speed up the airstream. This approach keeps the note from cracking, but it produces a very sharp note with a thin sound. A more useful strategy for these notes is to aim the air precisely using the jaw and lips, but keep the aperture fairly relaxed and open, not putting too much pressure on the airstream.

The human element

Oh, how I wish that my intonation could be absolute and perfect, like a synthesized keyboard's. But wait a minute: I wouldn't actually want to sound like a synthesized keyboard! The digital revolution has taken the form of synthesized and sampled instruments, even entire orchestras that can be played from a single keyboard — with perfect intonation, no less. The only problem with these perfect, digitized versions of live musicians is that they tend to sound a little *too* perfect; if you listen closely, you can tell that it's not a real orchestra playing. Those little fluctuations of pitch and emotion, that intangible human element, can't be replicated on a machine, no matter the skill of the person manipulating it. So your intonation will never be perfect — and that's the beauty of it! (That's not an excuse for playing badly out of tune, though.)

I also have some quick, easy fixes for both of these notes coming in the last section of this chapter, so stay tuned!

Loud and soft: How dynamics affect intonation

The two things you need to remember regarding dynamics and intonation are

- As you play louder, the flute tends to go sharp.
- As you play softer, the flute tends to go flat.

These two points are pretty simple, but they're incredibly important in developing good intonation. Variety of dynamics is an integral part of making music, so you always need to be aware of your dynamic level and how it's affecting your pitch. A particular note that has a tendency to go sharp, for example, won't be quite as sharp if you're playing it softly. But play that sharp note loudly, and you've got a double whammy: sharp on top of sharp equals really, really sharp — maybe even excruciatingly sharp.

Musical phrases often taper dynamically at the end so that you're playing pretty softly at the ends of many phrases, which creates the tendency to go flat. Because you're more likely to run out of air at the end of a phrase than at the beginning, you may also be blowing less air than you normally would at the end of a phrase. Playing softly and running out of air at the same time is another double whammy: Flat on top of flat equals very flat. Suppose that the last note of the phrase you happen to be playing is also a note that has a tendency to be flat — then you've got three strikes against you. So you need to be very aware of your intonation as you reach the ends of musical phrases.

The flute and the clarinet are adversaries!

In this chapter, you're finding out about the flute's tendencies when it comes to pitch. But don't assume that these pitch tendencies are the same for every instrument. Woodwind instruments, in particular, all behave a bit differently where intonation is concerned. For example, the clarinet goes flatter as it plays louder, and sharper as it plays softer. Because the clarinet and the flute go in opposite directions pitch-wise when they play louder or softer, dynamic changes in an ensemble can be challenging to play in tune. However, in music as in life, they do sometimes have to work together (in musical ensembles, in this case) and find a middle ground where they can indeed work and play well together. The key is flexibility and compromise. See the last section in this chapter on solutions for playing in tune to develop your own pitch flexibility. After that, the compromise part is up to you!

It's all in the approach: Playing into a note from above or below

How you approach a note in a melody can determine whether you play it sharp or flat. Playing a note within a musical line can be very different from just playing it all by itself. Use the following steps and the musical example in Figure 15-2 to see just how differently a note can react when you play it within a certain context. The musical example in Figure 15-2 is an excerpt from *Minuet de L'arlésienne* by Georges Bizet (1838–1875).

1. **Power up your tuner and place it on your music stand so that you can see the display as you play.**

2. **Use the tuner to check your tuning notes.**

   Make sure that you're tuned to A=440.

3. **Play each note marked with an asterisk (*) in Figure 15-2.**

   Attack each note separately and hold it out at about a *mf*, checking your pitch with the tuner on each one.

4. **Play the music in Figure 15-2 as written, watching the tuner as you play, especially on the notes you already checked in Step 3.**

   You're probably finding that the pitch on the asterisked notes changes from Step 3 to Step 4.

If you're having trouble determining where your pitch is on the eighth notes, just hold the asterisked notes out a little bit longer until you can get a readout from your tuner.

If your pitch stays constant from Step 3 to Step 4, you're probably already changing your embouchure instinctively to adjust for pitch. Good for you! But try this step again and see whether you can keep yourself from adjusting, just to see what the pitch tendencies are if you don't.

Minuet de l'Arlésienne

Figure 15-2: Excerpt from *Minuet de l'Arlésienne* by Georges Bizet.

The most obvious change in pitch from Step 3 to Step 4 is that some of the asterisked notes come out substantially flatter in Step 4. The notes that you're leaping to from below will be lowest in pitch. The wider the leap — that is, the longer distance you have to travel to get to the upper note — the flatter that note will usually be. This tendency has to do mainly with the way you direct your airstream: Coming from the note below, you're already aiming your air lower to achieve the lower note, so going higher as you're slurring from below requires a little more adjustment than playing the higher note straight-on.

Luckily, the high E♭ and G already have a tendency to be sharp (see Figure 15-1), so those notes in this example don't go as flat as they might have. But check out the B♭, the last asterisked note: That one probably sounds flatter than all the rest.

Articulation and intonation

If you complete the set of steps in the previous section, you know first hand that articulated notes usually go sharper than notes that you slur into: The notes that you play separately and tongue in Step 3 are lower in pitch when you slur into them in Step 4. Refer to that same set of steps and play those articulated notes (high E♭ and G, middle F and B♭) while carefully watching your tuner. Most likely, your pitch will change from the beginning to the end of the note: When you articulate at the beginning, you get a little burst of air, and the pitch is momentarily on the high side; then, as the air evens out and tapers off, the pitch lowers to about where it should be. It may even go a little flat at the end of the note. If you build up a lot of air pressure behind your tongue and then release it as you articulate, you get an even more intense burst of air at the beginning of the note, and the pitch is even sharper. (See more about tonguing in Chapter 10.)

Be aware of how your tonguing affects your pitch: The harder you tongue, the sharper the beginning of the note will be.

Solving Tuning Issues

In this section, you can find solutions to all the intonation challenges I describe so far in this chapter. Whenever and wherever your pitch threatens to wander, you can corral it and bring it back to where it needs to be using the techniques listed here.

After you get familiar with these methods, use them creatively wherever you find a pitch problem. Use your tuner and your ears as your guides. These techniques — as well as little tricks you'll naturally develop on your own — will become second nature to you as you advance as a musician.

Embouchure

Manipulating the direction of your airstream is just as important a factor in getting around all the notes — and ranges — of your instrument as changing your fingerings. But it can also help you bend the pitch higher or lower on just one note, as well. As you develop your embouchure, you try aiming your airstream in different directions by moving your jaw and lips forward and backward to find your best embouchure placement for a particular note. Now it's time to get a little more flexible within your basic embouchure placement: You can also move the airstream up or down, raising or lowering a note's pitch *to get it in tune.*

You're probably already making small embouchure adjustments for pitch without even being aware of it — see whether you can catch yourself doing it sometime. It's the same motion you use to go up from the low to the middle octave or back down (see Chapter 11); it's just a smaller motion. So instead of bringing your jaw and lips forward to get up to the next octave, for example, you move it only far enough to raise the pitch of the note you're playing. Conversely, to lower the pitch, you drop the jaw and aim the air lower.

When you're playing softly, make your aperture a little smaller in order to speed up the air a bit on its way to the embouchure hole to help keep the pitch up. On the other hand, when you're increasing your volume level by giving more air, create as much space as possible in your aperture as well as in your mouth and throat, to slow the air down a bit on its way to the embouchure hole as you drop the jaw to aim the air lower to help keep the pitch down.

Follow these steps to practice playing in tune at various dynamic levels:

1. **Power up your tuner and place it on your music stand so that you can see the display as you play.**

2. **Use the tuner to check your tuning notes.**

   Make sure that you're tuned to A=440.

3. **Play a B on the staff, beginning the note very softly at *pp*, increasing your volume very gradually until you get to a *ff*, and getting softer gradually until you're back at *pp*.**

   Check your pitch with the tuner as you go and make embouchure adjustments as needed so that you're playing in tune the whole time.

Practice these steps regularly and eventually on every note in your range. You don't have to practice all the notes at once, though — the idea is to train your embouchure to be able to make the necessary adjustments as you get louder and softer.

Work on developing flexibility in your jaw and lips so that you can adjust pitch quickly whenever necessary.

Try playing through the longer excerpt from Bizet's *Minuet de l'Arlésienne* in Figure 15-3, adjusting for pitch along the way while checking yourself with your tuner. You may want to play it through once at a consistent *mf* before you observe the dynamics as written — playing loudly and softly where indicated will add yet another layer of challenge to your pitch puzzle.

You can raise the pitch of a note at the end of a phrase by moving the footjoint end of the flute away from you slightly. This movement changes the angle of the headjoint just enough to raise the pitch. It's a very helpful trick, but it's no substitute for a flexible embouchure and good breath support!

Breath support

Using good breath support (see Chapter 5) is an essential building block for good flute playing. You can really tell whether or not a flutist has good breath support if you listen for intonation. Without the breathing muscles supporting the airstream evenly, intonation becomes uneven, and pitch has a tendency to drop, especially at the ends of phrases. If you keep your air even and supported, your overall intonation will be better right off the bat, and the embouchure adjustments you make for pitch will be much more effective. Refer to Figure 15-3 and concentrate on breath support as well as embouchure adjustments.

TRACKS 74 & 75

Minuet de l'Arlésienne

Andantino Quasi Allegretto

Bizet

Figure 15-3:
Extended
excerpt
from
*Minuet de
l'Arlésienne*
by Georges
Bizet.

As I point out in Chapter 13, vibrato is by definition a constant, minute fluctuation in pitch. If it gets out of control, it can really interfere with your intonation, so keep your vibrato subtle and not too wide.

Alternate fingerings

For most of the problem notes listed in Figure 15-1, earlier in this chapter, you can use alternate fingerings to correct pitch. These fingerings are best used for certain applications only: For instance, a fingering that makes a sharp note a lot flatter should be used during loud passages only, because if you use it for soft playing, your pitch will just end up being too low.

Get to know the fingerings in Figures 15-4 and 15-5 and peruse the Alternate Fingerings chart in Appendix A regularly. Figure 15-4 lists fingerings that help you lower sharp notes, especially when you're playing loudly. Figure 15-5 lists fingerings to use for getting the pitch a bit higher on flat notes, especially when you're playing softly. Figures 15-4 and 15-5 contain the alternate fingerings you'll want to use the most often, but I include other useful ones as well in the Alternate Fingerings chart in Appendix A. Using these fingerings as necessary will take some getting used to. You probably won't want to put them all into practice at once, but keep going over them and reminding yourself that they're available. You never know when they may come in handy — and believe me, they will!

These aren't one-size-fits-all fixes: Because all flutes and all embouchures are different, you've got to test out the notes using these fingerings on your own flute, checking them with a tuner to determine whether they'll work for you.

Playing the high E without RH 4, shown in Figure 15-4, has more applications than just lowering the pitch: It also keeps the E from cracking when you're slurring into it from a high A.

Try it out using the following steps:

1. **Play a third octave A.**

2. **Slur from the high A to the high E below (using normal fingerings).**

   The E will probably be tough to get out in this context: Because the E is on the same harmonic series as the A, it tends to stay on an A instead of going to an E, even though you're changing the fingerings. (This problem is mostly solved for you, though, if your flute has a split E or a lower G insert — see Chapter 3 for details.)

3. **Play a high A again, with the normal fingering, but as you switch fingerings to play the E, take RH 4 off at the same time.**

   Your fingering for the E is now the same one listed in Figure 15-4. You shouldn't have any problem getting the E to speak using this particular fingering.

The fingering for the 3rd octave F♯ in Figure 15-4, using RH 2 instead of RH 3, is adjustable to a wide variety of pitches if you have an open hole flute. All you have to do is move the RH 2 (middle) finger around on the key, leaving the key itself down but uncovering some or all of the hole on top of the key. The more of the hole you uncover, the higher the pitch gets. (This trick works only on flutes with open hole keys — see Chapter 3 for more on open and closed hole keys.) As an added bonus, the high F♯ using RH 2 is more stable than the traditional, RH 3 fingering, so you'll have less trouble with it cracking. It's too low for use in very soft playing, though.

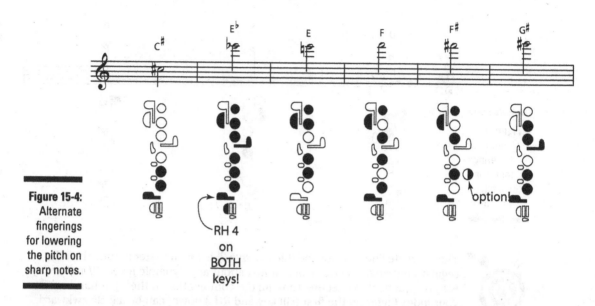

Figure 15-4:
Alternate
fingerings
for lowering
the pitch on
sharp notes.

In Figure 15-5, the D and A fingerings require an open hole flute, because you're uncovering, or *venting,* just a small portion of the hole on top of the LH 2 key, while leaving the key itself depressed. I notate the venting in the fingering chart as a circle that's only half filled in. Again, these fingerings are adjustable: You can vent as much or as little as needed — the pitch goes sharper the more you uncover the hole.

Perfect pitch versus relative pitch

I've got perfect pitch! is probably the most coveted, overstated, and ultimately overrated statement ever made by musicians. You may have heard the term perfect pitch used in passing before. It sounds impressive, but here's the actual definition: *Perfect pitch* is the ability to name or sing any note out of the blue, with no other pitch provided for reference. It's pretty cool, and not very many people have it. However, relative pitch, the ability to name

or sing any note with the use of a played or remembered reference note, is an extremely useful musical skill. Relative pitch has more to do with knowing the distances between notes than picking notes out of the blue. Many people have *relative pitch,* and it's a skill that you can develop further through musical training. A finely honed sense of relative pitch is essential in order to become an accomplished musician. Perfect pitch is helpful, but not required.

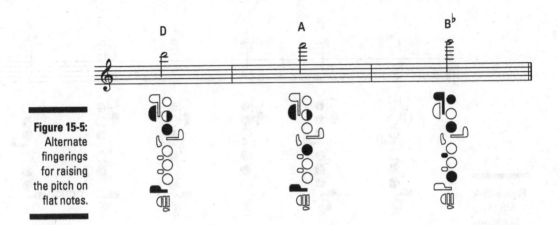

Figure 15-5:
Alternate
fingerings
for raising
the pitch on
flat notes.

The alternate fingering for the third octave B♭ is much better in tune than the regular fingering. You can use it at just about any dynamic level. It's not always easy or practical to execute, though: the combination in the right hand, with your index finger on the first trill key and RH 3 down, can be a little awkward. For good pitch on your high B♭, use the alternate fingering whenever you can, especially in slow passages, when you have time to get to it.

Now play the example in Figure 15-6 while checking in with your tuner, using embouchure adjustments, breath support, and alternate fingerings to get your pitch as close as possible to 0 on each note.

Figure 15-6:
Checking
your
intonation
using a
series of
octaves.

Chapter 16

Faster Tonguing and Getting Your Trills

In This Chapter

▶ Using double, triple, and flutter tonguing techniques

▶ Trilling evenly and correctly

▶ Taking on tremolos

The flute is one of the most agile of musical instruments — when you look at the amount of truly virtuosic music that composers write for it, you realize that its technical capabilities are just about limitless. If your fingers and tongue can move at lightning speed, the flute will readily come along for the ride.

Because the flute doesn't have the resistance of a reed (see Chapter 2 for details), it's the most responsive of the woodwind instruments when it comes to tonguing. Consequently, the flute is the perfect instrument for applying advanced tonguing techniques, such as double and triple tonguing, to get some spectacular musical effects. (Many reed players don't double or triple tongue at all.) Trills and tremolos are musical ornaments that quickly go back and forth between two notes. Trills go back and forth between two notes that are pretty close together, while tremolos use two notes that are farther apart. Both of these ornaments are a great workout for your fingers, because they require rapid, even movement, coordination, and precise timing.

In this chapter, you prime both your tongue and your fingers for speed, giving your technique a real edge, while at the same time honing the necessary skills for intermediate-to-advanced music making.

Mastering Double and Triple Tonguing

The concept of *double tonguing* is pretty simple: Instead of articulating using only a D consonant, as in single tonguing (see Chapter 10), you alternate D and G consonants (G as in the beginning of the word garden, not the name

George), which allows for increased speed: Because your tongue is alternating from front to back, it doesn't fatigue as quickly, so it has greater endurance as well, allowing for extended passages with rapid articulation. *Triple tonguing* is just a variation on double tonguing: It uses the same basic techniques, but alters the sequence of the consonants or displaces the rhythm so that you're ultimately articulating fast triplets.

When you first try the tonguing techniques in this chapter, you may find yourself feeling more than a little tongue-tied. But whatever you do, don't give up! For the vast majority of players, double and triple tonguing don't come easily, and necessitate weeks to months of slow, steady practice in order to finally be able to use them in actual playing. But all the practice time is totally worth it: being able to articulate sixteenth notes at a metronome marking of up to ♩=152 means that there's a lot more music you'll be able to play. The more music you can play, the better, right?

Double or nothing: Double tonguing

To tackle double tonguing, you need to make sure that you have a good grasp on single tonguing first (see Chapter 10 for more on single tonguing), and that you're single tonguing eighth notes up to a metronome marking of ♩=168. If you've gotten your single tonguing up to around this speed, and you're articulating pretty evenly, you've acquired enough facility to be ready for double tonguing.

To get the full effect of double tonguing, listen to a recording of the *Volière* (Aviary) movement of *Le Carnaval des Animaux* (Carnival of the Animals) by Camille Saint-Saëns. (You may want to check out the *Volière* recording of a young Paula Robison, which I mention in Chapter 21.) That piece uses double tonguing in the most amazing and descriptive way — it's not easy to play, but it sounds just like birds flitting around without a care when it's played well.

Getting started

When you're double tonguing, you alternate the consonants D and G. So as you play, you need to think of the syllables "Duh Guh Duh Guh." (Don't actually vocalize the vowel sound; just form your mouth into an "uh" shape as you play.)

Because you've been single tonguing for a while before you get to double tonguing, your tongue is already pretty used to using the "Duh" syllable as you play. What you do need to practice is the "Guh" part of double tonguing. Your tongue is made up mostly of muscle, and you can train and strengthen it just like any other muscle in your body. Because the back of your tongue isn't very involved in the single tonguing process, you need to specifically strengthen the muscles in the back part of your tongue in order to allow for smooth, even double tonguing.

To jump-start your double tonguing, follow these steps:

1. **Play a middle B (the one on the staff) and hold it out.**

2. **Start single tonguing using a "Duh" syllable.**

   Keep the notes as long as possible — think of just breaking up the one long note with light tonguing, but don't stop your air flow as you articulate.

3. **Play the B again, but this time, articulate using a "Guh" syllable.**

   Tongue lightly, using the back of your tongue instead of the front. Your tongue should hit the roof of your mouth just about where it does when you say words like "gas" or "goofy." Make sure that your tongue goes back down after you're done with the G; that way, you'll keep your air passageways open so that you can keep producing a resonant sound throughout. Practice this step for a while, until you start to feel comfortable with the "Guh" articulation.

4. **Slowly alternate the "Duh" tonguing with the "Guh" tonguing.**

   Try to match the front and back tonguing so that they sound the same. At first, you may find it tricky to tongue as lightly in the back as you do in front — think about using very little surface area of your tongue in the back. After all, you're only using the very tip of your tongue in the front. It really doesn't take much effort to separate the notes while keeping the air going. Less is more!

Practice this exercise daily until you feel pretty comfortable with slowly alternating "Duh" and "Guh." You may want to just *say* "Duh Guh" a few times without the flute first; then take out the vocalization and use the "Duh Guh" syllables while playing the flute afterward.

Evening out your double tonguing

When you're successfully making sounds on the flute with the "Duh Guh" syllables (see preceding section), it's time to gain some rhythmic control over your tonguing (I demonstrate these steps at several different speeds on Track 76 of the CD):

1. **Set your metronome to 120.**

2. **Matching the metronome beats exactly, articulate quarter notes on a middle B, using the "Duh Guh" syllables.**

   You should be articulating by repeating the consonants DGDG. Each consonant should fall right on a metronome beat.

3. **Increase the metronome speed to 130.**

   Make sure that your articulated quarter notes stay even by matching the metronome clicks. Some metronomes don't go to certain speeds — they may jump from 120 to 126 to 132, for example, without giving you an option for the numbers in between. If your metronome is like this, just use the next closest number, so you're upping the speed by about 10 at a time. The idea is, of course, to increase the speed gradually.

4. **Continue increasing the tempo by 10 at a time, playing exactly with the metronome, until you reach 200.**

   Inching the metronome upward and practicing the same thing over and over is tedious, but it's the only way to really train yourself (and your tongue) to master the double-tonguing process. Remember, mindful repetition is the key to good practice!

5. **When you're double tonguing quarter notes with the beat at 200, take the metronome down to 100 and start articulating even eighth notes; then take the metronome speed up by 10 at a time from there.**

   If you notice your tonguing becoming uneven — that is, if the eighth notes are starting to be unequal in length — go back down to the tempo where they were even and practice there for a while. Then take the tempo up again, and you'll likely hear some improvement.

   You may need to stay at that slower tempo for a few days' worth of practice sessions to get your bearings and let your tongue muscles settle in before you move on to the next tempo. But things will start to even out as you strengthen those tongue muscles.

6. **When you're double tonguing eighth notes with the beat at 200, take the metronome back down to 100 and start articulating even sixteenth notes; then take the metronome speed up by 10 at a time from there until you reach 150.**

   You should be articulating four even notes per beat, using the consonants DGDGDG. (Think dugudugudugu really fast.)

 The main tendency when it comes to unevenness in double tonguing is to make the "Guh" syllable longer than the "Duh." I'm not sure quite why, but invariably, when I hear uneven double tonguing in my students, it manifests itself that way around, so it ends up sounding a little bit like "duh GUUHH duh GUUHH." You may have trouble hearing whether or not your double tonguing is exactly even while you're playing, but if you record yourself, your evenness, or lack of it, will become abundantly clear. If you find yourself in the duh GUUHH predicament, you can help turn it around by practicing the skewed rhythm the other way around: Think about playing a dotted eighth/sixteenth note combination, for example, and think DUUHH-guh-DUUHH-guh. Then try playing even eighth notes again — more than likely, they'll be much more even than when you started.

Practicing your new tonguing skills

If you followed the last two sets of steps, your double tonguing is really coming along. For a few weeks, incorporate the previous set of steps into your daily practice routine, using other notes besides just the middle B — try notes throughout the range of the flute. Be sure to practice the "Guh" syllable by itself a lot to train the back of your tongue so that your double tonguing can become easy and fluid.

The point of double tonguing is to be able to execute fast, articulated passages. In order to be able to articulate at any given speed, though, you need to gauge your tonguing techniques: You want to have the ability to single tongue quickly enough, and double tongue slowly enough, so that there isn't an articulation speed in between that you can't handle. So practice your quick single tonguing and gauge it to your slow double tonguing to be sure that you're ready for any tempo.

When you practice your double tonguing, you're building your tonguing muscles. Reaching muscular failure is a part of that, as it is in weight training. Your tongue will tell you in no uncertain terms when you have to take a break, but your endurance will improve with every practice session.

An Andersen Etude

At this point, you want to put your new tonguing skills into practice by putting them into a musical context. The study in Figure 16-1, from *24 Etudes, op. 33* by Joachim Andersen (1847–1909), gets you double tonguing on repeated notes at a moderate tempo. (I've marked the appropriate consonants to use for articulation in the first measure, and you can take it from there.) Make sure that your articulated sixteenths are even.

Here are a few tips to keep in mind as you play the study:

- You may want to play the whole etude in Figure 16-1 at *mf* first so that you can concentrate on notes and articulation, before you add the dynamics.

- You may have noticed that there isn't one good place to take a breath in the Andersen etude. Because it has no piano accompaniment, you can cheat the rhythm a little bit here and there by breathing where you need to while still making some musical sense out of the phrase.

Track 77

24 Etudes, op. 33, No. 21

Andersen

Track 77 *(continued)*

Figure 16-1:
Etude #21
from *24
Etudes,
op. 33,* by
Joachim
Andersen.

A Gariboldi Etude

After you get pretty comfortable with double tonguing on repeated notes, you're ready to tackle passages in which you're double tonguing through changing notes, as in Figure 16-2. Play this etude by Giuseppe Gariboldi (1833-1905), from his *30 Easy and Progressive Studies.* Notice that when you have an eighth note and sixteenths following, you use D on the eighth and then start over with D on the first sixteenth, and then you alternate D and G on the following sixteenth. The consonants are marked in for you in the first four measures of the etude.

Figure 16-2:
Etude
#30 from
*Easy and
Progressive
Studies*, by
Giuseppe
Gariboldi.

Here are some tips for playing the etude:

- Use the D syllable on the rhythmically strongest beats or parts of beats, or on any note you want to emphasize. For the weaker parts of the beat, like the second and fourth sixteenths of a group, use G.

- Make sure you keep blowing air through the lines and giving good breath support as the notes change. Your air should travel through each phrase evenly while the tongue just divides the sound to separate the notes. Even when you're playing staccato (short note lengths), as in the Gariboldi etude in Figure 16-2, your breath support should extend through each group of notes. (For more on breath support, see Chapter 5.)

The second movement of J.S. Bach's Sonata in C major

The second movement of Johann Sebastian Bach's *Sonata in C major, BWV 1033*, requires most players to double tongue in order to reach the tempo of **Allegro.** (For more on tempo markings in music notation, see Chapter 4.) Start practicing this movement (see Figure 16-3) slowly and shoot for an ending tempo somewhere between ♩=120 and ♩=132.

Here are a few tips on playing this movement:

- In the Baroque period of music, which coincides with Bach's dates (1685–1750), articulations were largely left up to the performer, so you could theoretically add slurs here and there in this movement. However, because you're working on your double tonguing, go ahead and articulate the sixteenth notes as written here for now.

- For those sixteenth note passages where you start on the second sixteenth note of the beat, I recommend starting with a G consonant so that your pattern is GDG DGDG (gudugu dugudugu). This applies to the first beat of measure 29 (letter D), the third beat of measure 33 (five measures after D), the first beat of measure 37, and the first beat of measure 39. The consonants are marked in these measures so that you can follow them.

- Your air is what produces the sound, not your tongue! Even though your tongue is working pretty hard, try to keep it relaxed enough so that it doesn't take over and block your airstream. If you feel your tongue tensing up and start losing your sound, just slur through the sixteenth note passages for a little while to find your sound again. Then start lightly tonguing while keeping your air going.

- For a real challenge, try practicing all or part of this movement using only the "Guh" syllable to strengthen the muscles in the back of your tongue!

Tracks 79 & 80

Sonata in C Major, movement 2

J. S. Bach

Tracks 79 & 80 *(continued)*

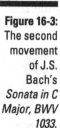

Figure 16-3:
The second
movement
of J.S.
Bach's
*Sonata in C
Major, BWV
1033.*

Three's a crowd: Triple tonguing

The term *triple tonguing* sounds really impressive — you'd think that it would be much harder than double tonguing, like some sort of Holy Grail of tonguing. Luckily, triple tonguing isn't really harder than double tonguing. It's just a variation on double tonguing, used to accommodate groups of three notes rather than two, like triplets or time signatures such as $\frac{6}{8}$ and $\frac{9}{8}$, where you find eighth notes in groups of three. (For more on time signatures, see Chapter 4.)

You can triple tongue in one of two ways (see Figure 16-4):

- The first method places the emphasis squarely on the beginning of each group of three by always putting the D consonant there, which helps to get the feeling of the triplets. The pattern is DGD DGD DGD DGD.

- The second method is a little trickier, but very useful in extremely fast passages. It's really just displaced double tonguing: The order of consonants is the same as in double tonguing, but the emphasis shifts. The pattern is DGD GDG DGD GDG. You can definitely get more speed with this method than the previous one, and it allows all the notes to be even. But I find that it doesn't work very well at a slower tempo because you tend to lose the feeling of the triplet.

Option1: Traditional triple tonguing

Option 2: Displaced double tonguing

Figure 16-4:
Two ways
to triple
tongue.

Triple tonguing is all about coordination. If you're pretty comfortable with double tonguing, it's just a matter of putting the consonants together a little differently, but it may take some time to get used to it. The main thing is to concentrate on those groups of three notes. Give the first note of the three a lot of emphasis at first — the accent will ground you in the rhythm. (And keep trying — you'll get it!)

To try out your triple tonguing, work on the study in Figure 16-5, from *24 Etudes, Op. 30* by Joachim Andersen. Start the etude with DG and then play the rest of the triplets with the first method, DGD DGD. The consonants are marked in for you at the beginning of the excerpt.

If you have trouble getting through the whole excerpt, don't despair — your tongue and coordination will need a bit of training to grasp the new order of the syllables. Just do a couple of measures now and come back to it later.

To practice the second method of triple tonguing (DGD GDG DGD GDG), also referred to as displaced double tonguing, play repeated sixteenth-note triplets on each eighth-note beat, as shown in Figure 16-6. Because you'll need to articulate at warp speed for this exercise, I recommend using displaced double tonguing.

Displaced double tonguing is really an exercise in coordination, but once you've got it, you'll never forget it. Start slowly, accenting the beginning of each triplet.

Track 81

24 Etudes, op. 30, No. 8

Figure 16-5: Excerpt from etude #8 from *24 Etudes, Op. 30* by Joachim Andersen.

Track 82

No. 8 from 24 Etudes, op. 30, No. 8

Andersen

Figure 16-6:
Practicing
displaced
double
tonguing.

Presto ma non troppo ♩ = 120

d g d g d g   d g d g d g d g d g d gd gd gd g d g   d gd gd g g d gd g   *etc.*

Figuring Out Flutter Tonguing

Flutter tonguing, more of a cool effect than a tonguing technique because it doesn't actually serve the function of separating notes, comes up in more contemporary repertoire and gets you rolling an R and playing at the same time. Although flutter tonguing still uses your tongue, it's completely different from double tonguing or triple tonguing. In flutter tonguing, you're not depending on the tongue to start the note; rather, the tongue creates an undulating effect in the sound of the entire note or phrase you're flutter tonguing. It's a little bit like listening to someone gargle mouthwash, except that the flute sound replaces the vocal sound, and, of course, there's no mouthwash. If you speak Spanish, Italian, German, or French, you're starting out ahead of the game in the flutter tonguing department.

You can flutter tongue one of two ways:

✔ Roll your R, exactly like you do when you say an R in Spanish or Italian but without using the vocal cords, while playing a note at the same time. (When you roll your R in Spanish or Italian, the tip of your tongue rolls on the roof of your mouth.)

✔ Say an R the way you would in German or French but without using the vocal cords, while playing a note at the same time. (German and French Rs use the back of the tongue rolling against the roof of your mouth, near the uvula.)

In animal terms, you can compare the front fluttering (Spanish/Italian) style of fluttering to a cat purring, whereas fluttering in the back (German/French) is a bit more like a growl.

With both of these flutter tonguing strategies, the air is driving the tongue. If you don't have a lot of air going, you won't be able to continue the effect. If you have trouble rolling your Rs, start with a D sound, and curl your tongue upward slightly from there as you forcefully blow out air — if you try this method enough times, it should give you an R rolled in the front.

Neither flutter tonguing method gives you a perfect flute sound, but that's not really what you're going for here. Flutter tonguing is meant to be an effect that's a little rough around the edges. Rolling in front gives you less control over your embouchure and airstream than rolling in back does, so flutter tonguing in the back is the best solution for fluttering on the lowest notes, but otherwise, choosing your fluttering method is just a matter of personal preference.

Composers have a few different ways of notating flutter tonguing, but usually you see the letters *fl* or *flz* somewhere in the vicinity of the passage to be flutter tongued. (The Italian term for flutter tonguing is *frullato,* while the Germans say *flatterzunge.*) You also may see a wavy line above the passage or a few lines on the note stems. Sometimes the word *tremolo* is used to indicate flutter tonguing, even though it's not exactly a correct use of the word. (See the tremolo section in this chapter for details.)

Composers started using flutter tonguing around the beginning of the 20th century. Many jazz musicians use it regularly as well. The French composer Maurice Ravel (1875–1937) seems to have been fond of the flutter-tonguing effect — he used it quite a bit in his orchestral pieces.

Figure 16-7 shows the rather prominent third flute solo in Ravel's *La Valse*. In this part of the piece, the flute's flutter-tonguing texture comes out nicely over the strings. (Ravel uses the word tremolo to indicate the flutter tongued passage.)

Track 83

Figure 16-7:
Flutter
tongued
passage in
La Valse by
Maurice
Ravel.

Playing Trills

When you play a *trill*, you rapidly move back and forth between two notes that are a half step or a whole step apart. A trill is an ornament, used to enhance or emphasize a certain note. Trilling notation follows a few basic rules:

- ✔ The note to be trilled usually has a *tr* abbreviation above it, sometimes with a wavy line following the letters.

- ✔ The note you see is the lower note of the trill. From that note, you trill to the next note higher. Go by letter: An A trills to a B, and a E trills to an F, for example

- ✔ Unless you see a small accidental sign above the trill, stay within the key signature — if a B♭ is in the key, you trill A to B♭ (not B♮), or if an F♯ is in the key, you trill E to F♯ (not F♮).

You can find trills in just about any kind of music. The basic idea never changes — you're always going back and forth between two notes — but what happens before and/or after the trill can vary according to what period of music you're playing. (For more on musical periods, see Chapter 14.) First, though, you need to get your fingers around the actual technique of trilling.

Getting even: The challenge of trills

Trilling involves wiggling your fingers in a rapid yet coordinated fashion. You've got to be able to trill evenly, or your trills will sound sloppy, which will detract from your music instead of enhance it.

Use the finger-wiggling examples in Figure 16-8 to get your trilling started on the right track:

1. **Work on the first line with the metronome marking set as indicated.**

   The first line counts a trill out for you in sixteenths and then in 32nd notes.

2. **Play the second line, trilling as quickly and as evenly as you can.**

   The second line shows the trill the way it's usually notated. Use the metronome as you're working on the second line as well so that you can count the length of the trilled notes to get the feel of switching from one trill to the next without a break.

All the trills in Figure 16-8 use the normal fingering for each note because you only need to move one finger to switch notes, so you don't have to worry about specific trill fingerings yet. I get into specialized trill fingerings later in this chapter and in Appendix A.

You may want to practice each trill separately before you put the whole example in Figure 16-8 together. You can work on the first measure of the first line, then skip to the first measure of the second line, and then move up again to the second measure on the first line, for example.

Keep your fingers close to the keys as you trill — all that wiggling often causes a lot of waving around of the fingers, which is unnecessary and definitely unhelpful!

Track 84

Figure 16-8:
Counting out your trills and then letting them fly.

Trill fingerings: How trilling!

Not all trills are quite as easy to play as the ones in Figure 16-8, for obvious reasons: It would be nice if you only had to move *one* key every time you wanted to move a whole step or a half step. But, flute fingerings being what they are, you have to get a little tricky when it comes to trilling. I include the best and most practical trill fingerings available in the comprehensive trill fingering chart in Appendix A.

A trill fingering chart is exactly like a regular fingering chart, but the keys on which your fingers move up and down to execute the trill are marked with an X instead of filled in.

Try some of the most commonly used trill fingerings in Figure 16-9: The charts are right under the notated trills. While you're at it, I sneak in another exercise to work on your trilling chops, this time in dotted rhythms. Try out the trills using the top line first and then practice them rhythmically by playing the second line. (I demonstrate all the trills in this example, as well as the rhythmic trilling exercise, on Track 85 of the CD.) Make sure that you're getting your most resonant sound on the lower note, which is the longer one in the dotted rhythm exercise. Keeping your airflow even helps you keep control over your fingers as well.

Trilling speed

Trills can vary in speed according to the tempo of the music you're playing. Fast, lively music calls for rapid trills, while using a slower trill when you're playing a slow, emotive piece is more appropriate. A trill doesn't have to be the same speed from beginning to end, either: If you're playing a particularly lengthy trill, you can start slowly and increase the speed gradually, if that feels right to do in context. So get creative with your trills and let them enhance your music making.

When you see a trill, don't assume that you can easily figure out the fingering yourself. Sometimes a fingering that you find on your own seems right and works readily, but it may not be the option that gets the best intonation on the upper note. Always look up the fingerings on the chart in Appendix A until you've got them committed to memory.

Track 85

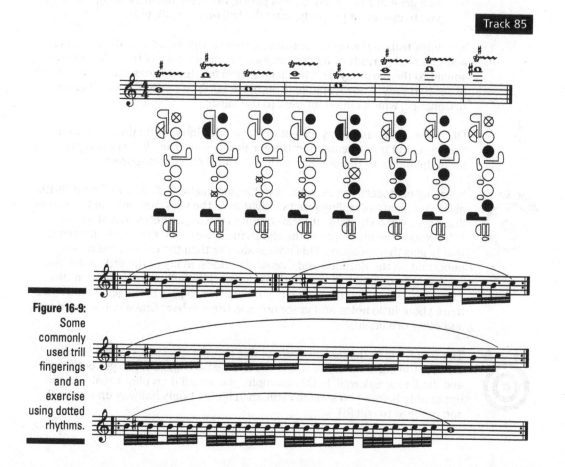

Figure 16-9: Some commonly used trill fingerings and an exercise using dotted rhythms.

A matter of style: Historically correct trills and other ornaments

Trilling in music of the Baroque and Classical periods (any music written before 1825) carries with it a special set of rules. While you could read books on the subject of Baroque and Classical trills and ornaments — and believe me, there are plenty — you can sound like you're well-informed on the subject of 18th and 19th century ornamentation if you follow a few guidelines:

✔ Most trills should start from the upper note. (Example: If you see an E trill, start on an F before you go on to wiggle E to F.)

✔ Play the upper note right on the beat where the trill begins, not before the beat.

✔ If the composer wrote the trill in a fast tempo and/or on a short note, you have the option to disregard the previous two rules and just start the trill on the main (lower) note. If you have time to squeeze in the upper note, as a general rule, go ahead and play it; but if the music is going too fast for you to execute it properly, start the trill on the main note.

Starting a trill on the upper note had a special significance in the Baroque and Classical periods of music. Usually, the upper note of the trill was dissonant to the harmony, and musicians lived for those notes that were outside of the harmony. They would lean on these notes in particular to bring out the dissonance, which added interest to the music.

Of course, there are many exceptions and additions to the three rules I mention here, but if you remember these rules to start, they'll carry you pretty far in the music of Handel, Bach, Mozart and their contemporaries.

Speaking of Mozart, the excerpt from his *Andante in C, K. 315,* in Figure 16-10, gives you plenty of trilling practice right from the very first note. In the second line, I give you a rhythmic interpretation of the upper notes that start the trills. Notice the little note in the eighth measure of the excerpt — it's the G that begins that measure. This note is smaller than the others, but no less important: in the Baroque and Classical periods, many of the little notes that you see take on one half the rhythmic value of the following note, as in this example — I give you the actual rhythmic value to play in the line below. (See more about little notes and grace notes in the sidebar "Grace notes, mordents, and other ornaments.")

The D to E trill in the last measure of this excerpt works best when you lift LH 1 for the duration of the trill — it's the best compromise to get both the D and the E to speak well. In this example, you would then play a real E as the upper note before you start the trill, then lift LH 1 only halfway up for the D, and proceed to trill RH 3.

Take a look at Figure 16-11, which contains trills, grace notes, written-out Nachschlag's, and mordents. I label the first few for you, so you know which is which. Play this highly decorated excerpt from *Andante and Scherzo* by Louis Ganne (1862–1923), and enjoy! (Remember to look up the trill fingerings in Appendix A.)

In Figure 16-11, you use the right hand trill keys for a few of the trills. Keep in mind that you can use your index finger or middle finger (RH 1 or 2) to operate the first trill key, and you can use your middle finger or ring finger (RH 2 or 3) to operate the second trill key. Which one you should use depends on what notes you need to play right after the trill. For example: In the sixth measure, you use the second trill key to trill the B to C♯. Use RH 3 to execute that trill so that it's easier for RH 1 to reach the A♯ right after the trill.

Tracks 86 & 87

Andante in C, K. 315

Mozart

Andante ♪ = 80

Figure 16-10:
Excerpt
from W.A.
Mozart's
*Andante in
C, K. 315,*
including
a rhythmic
interpreta-
tion of the
trills in the
second line.

Track 88

Andante and Scherzo

for Flute and Piano

Louis Ganne

Figure 16-11: Excerpt from *Andante and Scherzo* by Louis Ganne.

Tackling Tremolos

Tremolos are just like trills, but the notes are farther apart than just a whole or half step. (*Tremolo* is Italian for "trembling," which is a pretty accurate description of what a tremolo sounds like.) You don't see them very often, but my experience has been that they tend to pop up when I least expect them, and it's usually when I don't happen to have a fingering chart handy.

Composers typically write tremolos as a dramatic effect, usually in an accompanying line. (That ominous music you hear in spy movies or horror flicks usually involves tremolos.) They also occasionally appear in the flute solo repertoire. You can play tremolos at various speeds, like trills, but you sometimes come across a measured tremolo, in which you alternate the two indicated notes in certain rhythms like sixteenth or 32nd notes. I give you a few examples of tremolos, including their fingerings, in Figure 16-12.

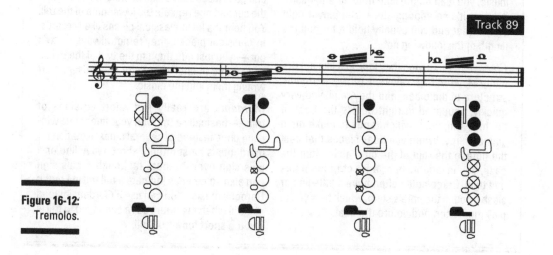

Figure 16-12: Tremolos.

Most of the tremolos you run into involve two notes that are an interval of a third apart — a note on one line of the staff will move up to a note on the next line, or a note on a space will move to the next space, as all the tremolos on Figure 16-12 do. The tremolo fingering chart in Appendix A covers more tremolos in intervals of a third, which are the ones you'll most often see.

Sometimes tremolo fingerings are pretty obvious, and sometimes they can be a bit tricky to figure out. The ones that aren't as obvious are almost always based on the harmonic series, like the last tremolo in Figure 16-12. (See Chapters 2, 11, and 14 for more on the harmonic series.) Feel free to get creative with tremolo fingerings — there really aren't any absolutes here. The general rule is to use a normal or harmonic fingering on the lower note and wiggle a few fingers to get the upper note to come out. As long as you're getting a true-sounding note for the lower note and some semblance of the right pitch on that upper note, you're doing just fine.

Grace notes, mordents, and other ornaments

When you see little notes like the ones in the eighth measure of Figure 16-10, you're dealing with another ornament. As with trills, how you play those notes depends on when they were written. Many of the little notes you see in Baroque and Classical music are actually appoggiaturas, and, like the upper notes on trills, have to do with enjoying the dissonance to a chord. *Appoggiatura* is an Italian word that means "leaning." In Baroque and Classical music, you lean on the little note, or emphasize it, when it's an appoggiatura. You play it right on the beat and you usually hold it for half the length of the following note.

Grace notes, although they look just like appoggiaturas, aren't as relevant to the harmonic structure of the piece, and they're played very quickly, squeezed in right before the beat of the following note, which tends to make them sound chirpy. When you hear pieces that cast the flute in the role of the bird, as is often the case, you invariably hear a lot of grace notes and trills. Grace notes often have a little line or slash through the note's stem, which tells you to play them short and before the beat.

I love the Nachschlag. Okay, you don't have to even try to pronounce it, because it's not really necessary to say it and because you may just get the people around you responding with "Gesundheit!" *Nachschlag* is German for "second helping." (So you do need to learn to say it if you're having dinner with Germans and you're very hungry.) But in music, the Nachschlag is a "second helping" on a trill. It's made up of two grace notes at the very end of the trill — the first one goes just below the main note of the trill, and the second one repeats the lower note of the trill. You hear it a lot in classical pieces like Mozart's. In classical pieces, they're not always written out — you just add them to the end of the trill as you see fit. In later repertoire, composers start writing them into the music.

Mordents are really just short versions of trills — basically a trill with your finger just wiggling once instead of several times. Notation for mordents is most often a short, wavy line or a plus sign over the note (although a plus sign can also sometimes indicate a full trill in French Baroque music). You can use a mordent instead of a trill when the note you're supposed to trill is just too short for a true trill.

Part IV

Darn Tootin': An Accompaniment to Your Growing Skills

The 5th Wave   By Rich Tennant

©RICHTENNANT

"Funny, I've never even heard of a a flute tonguing competition."

In this part . . .

It's time to start tapping into your full potential on the flute. If your skills are at the point where you're getting around the instrument pretty well and you've played a number of intermediate-level pieces, you're ready to start thinking about putting in some more quality practice time with warmups, scales, etudes, and more advanced repertoire.

In this part, I guide you through establishing an advanced practice routine so that you can start tackling some of the masterpieces of the flute repertoire. I also tell you when you've reached the point where a teacher can be helpful, and how to go about finding one if you're so inclined. As your playing progresses, you may want to play in an ensemble, so I get you going on all the possibilities from duets with a friend to playing in an orchestra. I put you in touch with flute clubs and other great ways to meet other flutists and find out more about flute playing. And last but definitely not least, I tell you everything you need to know about maintaining and caring for your flute, and finding a good repair technician when that becomes necessary.

Chapter 17

Revisiting the Practice Studio: Establishing a Routine

· ·

· ·

*I*f you've been playing the flute for a couple of years or so, and you're pretty comfortable with the material covered in Parts I, II, and III of this book, you may be wondering how you can keep building on what you've accomplished already (which is commendable, by the way). You want to get your sound, technique, and musicianship to the point where you can start working on some of the more difficult (and wonderful) pieces of music that you may have heard on recordings or in live concerts.

If you're planning on playing more advanced repertoire, you'll want to start working on an advanced practice routine. Getting a good warmup ensures that you get a consistently good sound, whether you're practicing by yourself or performing in a concert. Practicing melodic studies, technical studies, and etude books in a targeted and concentrated manner gives your flute playing a real workout and prepares you to play even virtuosic music with confidence, enabling you to focus not just on getting it right, but on playing it beautifully.

Think of this chapter as a personal trainer for your flute playing. You get suggestions on what kinds of warm-ups, exercises, and etudes to practice, and advice on how to start working on them. And your reward after all that practice: You get to practice — and play — some of the most profoundly soulful, or sweetly charming, or kookily operatic, or superficially virtuosic music in the classical literature, depending on which pieces you choose from my list of advanced flute repertoire at the end of this chapter. I also give you tips on where to find sheet music for all the practice books and pieces I recommend to you in this chapter.

Warming Up: Don't Sprain a Lip!

As your flute playing gets better and better, warming up becomes more essential to playing with your very best sound. As a beginner, you were just getting used to where to put the embouchure to get a sound out of the instrument. As you progressed to the intermediate level, you became more aware of the subtle nuances of the embouchure and their effect on every aspect of your playing.

When you've been playing for awhile, you settle into an embouchure that works for you, but you may not be getting the same result in every practice session. One day, things may come very easily, your sound is full yet malleable, and everything is responding nicely. The next day, you may be experiencing some frustration: You take your flute out of the case to practice, and, without warning, even though you were sounding fantastic the day before, you can't seem to get your embouchure in the right place today. Nothing is quite working right, and you can't figure out why. Part of the reason you're frustrated is that yesterday's stellar playing set up a heightened expectation for today's practice session.

But there's also another answer: warmups! Spending 15 to 30 minutes playing specific, slow exercises to warm up your embouchure really helps keep your sound consistent from one day to the next. Remember that your embouchure is made up of various small muscles, and practicing trains those muscles, much like an athlete trains for a sport. And what do athletes do before they practice or play? They warm up, of course. Athletes warm up their muscles in order to perform better and avoid injury. Mind you, I've never heard of a flutist actually spraining a lip or tongue muscle, but the general consensus among flute players is that warming up slowly does improve your performance.

Harmonics

Playing a series of harmonics is the best way to isolate your embouchure and feel it moving through several intervals without the added distraction of changing fingerings. The upper harmonics also add resistance because you have more keys down than you normally would to get those pitches. Working to open up your sound in spite of this resistance creates powerful changes in your sound.

In Chapter 11, you start getting around the harmonics series to guide your embouchure from the low notes to the higher ones. In Chapter 12, you use harmonics to gain resonance in your sound. Here, I give you part of a series of harmonics created by my teacher, William Bennett, to whom I am greatly indebted. (For more on William Bennett, see Chapter 21.) This harmonics series (shown in Figure 17-1) is a perfect warmup. It's the first thing I play when I get my flute out of the case at the beginning of the day. On Track 90 of the CD, I demonstrate the first 12 measures of the A section and the first 12 measures of the B section.

Track 90

Wibb's Harmonics

William Bennett

Track 90 *(continued)*

Figure 17-1:
Warming
up with the
harmonic
series.

This harmonic series primes your embouchure to produce your best sound. The first part of this exercise, which starts at the big letter A, is all about resonance. Work through it using the following steps:

1. **Starting at letter A, lift the air slowly, moving your jaw and lips forward to get to the next harmonic.**

   Go for a full, round sound and optimal resonance. (See more about resonance in Chapter 12.) Be sure not to squeeze your aperture as you go up — it may get a bit smaller to speed up the air very slightly, but that should just be a byproduct of bringing your lips forward.

2. **Hold the top harmonic of each group as long as necessary to achieve your most open sound.**

   Lift your soft palate, keeping your throat open and creating lots of space inside your mouth. (You can find out more about lifting the soft palate in Chapter 12.) Check your alignment in the mirror, making sure that you're keeping the back of your neck long and your shoulders as relaxed as possible. (See more about posture and alignment in Chapter 5.)

3. **As you descend back down to the fundamental note, try to match the embouchure placement you used for each note on the way up.**

   Again, play each note with as much resonance as possible as you move the airstream downward. Don't exaggerate the downward motion, though — move only as much as you need to so that the sound effortlessly falls to the lower note.

4. **Follow Steps 1 through 3 until you reach the end of the A section, at the double bar before the big letter B.**

After you complete the first part of Figure 17-1, go on to the second section, which starts at the big letter B. This section is all about the diminuendo. Follow these steps as you work through it:

1. **At letter B, you're starting with the highest harmonic you were playing at the end of the A section, which is a sounding D♯ harmonic played with a G♯ fingering.**

Start with the same big, full sound that you're producing throughout the A section. (You *are* producing a big, full sound throughout, right?)

2. **While you're still playing the first note, make a big diminuendo while also aiming the air as necessary to arrive at the lower harmonic.**

   Don't go too low: Because you're playing softer, you have to keep the air aimed a bit higher than you normally would in order to avoid going flat. It's a tricky little balancing act — just listen closely and be very aware of what you're doing. Play as softly as you can at the end of the note while staying aware of your pitch and staying *on* pitch.

3. **Now repeat the G♯ you were just playing softly, but go back to the open, resonant, *mf* sound and from there, diminuendo again as you're dropping to the lowest G♯.**

   End very softly and adjust for pitch as you did in Step 2.

4. **Repeat the lowest G♯, this time at *mf* again, and get softer as you lift your air, going up the octave to the next G♯.**

   Because you need to get to the next octave, you're lifting the air. But because you're playing softly, you need to lift the air even more. So come very far forward with the jaw and lips.

5. **Repeat the middle G♯ at a *mf* and diminuendo again, up to the sounding D♯ harmonic.**

   Lift the air like crazy! Concentrate on the inside of the lip and bring it forward. By the time you're playing very softly on this note, your aperture will be a bit smaller than when you started at letter B, but it should never feel like you're forcing or pinching it.

6. **Continue on to the next diminuendo group, starting on a sounding D harmonic played with a G fingering.**

   Work the rest of the diminuendo series as you did in Steps 1 through 5.

As you're working through this harmonics warmup series, I'm sure you won't have any problem realizing that your embouchure is getting a serious workout. In the A section, you create a big sound and start to move the embouchure to go from low to high and back again, and in the B section, you're moving your embouchure to accommodate loud and soft fundamentals and harmonics. When you're playing soft, high harmonics, you have to come very far forward to keep the pitch true — all this movement really primes your embouchure for the flexibility you need when you're playing at extreme dynamic levels. You can use your open, resonant sound from the A section as a point of reference to make sure that you're staying fairly relaxed and open when you're playing more softly in the B section. By working with harmonics on a regular basis, you encourage your embouchure to consistently place notes exactly where they need to be.

Long tones

Long tones are simply notes held long enough so that you can hear, see, and feel exactly what you're doing. Long tones are different from harmonics in that they all use the real fingerings, so they're true notes.

Many flutists have written books on how to practice long tones, but the gold standard is still *De la Sonorité* (ed. Leduc) by Marcel Moyse. *De la Sonorité* is French for "Of the Sonority." The exercises in Moyse's book are simple but efficient, and are very well thought-out. Every section is targeted for a specific purpose, whether it's loud playing, soft playing, crescendos and diminuendos, or flexibility. The book includes lots of instructions and advice, as well.

If you don't want to buy a book on long tones, but still want to practice long tones, make up your own exercises — the simpler and slower, the better. One of my favorite things to play after I go through the harmonic series is to just play slowly up and down the range of the flute chromatically (all half steps, not skipping any notes). Play the simple chromatic scale series in Figure 17-2 slowly, concentrating on producing your most resonant sound, slurring smoothly, and matching the sound quality from one note to the next.

Track 91

Figure 17-2: A chromatic long-tone exercise.

I've marked two different sets of dynamics on the long-tone exercise in Figure 17-2: The first set is for the first time through, and the second one is for the second time you play it, when you take the repeat. Always vary the dynamics on long tone exercises and check your intonation with a tuner while you're at it!

Marcel Moyse

Marcel Moyse (1889–1984), a legendary French flute player and teacher, wrote many studies and exercise books. The last time I checked, 22 of them were still in print and available for purchase. His books are comprehensive and methodical, but the ideas in them are extraordinarily creative and, above all, musical. The list of Moyse's former students reads like an international "Who's Who" of flute playing — it includes Sir James Galway, William Bennett, Trevor Wye, Paula Robison, Carol Wincenc, Aurèle Nicolet, and many others. I'm actually "descended" from him in the genealogy of his school because I studied with William Bennett.

I once had the honor of attending one of Moyse's masterclasses in Brattleboro, Vermont, and I shall never forget it. (For more about master-classes, see Chapter 18.) At the time, he was already in his 90s, but his intense passion for music shone through in everything he did, and he was still teaching with great intensity, energy, and even the occasional expletive. (When Moyse wasn't happy with your playing, he let you know in no uncertain terms!) The following quotation, from the Marcel Moyse Society's web page (www.moysesociety.org), sums up his spirit perfectly:

"I long ago observed that the real beauty of the sound comes from the generosity of the heart."

— Marcel Moyse

Melody books

After you're warmed up with the harmonics series and a few long tones, play a slow melody or two to start putting your resonant sound into the context of musical phrases and to further address embouchure issues you'd like to improve upon.

True to form, Marcel Moyse wrote some incredibly useful melodic studies. Some of them appear at the end of *De la Sonorité,* but his books *Tone Development Through Interpretation* (McGinnis & Marx) and *24 Little Melodic Studies with Variations (Easy)* (Leduc) both contain melodic studies from beginning to end.

The *24 Little Melodic Studies* (flutists also lovingly refer to these as "the 24") are short melodies, each of which poses a problem for you to solve. After you've worked on the melody to your satisfaction, you progress to the variation, which takes the difficulty a step further to make it even more challenging — and gives you another puzzle to solve. (Don't let the word "Easy" in the title fool you — they may look easy, but if you work on them properly, you can really hone your embouchure and articulation skills with these studies!)

Tone Development Through Interpretation is ingeniously divided into eight sections, each of which concentrates on a different area of flute playing. Some sections are about a particular register or dynamic level, and others address subjects such as suppleness, expression, or color. All in all, it's a fantastic book for working on various aspects of sound production, embouchure, and overall musicianship. Woodwind players (not just flutists) from all over the world used to come to Moyse's classes to play these melodies for him and get his feedback.

John Wion (1937–), retired New York City Opera principal flutist, wrote a book called *Sing!* (Falls House Press), in which he transcribes various opera melodies for flute and provides you with piano parts for all of them. Like *Tone Development Through Interpretation,* this book is quite useful for working on sound production, embouchure, and musicianship. You also get to know some wonderful opera melodies along the way!

Giulio Marco Bordogni (1789–1856), an Italian opera singer, published many studies during his lifetime, many of which are now available transcribed for various instruments, including the flute. Check out *Melodious Etudes for Flute* by Bordogni & Clark (Boosey & Hawkes).

You can find melodic studies in just about any music you play — the aforementioned books are great additions to any flutist's library, but all they really do is give you tools to concentrate on certain aspects of your sound production and tone color during your practice sessions. If you keep your eyes and ears open as you play and listen to music, you can find melodies to practice just about everywhere. Figures 17-3 and 17-4 are a couple of examples to get you started.

Figure 17-3 is an excerpt from the opera *Carmen* by Georges Bizet. It's the *Entr'acte* (French for "Interlude") that precedes the third act of the opera. It starts out with just the flute and harp presenting this gorgeous melody.

Track 92

Carmen Entr'acte

Bizet

Andantino quasi Allegretto ♩ = 76

pp

Figure 17-3:
Excerpt
from the
Entr'acte
from
Georges
Bizet's
opera,
Carmen.

This melody is a great opportunity to work on embouchure placement in the middle and high registers. Although this excerpt is marked *pp* as it appears in the original score, you can play it out a little bit more because it's a flute solo that has to project from the depths of an opera pit to the back of a big concert hall. Let your flute sing through the intervals as you keep your air flowing, making embouchure adjustments as appropriate. Try using the alternate fingering for high B♭ that I give you in Chapter 15 (you can find it in the Alternate Fingerings chart in Appendix A as well) to play the B♭ in the ninth measure of this excerpt — that way, you won't have to move the embouchure so far forward to get it in tune. In the tenth measure, you may want to use the second trill key to get quickly from the C to the D as you play the grace notes, instead of using the normal fingering for D. (Or, if you happen to have a C♯ trill key, use the C-D trill from the C♯ trill key fingering chart in Appendix A.) Watch your pitch on the very last note — that E♭ tends to be quite flat, so you have to angle the air up to get it in tune. (See more about pitch in Chapter 15.)

The melody in Figure 17-4 is an excerpt from *Pavane, op. 50* by Gabriel Fauré. (A *Pavane* is a slow dance using very basic steps, like a procession.)

Track 93

Figure 17-4:
Excerpt from *Pavane, op. 50* by Gabriel Fauré.

Pavane

Fauré

Andante molto moderato ♩ = 84

p

Fauré's *Pavane* for orchestra starts with the flute playing the haunting melody in Figure 17-4, accompanied by pizzicato (plucked) strings — the flute almost sounds like it's floating over the accompaniment, like it's having one of those eerie flying dreams. Find a recording and listen to it — you'll see what I mean!

Play this unforgettable melody with an evocative tone color — maybe something that sounds a little melancholy and distant. Try playing with forming different vowel shapes in your mouth to vary your sound. (More on tone color in Chapter 12.) Slur smoothly from note to note to create a long phrase that sounds almost like it's suspended in mid-air. To take this tone color throughout the range of the flute, start it on a G, and play the same melody in a new key. Then play the melody starting on a G♯, then on an A, and so on. That way, you can practice the same smooth legato and eerie tone color through the middle and high octaves. (I give you a couple of keys in Figure 17-5 to get you started.)

Figure 17-5:
Transposing
Fauré's
Pavane.

The Building Blocks: Scales, Arpeggios, and Technique Books

After you've warmed up your embouchure, it's time to get your fingers moving. You want to keep the beautiful sound and steady air flow you've honed in your harmonics series, long tones, and melodic studies, and slowly start building some speed, using the musical structures that you most often find in the pieces you're playing: scales and arpeggios.

When you come across a technically challenging passage in a piece of music, chances are that it contains certain musical building blocks upon which most western classical music is based.

It's like cooking a dish that you've never prepared before. Nothing elaborate or exotic —say it's a new spaghetti sauce recipe you're trying out. Chances are that you have many of the ingredients already on hand in your kitchen: tomato paste, olive oil, onions, garlic, wine, salt, pepper, oregano, rosemary, parmesan. (My husband is not going to be pleased with me giving away his family's sauce recipe so I left out the anchovies.) So all you need to do is make a quick trip to the market to perhaps get some fresh tomatoes and a few other vegetables, and perhaps some ground beef, if you're so inclined.

When you were setting up your kitchen for the first time, you made sure you had the basics, such as salt, pepper, and olive oil. As time went on, you accrued spices and started to stock things like tomato paste and oregano in your pantry. It would be a real drag if you had to go out and buy every single ingredient for your recipe every time you wanted to try a new recipe! That's what it's like to cook up a nourishing and delicious flute repertoire.

Think of your scales, arpeggios, and other technical studies as the basic ingredients for your spaghetti sauce. What you're doing when you practice these basics regularly is setting up your technique (your kitchen) with all of the basic patterns that you'll come across in music, such as scales (salt, pepper, olive oil). As time goes on, and you've mastered the scales, you start to add arpeggios to your regimen (oregano, tomato paste) so that you're better prepared to play more difficult passages. The sky's the limit on the types of patterns you can practice — that's why so many people have written technique books. But what, and how much, you do depends on how well-stocked a technical reserve you want, or need, to have for your own personal goals. (Personally, I use spaghetti sauce out of a jar if I ever cook at all, so that tells you how well my pantry is stocked!)

Every once in a while, you could come across a piece that uses unconventional harmonies and scale patterns. That's when you need to spend time practicing those unusual combinations (or going out to find dried morel mushrooms and anchovies). But most of the music you play will end up being based on the types of combinations you can find in technique books. If you've got those ready to go, you end up spending less time practicing in the long run, because you've already got your very own recipe for success readily at hand.

Making scales a daily habit

Play your major and minor scales every day. That's all I have to say on the subject, really. It's that simple. Okay, next topic?

All right, while I'm at it, I'll elaborate a little bit further: Refer back to the Circle of Fifths in Chapter 4 and practice the major and minor scales all the way through the flute's range. In Figure 17-6, I give you a couple of different ways to practice a D major scale.

Figure 17-6:
Practicing
a D major
scale.

TIP

Here are a few tips to keep in mind:

✔ As you practice the D major scale up to the fourth octave D, you can put your right-hand pinky down on the C key anytime after you play the C♯ above the staff; it won't affect the sound of the high notes too much. That way, you have one less finger to worry about placing right when you hit that fourth octave C♯ and D.

✔ Try going through all your scales using the types of patterns I feature in Figure 17-6, instead of just taking them straight up and down from tonic note to tonic note. Using your metronome, start slowly and build your technique by gradually increasing the tempo.

✔ If you need a crash course in scales and key signatures, or even just a quick review session, read the section on key signatures in Chapter 4 of this book and/or purchase a copy of *I Love Scales* by Robert Winn (Mel Bay). The title of this book alone is worth the price of admission, but it also covers basic music theory and takes you through all of the scales one by one. It also includes melodies based on many of the key signatures.

Practicing arpeggios

Arpeggios break up a chord structure into separate notes. More often than not, technical passages are made up of some sort of broken chord structure. That's reason enough to practice arpeggios, and you can practice a seemingly endless array of them. Technique books always include enough arpeggios to keep you practicing for quite a while.

Figure 17-7 is an excerpt from the second of *Seven Daily Exercises for Flute, op. 5* by Mathieu-André Reichert (1830-1880). The original exercise is two pages long, and goes through all the major and minor keys using arpeggios.

7 daily Exercises, op. 5, No. 2

Figure 17-7:
#2 of
*Seven Daily
Exercises
for Flute,
op. 5* by
Mathieu-
André
Reichert.

This is a technical study, but you don't get extra credit for going fast if you compromise your sound. Lift the air to the top note of each arpeggio and keep your beautiful, singing sound throughout. Vary the dynamic level to suit your goals — or your mood!

Finding the right technique book for you

While an amazing array of flute technique books are available on the market today, they all have two things in common: scales and arpeggios. If you work through the exercises in the SmartMusic computer accompaniment program (see Chapter 5), it will keep you busy working on your technique for a long time without you ever touching a book. I'd love to be able to tell you that this book contains everything you'll ever need, but there's a world of study now opened up for you. I will tell you that this book is the best place to start, though (but again, I'm biased).

Here are several technique books that I've found endlessly useful for myself and my students:

- *Daily Exercises* (Leduc). This book was cowritten by two of Marcel Moyse's teachers, Paul Taffanel (1844–1908) and his student Philippe Gaubert (1879–1941). It's methodically laid out and takes you through endless combinations of scales and arpeggios, in all the keys, with all sorts of different articulations.

- *Daily Exercises* (Leduc). Like the Taffanel-Gaubert *Daily Exercises*, Marcel Moyse's exercise book is a well-organized journey through scales and arpeggios in all keys. Moyse, again true to form, adds yet another level of challenge. He suggests a grueling practice schedule based on a lettering system used throughout the book. I tried it once, to no avail. My fingers nearly fell off. Man, that guy was tough. But the individual exercises in this book can give your technique a major boost when practiced judiciously.

- *Seven Daily Exercises, op. 5* (Leduc). Mathieu-André Reichert wrote musically pleasing scale and arpeggio combinations in this exercise book. Each exercise is two pages long, but because there are only seven of them, this book isn't too overwhelming in scope.

- *The Flutist's Vade Mecum* (Progress Press). Walfrid Kujala (1925–), the legendary retired Chicago Symphony Piccoloist, has penned a number of excellent books on flute-related subjects, and this one is destined to be a classic. He gives the reader practice tips and guides as well as helpful fingerings for the plethora of finger combinations that appear in this book. The "Basic Scales and Arpeggios" section is unmatched in its efficiency. He takes you through each key using the same sequence, but varies the articulations with each key.

✔ ***Practice Books* series (Novello).** As well-known for his Practice Books as he is for his playing and teaching, Trevor Wye (1935–) seems to have followed in the footsteps of his teacher, Marcel Moyse, when it comes to prolific publishing. His Practice Books series includes *Tone, Technique, Articulation, Intonation and Vibrato, Breathing and Scales,* and *Advanced Practice.* You can buy each book separately, or get them all in one volume with the *Omnibus Edition.* The *Technique* Practice Book, like all the other practice books, is cleverly laid out and includes lots of helpful tips and advice, with some wry British humor thrown in for good measure.

✔ ***Daily Exercises for the Flute* (Schirmer).** André Maquarre (1875–c1936), Principal Flutist with the Boston Symphony Orchestra from 1898 to 1918, wrote this basic yet challenging collection of exercises. This book is a tried-and-true staple in many a flute teacher's studio.

Taking Your Skills Further: Etudes and Studies

If you've looked at several books of studies and etudes, you may wonder what the difference is between an etude and a study. They both seem to go on for a page or so, and they all involve a lot of repetitive patterns, such as technical studies, although they feel — and sound — like music.

The answer is simple: *etude* is the French word for "study." There is no difference — I suppose you could say that "etude" is just a fancy word for "study." Etudes (or studies) are little pieces that incorporate and work on various technical and musical issues. They're usually geared toward a certain level of playing, and most etude books methodically go through the key signatures in progressive order.

Some good reasons for practicing etudes

In the same way that a painter might do a study in pencil before he starts his big painting, musicians play studies so that they can hone their technique and endurance before they start on the great pieces in the repertoire.

You should practice etudes because

✔ They improve your facility in every key, throughout the range of the instrument.

✔ Playing repetitive technical passages in a musical context builds endurance so that you can sail through lengthy and/or difficult sections in your solo repertoire with relative ease.

- An etude typically lets you focus on one or two challenges at a time, and you get to repeat those challenges over and over so that you've mastered that particular difficulty by the time you're done working on the etude.

- If you practice your etudes for long enough, your neighbors may just pay you to *stop* practicing. (That one hasn't happened to me yet, but I keep trying!)

Studies as music

A good number of piano etudes are deemed concert-worthy, like those by Frédéric Chopin (1810–1849) and Franz Liszt (1811–1886). Flutists play far fewer of their etudes in concert, but many of them are actually quite listenable. Flute players have called Joachim Andersen, Danish flutist and composer of numerous flute etudes and pieces, "the Chopin of the flute," and with good reason: Although looking at one of his studies can seem daunting due to the epic number of notes on the page, a melody is always hidden in there somewhere. The flutist's job is to find the melody and bring it out, playing it in a musically convincing way in spite of all the supplementary notes swirling around it. This particular challenge makes practicing your technique into more of a musical proposition than just practicing random patterns, but it also has an added benefit: Provided that you've learned the notes well, concentrating on the musical phrase created by the melody actually makes the technical aspect of the etude easier.

Figure 17-8 shows you a classic example using the second etude from Andersen's *24 Etudes for the Flute, op. 33.*

Underneath the etude in Figure 17-8, I indicate Andersen's hidden melody in the first 16 measures. Play through it, find it in the etude, and bring it out as you play. See whether you can play the phrase musically, not just emphasize each melodic note equally.

Suggested etudes:

- *Melodious & Progressive Studies for Flute* Books 1, 2, and 3 (Southern Music). All three of these popular books, meticulously compiled and revised by Robert Cavally, former flutist with the Cincinnati Symphony Orchestra, are collections of etudes by various composers, including Andersen, Gariboldi, and Köhler. Each book gets progressively more challenging.

  Note: I don't list a publisher on the following etude books because there are many available, and they're all similar in quality. (For more on editions, see the sidebar later in this chapter.)

- Joachim Andersen: *18 Studies for Flute, op. 41; Twenty-Four Etudes for Flute, op. 33.* Opus 41 and opus 33 are the entry-level Andersen etude books. (For the very advanced flutist, opus 15 and opus 63 are the most challenging of Andersen's etudes.)

Track 94

Twenty-Four Etudes For the Flute, op. 33, No. 2

Andersen

Figure 17-8: Etude No. 2 from Joachim Andersen's *24 Etudes for the Flute, op. 33.*

- Benoît-Tranquille Berbiguier: *18 Studies.* Although still technically challenging, these aren't quite as difficult as the Andersen etudes. He does have you do a lot of jumping all over the range, though, which is a great workout for your embouchure.

- Nicholas Platonov: *30 Studies.* These are relatively obscure, but they're a great find. They're at a comparable level to the Andersen etudes, at a medium level of difficulty — these are good to play after you finish Andersen op. 33 and 41.

- Sigfrid Karg-Elert: *Thirty Studies, op. 107.* These also go by the name *Thirty Caprices, op. 107.* Karg-Elert, a late Romantic era German organist and composer, wrote a lot of variety into these little pieces, such as sudden tempo and dynamic changes. He composed these studies specifically to prepare flutists for more complex, modern harmonies, so you come across many accidentals here. There's even some flutter tonguing. You definitely won't have a chance to get bored: Most of the *Caprices* are pretty short (but intense) at just half a page each.

Making Music: Playing the Repertoire

After your warmups, melodic and technical studies, and etudes, you need to practice whatever pieces you're working on. Don't make the mistake, however, of thinking that your warmups, melodies, scales, arpeggios, and etudes aren't music. They're actually the very essence of music, and that's why practicing them is such good preparation for playing the flute repertoire. Practice your scales, arpeggios, and studies musically and with a beautiful sound, and you're ahead of the game when you start playing your repertoire.

Studying music

Before you start practicing any piece of music for the first time, you need to gather a few bits of important information. Follow the steps below to familiarize yourself with the piece before you begin to play:

1. **Take a thorough look at the title of the piece.**

   The title of a piece of music can tell you a lot about how to play it. Is it a Sonata? A Concerto? A Fantasy? Look up definitions for terms you don't know that appear in the title of the work. (For more on looking up musical terms, see Chapter 4.) If the composer dedicated it to a particular person, find out as much as you can about that person and think about how the dedication might factor into the music. Also pay attention to any subtitles — often, they indicate whether the music is supposed to tell a story.

2. **Get familiar with the composer.**

   Find out the composer's dates and nationality—an internet search usually yields this information. Then figure out what was going on at that time in history. Playing music of generations past can be like a trip to an art gallery: History influences art. You can really enrich your experience and your playing if you get some historical perspective. (Case in point: the movie *Amadeus*. If you've seen it, think about how it affected your perception of Mozart's music. If you haven't seen it yet, go rent it immediately!)

3. **Observe the tempo marking.**

   Often, the tempo markings are just there to tell you whether the piece is slow or fast, but sometimes they can tell you more about the character of the music. A piece or movement marked ***Siciliano*** is a particular type of dance, for example. If you're not familiar with the term, look it up. If you don't find it in a music dictionary, try a language dictionary. (*Hint:* It has nothing to do with music played at a mob wedding!)

4. **Look at the time signature.**

   Figure out its relationship to the tempo marking. For example, if you've got a piece in $\frac{4}{4}$ and the tempo marking is ***Adagio,*** will you be counting it in quarter notes (four beats), or will it be so slow that you'll be counting in eighth notes (eight beats)? Looking ahead to sections with faster note values, consider how fast you're going to want to play them, and gauge your tempo accordingly. (More about time signatures in Chapter 4.)

5. **Consider the key signature.**

   The key signature isn't just for remembering which sharps and flats to play in the piece — the key you happen to be playing in can even evoke a certain mood in the listener. So find out what key you're playing in and whether you're playing in major or minor. Then scout around and see whether the key ever changes. (See more about key signatures in Chapter 4.)

6. **Look for accidentals.**

   The more music theory you study, the more you know which accidentals to look for in certain keys. But if you don't know exactly what to look for, you can still do yourself a huge favor by being aware of accidentals before you start. Pay particular attention to accidentals you see popping up over and over again, and to areas that have a lot of accidentals — these types of clues tell you that the composer may have briefly switched to a different key without actually changing the key signature. (More on key signatures in Chapter 4.)

7. **Survey the dynamic markings.**

   Be especially aware of any sudden dynamic changes. (For more on dynamic markings, see Chapter 4.) See whether one section appears to be the loudest in the piece — it may signal a climactic point. If you have a historically accurate edition of a Baroque piece, you may see very few or no dynamic markings because adding dynamics was largely left up to the performer in those days (1685–1750). (See the sidebar later in this chapter for more on editions.)

8. **Think about breathing.**

   Sometimes the composer or editor marks in recommended places to breathe by placing a comma or a V-shaped mark in between note heads. Make sure that you know where they are — you can determine whether or not they work for you as you play the piece. Add your own breath marks as you go so that you map out a breathing plan. (For more about making marks in your part, see Chapter 18.)

9. **Scout around for any rhythmically or technically challenging sections.**

   Seeing lots of sixteenth or 32nd notes in an *Allegro* could very well mean that your fingers are going to get a workout. Seeing lots of sixteenth or 32nd notes in an *Adagio* could pose some counting challenges. Give yourself a preview of the sections that look problematic — you can even try them out before you start at the beginning of the piece, just to get an idea of what you're getting into. Remember when practicing a piece of music that you don't always have to start at the very beginning and work your way through sequentially. Always playing the piece in that order can actually detract you from learning the entire piece well.

10. **Study the keyboard part, if there is one.**

    You're playing one note at a time, and the pianist (or harpsichordist, or organist) is playing multiple notes with both hands. If you only learn your part and don't know anything about the accompaniment, you really only know one-third of the piece. So do as much as you can to know the accompanying part. That way, you can make musical decisions in the practice room that make sense with the whole piece, which will serve you well when you then play the piece with all of the parts present. You'll be able to count your rests more accurately, too, because you'll be ready for what the music is doing while you're resting and counting.

When you've done your homework using these steps, you're ready to delve into the piece by playing through it slowly and carefully. Try to be aware of any mistakes as you make them, because you don't want to keep repeating a wrong note or rhythm. As you get more confident with the material, start increasing the tempo as appropriate.

But above all, enjoy the process. Find out as much as you can about the music and try to figure out what the composer's intention was. Playing music can be like reading an absorbing novel, only this story is interactive. You get to make it your own, which, as you'll soon discover, is an artistically and musically enriching experience not to be missed.

Don't expect to keep improving with every single practice session. Even if you're practicing thoughtfully and conscientiously every day, you're going to experience ups and downs in your learning curve — maybe even a plateau every once in a while. Over time, though, you will definitely progress: In just a few months' time, you'll be able to look back to where you are now and know that you've accomplished a great deal.

Choosing pieces to play

Your first order of business should be to pick pieces that you like — practicing music that you enjoy listening to and hearing yourself play well can be a great motivator. That being said, give yourself a good mix of styles to play. If you love French Romantic music, work on one or two pieces out of the *Flute Music by French Composers* collection, and then start a Baroque piece, such as one of Vivaldi's *Il Pastor Fido* sonatas. Mixing it up keeps you fresh, and different styles of music present different types of technical and musical challenges, as well. Getting to know various styles of music ensures that you're becoming a well-rounded musician, not just a flute player — and making music is really what it's all about.

You should play music you love, but just because you fall in love with a piece of music doesn't mean that you have to immediately start playing it, especially if it's far beyond your technical capabilities at the moment. You want to challenge yourself, but not to the point of extreme frustration or burnout. You know best what your own level is — if you feel like the music is challenging but within your reach, go for it. If you realize that you're in over your head after you start working on a piece, switch to something a little bit easier and come back to it later. Your level will keep growing over time if you're practicing consistently, and you may find that in six months to a year the piece you used to struggle with suddenly seems a lot easier.

Suggested repertoire

In this section, I list some advanced pieces for you to play. They're all pretty challenging, but they should be technically accessible to you if you've been playing for three years or so. Some of them are pretty advanced in the area of musical interpretation. The Bach Sonatas, Mozart Concerti, and Telemann Fantasies in particular require a thoughtful and musically sophisticated player to really do them justice. If you decide to work on them, take your time and think about your interpretation — listen to lots of performances of music by these composers, and not just on the flute: Listen to J.S. Bach's Cello Suites and Brandenburg Concerti, for example; or to Mozart's piano concerti and operas.

For the truly adventurous: Avant-garde techniques and contemporary music

Some of the music written after the second half of the 20th century can sound pretty wild. That's because flutists and composers started experimenting with trying to create new sounds right around that time. These effects include key clicks, slap tonguing, extreme vibrato, singing while playing, *glissandos* (sliding around between notes), *multiphonics* (playing two or more notes at once — yes, it's possible!), *quarter tones* (notes in between half steps), creative amplification, and notes above the fourth octave D. Some composers, such as Luciano Berio, Pierre Boulez, Kazuo Fukushima, Katherine Hoover, Shulamit Ran, and Edgard Varèse use these extended techniques sparingly, while others really go for a totally avant-garde effect — you've really got to hear it to believe it. Robert Dick, a flutist, composer, and a pioneer in this field, has even written an instructional book on these techniques called *The Other Flute* (Robert Dick/Multiple Breath Music). Check out music and recordings by flutist-composers Ian Clarke and Matthias Ziegler, as well.

✔ Collections:

- *Sonatas, BWV 1020, 1030–1035* — J.S.Bach (Breitkopf/Kuijken, Bärenreiter, or Henle.) *Note:* Start with the G minor BWV 1020, E♭ major BWV 1031, or C major BWV 1033 Sonatas.

  You can hear the second movement of Bach's *Sonata in E♭ Major* on Track 61 of the CD, and I include the flute part in Chapter 12 so that you can play along with the CD accompaniment track (Track 62).

  You can hear the second movement of Bach's *Sonata in C Major* on Track 79 of the CD, and I include the flute part in Chapter 16 so that you can play along with the accompaniment track (Track 80).

- *12 Fantasias* — G.P. Telemann (Breitkopf/Kuijken)

- *Flute Music by French Composers*, Louis Moyse (Schirmer)

  You can hear excerpts from pieces in this collection on the CD: An excerpt from Gabriel Fauré's *Fantasie* is on Tracks 34 and 35, and an excerpt from Louis Ganne's *Andante et Scherzo* is on Track 88. The Fauré excerpt appears in Chapter 10, and the Ganne excerpt in Chapter 16.

- *Six Sonatas "Il Pastor Fido," op. 13* — Antonio Vivaldi (Hortus Musicus or Southern Music)

✔ Pieces:

- *Hamburger Sonata in G* — C.P.E. Bach (Schott)

- *Syrinx* — Claude Debussy

- *Sonate* — Paul Hindemith (Schott)

- *Danse de la Chèvre* — Arthur Honegger

- *Pièce* for solo flute — Jacques Ibert (Leduc)

- *Andante in C, K. 315; Concerto in G, K. 313; Concerto in D, K. 314;* W.A. Mozart (Bärenreiter or Novello). *Note:* I suggest that you play the Andante in C, K. 315 before you start working on either one of the Concerti.

  You can hear an excerpt from Mozart's *Andante in C Major, K.315,* on Track 86 of the CD, and I include the flute part in Chapter 16 so that you can play along with the CD accompaniment track (Track 87).

- *La Flute de Pan* — Jules Mouquet

- *Sonata* — Francis Poulenc (Chester Music)

- *Suite* — Charles-Marie Widor

When a piece is only available through one publisher, or when I have one or more preferred editions, I specify certain publishers. I don't list publishers for pieces that have several choices available when those choices are all comparable. (For more on choosing editions and finding sheet music, see the sidebar "A word (or two) about editions," later in this chapter.)

Finding sheet music

If you're like me, you'll amass quite a collection of sheet music over the years. If I hear a piece I like, I try to get my hands on the music so that I have it handy whenever the need (or fancy) arises. (Then again, I have a similar policy on shoes.)

Check out the sources in the following list to find the music you're looking for.

✔ **Local music shops:** If you've got a music shop that carries sheet music in your area, that's great. Try to make sure they stay in business by buying most of your sheet music there. However, if your local store doesn't have the music you need in stock and you don't want to wait for a special order to come in, which can take a while, I recommend ordering it from an online retailer.

✔ **Online retailers:** You can find lots of online sheet music retailers; just do an Internet search. But only a couple of sites specialize in flute music and have brick-and-mortar stores, as well:

- Flute World (www.fluteworld.com): If it's flute-related and Flute World doesn't have it, you'll have a hard time finding it anywhere else on the planet. New and used flutes, accessories, sheet music, books, and recordings are all available on its web site or in its brick-and-mortar store in Farmington Hills, Michigan. Flute World also offers flute repairs.

- Carolyn Nussbaum Music Company (www.flute4u.com): Like Flute World, this flute specialty house offers flutes, accessories, sheet music, books, recordings, and repair on all major flute brands and models. It's also a brick-and-mortar store in Plano, Texas, with a friendly and approachable staff.

✔ **Public domain sites:** Sheet music that is in the public domain is not protected by a copyright, so a few generous souls (and libraries) post music online for free download. My favorite place to look for public domain sheet music is the International Music Score Library Project (http://imslp.org/wiki/Main_Page). Also known as IMSLP / Petrucci Music Library, it's a public service site where anyone can upload or download public domain music.

✔ **Libraries:** Your public library may have sheet music available. If you can't find sheet music there, it probably does have books about music and recordings you can borrow, which should also prove useful. If you're affiliated with a college or university, check to see whether the school has a fine arts library or music library. And whether you use a public or university library, don't forget to check out book sales — you never know what you could find.

TECHNICAL STUFF

A word (or two) about editions

Sometimes one piece will be available from several different publishers, which can make shopping for music confusing. The earlier the music was composed, the more time editors have had to interpret, re-interpret, and, in effect, move farther away from what the composer originally intended. Generations later, historians do a lot of research to clean up all the editing that was done over time to get the music back to its original state. So you typically pay more for the cleaned-up, or *Urtext* editions of music by composers such as Handel, Bach, and Mozart. Personally, I'd rather play from the music that those composers originally wrote, so those are the editions I usually recommend.

With more contemporary music, most of the time you don't have to worry as much about which edition to buy. (Yet another good reason to look up composers' dates!) In this book, I suggest editions for earlier pieces and provide you with a publisher name for works that are only published by one company.

Chapter 18

Taking Your Playing to New Heights: Teachers, Ensembles, and Performances

. . . .

In This Chapter

▶ Tapping into your potential with teachers and masterclasses

▶ Getting it together with ensemble playing

▶ Preparing for great performances

. . . .

*I*f you've been practicing and playing steadily for a year or two (or more) and you've mastered the basics of flute playing, you may want to consider playing for someone besides yourself, whether it be for a teacher, for the congregation at your church, or even your family and friends in your own living room. Performing can really give your playing — and your confidence — a boost.

In case you're thinking about really dedicating yourself to your instrument and taking lessons, I tell you what a teacher can (and should) do for you, and I give you advice on shopping around to find the perfect one for you.

You also may be thinking about auditioning for a local band or orchestra, or getting together with one or more other musicians to play flute and piano pieces, flute duets, or music written for all sorts of other small ensembles. In this chapter, I guide you through the many ensemble options available to you, and share some personal insights about the joys — and challenges — of playing auditions for large ensembles.

Finding a Teacher

The word "teacher" may or may not have a good connotation for you. After all, it sounds an awful lot like going to school. But a good teacher can help you improve your flute-playing skills faster than you'd be able to do alone by constructively critiquing your playing, helping you choose studies and repertoire tailored to your needs, and giving you helpful tips according to the particular challenges you're facing in any given piece of music.

I'd like to think that I can tell you everything you'll ever need to know about flute playing in a single book. (And I think I've come pretty close with this one, if I do say so myself!) If you're alert and astute during your practice sessions, you can teach yourself effectively and make a lot of progress on your own. But at a certain point, teaching yourself becomes a little bit like cutting your own hair. A teacher, like your favorite hairstylist, has two things you don't: experience and perspective. (Think of it as the musical equivalent of having someone to make sure that you don't mess up the back!) No matter how many mirrors you watch or how high-tech your recording equipment is, seeing and hearing yourself objectively is extremely difficult. When you add a high level of experience to the teacher's perspective, magical things can happen. The teacher may catch a mistake that you've been overlooking, or pinpoint something in your embouchure that makes all the difference in your sound.

You can seek out a flute teacher at any level, whether you're a beginner or an advanced player. Every flute player is different because every person is different, so no two players have the same embouchure, technique, musical ideas, strengths, or weaknesses. And no two players make the same mistakes, either. The teacher's job is to guide you through your own personal journey as a flutist.

A teacher's experience and training can also help guide you through your musical development. As your technique and sound production improve and you begin studying more advanced pieces on your own, you'll probably find yourself becoming much more interested in musical styles and subtleties. A gifted teacher helps you sort out flute-playing styles for the various musical periods and shows you how to interpret the music to really make it sing.

Any time is a good time to start taking lessons; however, a particularly good time to look into this option is when you feel "stuck." Maybe you've hit a plateau with your playing, and the pieces you really want to be playing are just a little bit out of reach. Or you're working on a piece of music that's raising a lot of questions regarding technique ("Is this even remotely possible?") or style ("How do I decide where to slur or tongue in this Baroque sonata?"). Or maybe there's one aspect of your flute playing, such as double tonguing, that you've never quite been able to do well, and you're not sure why. Or you'd just like some help navigating your way through the vast classical flute repertoire ("Which of these hundreds of pieces is the most appropriate one for me to work on at this stage in my development?"). These are all great reasons to look for guidance from a professional — a good teacher can help put you on the fast track to success. (Or just tell you to practice more, which is also always an option!)

Finding teachers in your area

In finding the best teacher for you, consider both your skill level and your interests. Flute teachers often specialize in certain playing levels or styles. For example, one teacher's studio may be primarily dedicated to beginners, encouraging ensemble playing with flute choirs and studio recitals, while another may be an orchestral player and college professor who prefers to teach advanced repertoire and coach orchestral excerpts for those auditioning for professional orchestras. Or you may find a jazz player adept at teaching improvisation, or a piccolo specialist, or a flutist who mainly plays on historical instruments and loves to teach music from the Baroque and Classical periods. (For more on musical periods, see Chapter 14.) Remember, a large number of flutists are out there, so your chances of finding a teacher who shares your interests and can be helpful in addressing your particular challenges are very good indeed.

To find out about flute teachers in your area:

✔ **Talk to other flutists in your area.** If you don't know any flutists, you can get to know some by joining a local flute club or flute choir. Some flute clubs even feature teacher directories on their Web sites. (For more on flute clubs, see the sidebar "Connecting with other flutists," later in this chapter.)

✔ **Find out whether any colleges or universities near you have a music department.** The music department office may have a listing of university graduates who are flute teachers. Or you can contact the college's flute professor directly to see whether she teaches privately. If not, you will most certainly garner a recommendation or two to help you find private instructors in your area. Another good strategy is to attend university flute recitals (which are almost always free) and chat up the performer afterward. (Hint: Musicians love being approached after concerts, especially if compliments are involved!) Whether the performer is a professor, guest artist, or student, you can find out a lot by listening to the music and asking pertinent questions. You may even find a teacher that way — you never know whom you might meet!

✔ **Contact a high school near you and see whether they can put you in touch with their band director.** Band directors sometimes teach privately, but because they have to know how to play all the instruments in the ensemble, their flute-specific knowledge may be limited. However, most band directors will be able to recommend an area flute teacher, and some directors even have teachers of various instruments come to the school one or two afternoons a week to give individual lessons to the students.

✔ **Many music stores have in-store teaching studios and hire instrumentalists from the community to give lessons there.** The upside of this arrangement is that it's convenient for both the student and teacher, and you're always working in a professional environment, rather than going to somebody's house. Also, any instruments, music, or accessories you may need will likely be available right there at the store. However, the music store, being the middle man, takes a cut of the lesson fee, and you may find yourself being pushed into buying all of your musical accoutrements there as well. Of course, music store policies vary widely, so it's worth finding out what your local store has on offer.

✔ **Call the local branch of the musician's union (American Federation of Musicians, A.F. of M.) and ask for their teacher listings.** It may even have a Web site where you can search for teachers by instrument. If you live in a small town, find the A.F. of M. local in the nearest big city. Musicians in your town may still be members of that local and therefore listed on their roster.

Asking the right questions

Lesson fees vary widely, starting at around $15 to $20 for a half-hour lesson (good for beginners) to $70 to $100 and up for a full hour lesson (for intermediate to advanced players), and everything in between. Top-level star teacher-artists sometimes charge rates up to $200 per hour or so. Keep in mind that you do typically get what you pay for — the teachers who charge more tend to be the more experienced players and teachers. But you can also find fantastic teachers at lower rates. Keep the following points in mind as you compare teachers:

✔ Don't be afraid to shop around. Many teachers are perfectly fine with giving a get-to-know-you lesson on a trial basis, and some of them even offer a short session for free so that you can see how you work together.

✔ Get a sample lesson before you commit to ongoing lessons with a particular teacher, whether you end up paying for that first lesson or not.

✔ Discuss your goals, interests, and preferences with the teacher before starting regular lessons. Weekly lessons are the norm; however, if you work well on your own and just want to check in with a teacher every once in a while to make sure you're headed in the right direction, that can be a viable option as well, depending on your teacher's policies.

✔ Remember that the best players don't necessarily make the best teachers. The best flutist in town may be so busy playing gigs that there's little time left to dedicate to teaching — in that case, the teaching can sometimes become an afterthought. Someone who has set up a private teaching studio and dedicates their days mostly to teaching may be a better fit for you, particularly if you're a beginning or intermediate student.

You want to become the best flutist and musician you can be, not necessarily play exactly like your teacher. If you want to play with a beautiful sound like your teacher's, that's great, but your face and lips are unique, so your embouchure setup is not going to be exactly like anyone else's. Be wary of anyone who tells you that your embouchure should look exactly like theirs, or indeed that there is only one way to play a particular piece of music. Hearing your teacher play, attending concerts, and listening to recordings can be a wonderful way to find your own sound and interpretations, because you can develop your own personal preferences that way, but if you end up sounding exactly like the person you're emulating, there's not much point in making your own music. If a teacher is requesting that you play the notes, rhythms, and dynamics correctly as the composer wrote them, while at the same time finding your own musical voice, you're on the right track. But if you get the sense that you're being cloned, start looking for a different teacher immediately!

Masterclasses: Gleaning Tips from the Pros

The best way to get a lesson without actually having a teacher is to attend a masterclass. The term sounds intimidating — it conjures up images of old-school master teachers with thick European accents and an air of superiority. But these classes are a great way to glean valuable information from some of the top teachers around.

A *masterclass* is basically a public lesson — the masterclass participant (usually chosen some time before the class) plays a piece, and the teacher critiques and teaches right in front of the audience. Teachers who are invited to give masterclasses tend to be leaders in the field and accomplished musicians themselves. They often travel from city to city giving these classes, so they typically have a high level of expertise.

Making your mark: The pencil as musical tool

You should always use a pencil to mark your parts during rehearsals and lessons so that you can remember what your teacher/conductor/colleagues requested. Writing notes directly in your part during lessons gives you reminders about what the teacher said once you're practicing back home. (Most teachers will also let you record your lessons with an unobtrusive device — just ask before you switch it on.) If possible, bring a score and part for pieces being performed in any masterclasses you're attending, and make pencil marks accordingly when you hear an idea you don't want to forget.

Band and orchestra conductors are always asking for adjustments to dynamics, articulations, and all sorts of other stuff in rehearsals, so you'd be well advised to pencil in what they say right away — conductors don't take kindly to having to ask twice. When playing in an ensemble, you also may want to make a note in your part to indicate which instrument you're playing with at any given time or pencil in cues to help you come in correctly after a rest. If you miss an accidental when playing through a piece the first time, chances are that you'll miss it again unless you write flat, sharp, or natural signs in your part as reminders.

By the way, your pencil is also a useful tool in your practice studio: Mark in your preferred breath marks, slurs, accidental reminders, and anything else you don't want to forget into your part as you practice. One caveat: Mark clearly and concisely so that you'll know what's going on the next time you see your markings, and so that the next person who gets your band or orchestra part doesn't have to spend half of rehearsal erasing gobbledygook. (And believe me, I've been there!)

The really useful thing about masterclasses is that the teacher is focused on teaching the audience something as well as the student. So you get demonstrations and explanations that you wouldn't normally get if you were just a (flute-playing) fly on the wall observing somebody else's lesson. How the class goes is, of course, entirely dependent on the teacher, the musicians chosen to participate, and the involvement of the audience, so the experience can vary from class to class.

If you're an auditor (audience member) in a masterclass, you don't have to do anything but listen and absorb all the useful information, or take notes if you like. Workshops are another story: They are usually less formal than masterclasses and involve lots of audience participation, such as trying little exercises right on the spot. Workshops typically focus on one aspect or style of playing, such as sound production, Baroque music, contemporary techniques, or improvisation.

You can find masterclasses and workshops in your area by checking out the "Connecting with other flutists" sidebar later in this chapter.

Ensembles: Playing Well With Others

Playing in an ensemble, whether it's made up of two musicians or 200, can be an incredibly gratifying experience. Combining or interweaving your sound with someone else's playing to create a bigger musical picture is one of the greatest things you can do as a musician. Sure, you can make some pretty fantastic music on your own, but the experience of having harmonies and countermelodies happening around you as you play is unparalleled. And the interchange of the different instruments adds variety and interest for the listener, too.

Pianists: A worthy accompaniment

Although many great flute pieces don't include a keyboard accompaniment, the vast majority of the pieces you'll want to play are for flute and piano or flute and harpsichord. (A piano usually works fine as a harpsichord substitute.) Sometimes, the keyboard simply supplies the harmony and bass line to the flute's melodic lines, but composers also love to write countermelodies or back-and-forth interplay between the flute and piano.

If you're playing a piece for flute and piano, make sure that you prepare by studying the piano part and perhaps listening to a recording of the work before you get together with a pianist to put it all together.

Hopefully you already have a pianist friend who would just love to get together with you and play. But if not, ask your flutist friends if they can recommend someone. (To find new flute-playing friends, see the sidebar on connecting with other flutists later in this chapter.) Another option for finding a pianist is to contact your local university or music store for recommendations. If you do end up working with a professional pianist, make sure that you clarify the fees for rehearsals and performances so that there's no misunderstanding. (Professional musicians love what they do, but they still need to eat and pay the bills just like everybody else!)

Ideally, you want to build a rapport with a pianist so that you can get to know each other musically and personally, so try to find one you like and work with that one on an ongoing basis. That way, you can be comfortable and really enjoy making music together.

Duets, trios, and quartets: The more, the merrier

Playing flute duets with a friend can be addictive — good thing there's so much music for two flutes to choose from! You could play for weeks on end and still not run out of music. To find a duet buddy, check out the sidebar on connecting with other flutists — and join your local flute club, if you have one!

If you're at a beginning or intermediate level, get the *Selected Duets* collection, Volumes I and II, published by Rubank and edited by Himie Voxman. You can also start playing duets by Telemann, Quantz, and Mozart. If you're more advanced, look up duets by W.F. Bach, Kuhlau, Musczynski, and Hindemith, or pieces for two flutes and piano by Doppler. Flute trios and quartets are also a lot of fun, particularly if you have more than one flute-playing friend. And the more flutes are playing, the more you all get to work on your intonation (see Chapter 15), so it's great practice for larger ensemble playing, as well. Check out any of the flute trios by Hook (Rubank or Kendor), which are beginning to intermediate level. The flute quartet collection *Flute Symphony* (Rubank) is appropriate for intermediate players. For advanced players, all of the flute trios by Walckiers (Editions Musicus) are very good, and Casterède wrote a charming little piece called *Flûtes en Vacances* (Flutes on Vacation) (Leduc) for three flutes with an optional fourth flute. The quartets by Reicha (Amadeus or Hofmeister), Kuhlau (Southern), and Dubois (Leduc) are also outstanding.

Composers write music for all sorts of combinations of instruments. You can find a wide variety of *chamber music* (small ensemble music) if you dig around in the sheet music sources I list in Chapter 17. Some traditional chamber music combinations that include the flute are the Baroque *trio sonata* (2 flutes, or flute and oboe, or flute and violin, plus harpsichord and cello), the *woodwind quintet* (flute, oboe, clarinet, French horn, and bassoon), the *flute and guitar* duo, the *flute and harp* duo, and the *flute and string quartet* (flute, violin, viola, and cello). Also be aware that many instruments can be substituted for others — for instance, a harp substituting for a guitar, or a piano substituting for a harpsichord.

As long as you have friends and family who are musically inclined, you'll never be at a loss for having someone to play with.

Flute choirs: Safety in numbers

A flute choir is a group of five or more flutes, often including a variety of flute types, such as piccolo, alto, bass, and contrabass flutes. (Read more about different types of flutes in Chapter 22.) Because of the flute's incredible popularity (see Chapter 2), vast numbers of amateur flutists are looking for an outlet to play. Because the number of flutes in bands and orchestras are limited, and there's no limit on how many flutists can play in a flute choir, flute choirs have sprouted up around the globe, and consequently, more music for flute choir keeps getting published.

These days, flute choirs have a wide range of music at their disposal, including original works and transcriptions of pieces originally composed for band or orchestra. And what a cool sound they make — kind of like a giant calliope. You've really got to hear it to get the full effect!

Large ensembles: I'm with the band!

Playing in a large ensemble, such as a band or orchestra, can be incredibly exciting. When 30 to 100 or more musicians perform music together, the dynamic possibilities you can produce are almost limitless. Composers can write an accompanied solo for one instrument playing softly, or they can have all the instruments playing together at the tops of their respective dynamic levels to create a massive wall of sound. Participating in this process is a powerful and moving experience to which I simply cannot do justice in these pages. If you are fortunate enough to be part of a large ensemble, you need to be able to follow a *conductor* (the person waving the stick up front), which is not too hard to do if you have a good sense of rhythm and you prepare well by practicing your parts before rehearsals.

A *band* or *wind ensemble* is made up of mostly woodwind (see Chapter 2) and brass instruments (brass instruments include the trumpet, trombone, and tuba). Percussion instruments frequently participate in bands and wind ensembles as well. The main difference between a band and a wind ensemble is that wind ensembles are typically smaller and often feature one person per part, whereas bands are usually massive ensembles with several people playing the same part in each section. Generally, the music that bands and wind ensembles play is that of a few 19th-century composers and many 20th-century composers (plus lots of marches). They also often play transcriptions of orchestral works.

There's nothing quite like playing in an *orchestra*. Orchestras include violins, violas, cellos, and string basses, which make up the large string section. The woodwinds, brass, harp, keyboards, and percussion play behind the string section and are usually playing one person to a part. J.S. Bach, Brahms, Beethoven, Mendelssohn, Mozart, Strauss, Tchaikovsky, Stravinsky, and many other great composers wrote timeless masterpieces for the orchestra, so playing in an orchestra gives you the rare privilege of bringing such great masterworks to life.

Connecting with other flutists: Flute clubs, publications, Web sites, and e-mail lists

You can connect with other flutists in your area and beyond using a variety of resources:

✔ Check out the National Flute Association's Web site at www.nfaonline.org. Click the Resources tab, and you'll find a link to their listing of local flute clubs by state. You'll also see a Masterclasses link, where you can find a comprehensive list of masterclasses that are happening nationally and internationally. There's a Flute Events listing, as well. And while you're on the NFA Web site, why not join? The NFA is an organization that's dedicated to bringing flutists of all levels together, and it hosts an annual convention. The NFA publishes a magazine four times a year that's aptly named *Flutist Quarterly*. The organization also offers reasonably priced instrument insurance.

✔ If you've found a local flute club, that's great— you can start meeting fellow flute players and attending events. If you haven't found a flute club, start one! (I'm one of the founding members of the Greater Indianapolis Flute Club, and I can tell you from experience that there's no better way to get to know the flute players in your area.) The NFA publishes a booklet called "Guide for Flute Clubs," which tells you how

to start one. You can order it from the NFA Store section of the NFA Web site.

✔ *Flute Talk* magazine is an informative resource and a fun read for flutists of all ages and playing levels. It includes interviews with accomplished flutists, features on various performance styles, a column on piccolo playing, performance guides for flute repertoire, masterclass and event listings, and much more. Check out the Web site for more information: www.flutetalkmagazine.com.

✔ By subscribing to a flute-related e-mail chat group, you can virtually meet flutists all over the globe. Anyone can join and post to the list, as long as the message is flute-related. The two groups I subscribe to are Flute List (www.larrykrantz.com/fluteweb/fluteweb.htm) and Sir James Galway Flute Chat (http://launch.groups.yahoo.com/group/Galway-Flute-Chat). If you post a question here, one of the responses may come from Sir James himself! (If you subscribe to these groups, I recommend choosing the digest version so that you get one e-mail per day with all of the day's posts in it, instead of getting a large number of individual e-mail posts.)

You can find community bands, wind ensembles, and orchestras all over the country, in both big cities and smaller towns. Most are made up entirely of amateurs, and a few are semi-professional. Ask around, scan the local paper for performance dates, or do an Internet search to see whether there is one in your area. To play in a community group, you'll likely have to play an audition. Be sure to find out the expected level of playing and audition requirements. If it seems out of your league, just keep practicing for another year or two (or three?) until you're ready — there's no better incentive to practice than having a goal like an upcoming audition!

Performing: Playing for Your Peeps

Performing music is sharing yourself and your musical discoveries with your audience. And it's always a voyage of discovery for the performer, too — as soon as other people are listening to you, your perspective on your playing changes. You find yourself becoming more self-aware, more focused, and more conscious of every detail in the music. When you're properly prepared, performing can be a transcendent experience. And it's a culmination of all your hard work: After performing a piece well, you feel a real sense of accomplishment as you put that piece away for the time being and get ready for your next project.

Recitals and other performance opportunities

It doesn't really matter where or when you perform, just as long as you do it. Like anything else, if you put it off for too long, the prospect will just get more and more daunting. Set a goal, whether it's playing "Mary Had a Little Lamb" for your friends and family in the living room, performing a piece at a local flute club function, playing a full recital of music by great composers at a church or recital hall, or making your Carnegie Hall debut (I enjoyed that distinct privilege in 1989 playing in concert there with the Indianapolis Symphony Orchestra), and start planning. After you set a date, time, place, and plan your program, you'll be amazed at how motivated you are to practice.

If you're thinking about giving a recital, check out local churches or universities as venues. Universities often have nice large rooms or recital halls with pianos that you can rent for a fee, but churches are usually the less expensive option. (Churches also tend to have very forgiving acoustics!) If you have a piano in your living room, or have a friend who does, you've got the perfect setup for an informal house concert — invite your friends and family, play some great music for them, and have some punch and cookies ready for a gathering afterward.

When planning your program, remember to pace yourself. If you're performing more than one piece, make sure that not all the pieces are stretching your playing ability — give yourself a breather by programming easier pieces in between the more difficult ones. Pace your practice time, too: Practice the pieces slowly and in sections first, taking lots of breaks, and as you get closer to your performance date, start playing through each piece in its entirety. Then begin playing through your program in order, stopping only briefly between pieces. This approach builds your endurance so that your embouchure, tongue, fingers, and indeed your entire body won't give you an unpleasant surprise on the day of the performance. Think of it as working up to a marathon — you have to train for it progressively, not force your body to do all the work at the last minute.

Go ahead, take a bow!

When you've finished your performance and the inevitable thunderous applause begins, take a bow — you deserve it. Just bow your head and torso forward and think or say, "Thank you" to your audience. You're thanking them for the applause, and for letting you share your music with them. And don't forget to acknowledge your pianist, if applicable, by extending your arm out toward her with a graceful gesture.

Ensemble auditions

Auditions are a different experience from performing just one piece or even a full recital because you have a number of pieces to perform, but you only have a short time (typically 5 to 15 minutes) to audition. The people listening to you will have you stop and start, playing a technically challenging section from one piece and a few measures of a solo passage from another. So when you're auditioning, you're effectively sprinting (playing just a few of the more challenging sections of pieces) rather than running a marathon (playing through a full concert's worth of pieces).

An audition for a professional orchestra can be an extremely intense affair, comprising the most difficult passages from the entire orchestral literature — I've seen audition repertoire lists with 30 or more excerpts on them.

Because an audition is a different performing situation from a concert or recital, you need to prepare for it differently, too. You need to be able to switch your musical mindset from one excerpt to the next quickly, so after you've practiced all your music, go through the excerpts and/or pieces in random order. Get a friend to quiz you on them, kind of like they're using flash cards, and you'll get the feel of what your audition will be like.

Most ensemble auditions don't include a piano accompaniment, so you need to be able to play *as if* the piano or orchestra or band were playing along right there with you; in other words, you need to be able to hear the other parts in your head as you play. In the case of ensemble auditions, you need to know not only the excerpt or part that you're playing, but how the whole piece goes and what the other parts sound like. So if you're thinking about auditioning for an orchestra (whether it's your local community orchestra or the Berlin Philharmonic), attend lots of concerts, listen to recordings, and really get to know the orchestral literature. If you can study the full scores to the orchestral masterworks, so much the better, as a score will give you a broader sense of what the composer was trying to achieve with a particular piece as well as provide a solid frame of reference with regard to what's expected from you and from those with whom you'll be performing!

TIP

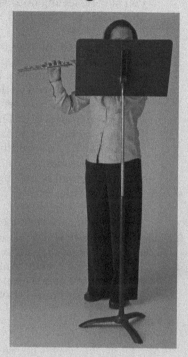

Music stands and performing

Unless you've got your music memorized, you'll need to use a music stand when you're performing or auditioning. (Memorizing music can be useful, but I usually opt to have my music in front of me when I'm performing. Whether or not you play from memory is just a matter of personal preference.) But be very conscious of how you adjust your music stand's height. For a performance or audition, your stand should be high enough so that you can see the music easily, but not so high that it obscures your face, as the hapless flutist in this photo has done — the audience wants to see you!

Performance anxiety

Everybody gets stage jitters. Vladimir Horowitz, legendary pianist, had to be physically pushed out on the stage before a number of his performances because he was terrified — but once out there, he always performed brilliantly. The celebrated singer Maria Callas once said "Every time I go out on stage, they are out there . . . to get me." Famous folk singer Carly Simon has admitted to having debilitating stage fright, and Oscar-winning actor Sir Laurence Olivier wrote about his bout with stage fright in his autobiography. If you ask me, any performer who says they never get stage fright isn't being entirely honest.

Okay, it's nice to know that all performers are in the same boat regarding onstage nerves, but how do you deal with it? Unfortunately, the answer isn't simple, because again, everyone's different. The old adage of imagining the audience in their underwear never really worked for me — I've already got enough to think about during a performance without adding that imagery to my consciousness — but it is true that a sense of humor and a realistic attitude, along with good preparation, can be a powerful antidote to stage fright. Being very aware of your body language can be helpful, as well — be sure that you're keeping your neck long and your body aligned so that any tension you may be feeling doesn't have a chance to feed on itself. (For more on body alignment, see Chapter 5.)

Being prepared for your performance is an essential ingredient to combating stage fright. The more secure you are in your playing, the more confident you'll be in performance. But don't expect perfection: If you're hoping to far surpass what you've done in the practice room just because you have an audience now, you set yourself up for disappointment and potentially an even greater level of self-imposed anxiety. Why do that to yourself? You're human, and humans make mistakes — that's only natural. (All the digital doctoring they do on recordings these days notwithstanding.) You want to play the best you possibly can, but not freak out over any little mishaps, or worse yet, be so afraid of making a mistake that you can't play beautifully because you're too stiff.

The phenomenal violinist Henryk Szeryng once told a student, "When you make a mistake — not *if* you make a mistake, but *when* you make a mistake — just play the next passage so beautifully that the audience will forget you ever made a mistake." That quotation really says it all. Don't be afraid of your mistakes in performance, and don't let on if you make one. Just go on to make some beautiful music. After all, that's why you're here!

Chapter 19

Repair and Maintenance: Taking Care of Your Instrument

Keeping your instrument in top playing condition is an important part of being a musician. The flute's mechanism is surprisingly durable, but it does need a little TLC every now and then — both from you and from an experienced repair technician. You don't want to wait until your flute is suddenly unplayable because of severe pad deterioration before you take it in for repair — that would be a little like waiting until you see smoke coming from under your car's hood before you ever take it in to a mechanic. Your flute, like your car, needs regular checkups to keep it running smoothly and to avoid any last minute emergencies —believe me, you don't want your flute acting up right before a concert or recital!

Giving Your New Flute a Little TLC

When you buy a new flute, it should be in perfect condition. But sometimes, even on a brand new flute, you can find a pad or part of the mechanism that may need a slight adjustment. If you're consistently having trouble getting a particular note to speak, take or send it back to the place where you bought it. The original dealer should be able to tweak it for you for free, depending on the warranty.

If you ship your flute for repairs, make sure that you pack it well and insure the package for the replacement cost of your flute and any headjoints, crowns, or other accessories you've included in the package. (Talk to your insurance carrier to determine whether or not you need to insure your instrument during shipping.)

If you're a flute-playing novice, ask an experienced flutist to play the flute for you a week or two after you buy it to check for any leaky pads, popped springs, or irregularity in the mechanism. No worries — sometimes even a new flute can come to you slightly out of whack, or things can shift around a bit in the first couple of weeks as you play it.

After you and your flute have settled in, you really don't have to do a lot in the way of day-to-day maintenance. Just make sure that you clean out the inside of the flute regularly to prevent moisture buildup — at the end of each practice session at the very least, or every hour or so if you're playing for longer stretches. If you're getting a lot of condensation, remove water bubbles intermittently during your practice sessions. (For more on cleaning your flute, see Chapter 7.) You should also periodically check the placement of your headjoint cork. (See Chapter 15 for instructions on how to check your cork.)

An annual *clean-oil-and-adjust procedure* (also known as a C.O.A.) is as important for the long-term well-being of your flute as regular oil changes are for your car. Once a year, a qualified repair technician needs to take your flute apart, clean off any buildup of dirt and dust in the mechanism, lubricate the metal-to-metal spots to prevent wear, and adjust the pads as necessary to correct any leakage between the pads and the tone holes. Prices for a C.O.A. vary by individual shop and according to your type of flute — expect to pay from $110 (for a student model flute) up to about $300 (for a professional model flute).

If you neglect your flute by skipping your yearly C.O.A., you'll find that certain notes will start sounding hooty and will speak less easily as the pads go out of adjustment, and over time the mechanism itself can get noisy and start sounding pretty clanky. Dirt and dust buildup in the rods can also cause the keys to *bind*, which means they may start sticking in a down or up position (and usually at really inconvenient times, let me assure you).

Keeping your instrument free from moisture buildup, checking the cork from time to time, and getting it into the shop for a C.O.A. once a year should keep your flute in tip-top shape. In between C.O.A.s, if you notice a note that you don't normally have trouble with becoming problematic — for example, not coming out easily or producing a strange sound —give your friendly repair technician a call to have your pads adjusted. Pad adjustments usually involve taking off the pad and putting a very thin paper or plastic shim on certain portions of it in order to reconcile the pad to hit precisely all the way around the tone hole when you depress it.

Combating Wear and Tear

The main issues you'll undoubtedly encounter with your own flute will probably involve the mechanism and pads. The tube itself probably won't change much unless you drive over it with your car like I once did — don't even ask.

You'll also probably find yourself fighting a lifelong battle with some manner of tarnish. Many repair technicians remove tarnish from silver with a 3M product called Tarni-Shield Silver Polish, which removes tarnish from silver without the use of harsh abrasives. If you don't like the look of tarnish on your flute (personally, I think a little tarnish gives my flute character), you can use a little Tarni-Shield as directed on the bottle. But be careful not to get any of the product on the pads or in the mechanism — you don't want to damage your pads or gunk up the mechanism just to have a tarnish-free flute.

In the final analysis, regular maintenance and a yearly C.O.A. will help keep complete overhauls at bay and keep you and your flute sounding your best.

Pads

Synthetic pads last far longer than traditional pads, but both are subject to wear. (See Chapter 3 for more on synthetic and traditional pads.) Over the course of a few years, the pad repeatedly hitting the tone hole under pressure from your fingers causes wear on the pad covering. Once the skin that covers the pad starts to split, the pad's ability to completely seal the tone hole becomes compromised, and the pad will need to be replaced.

But a pad doesn't have to be split to need replacing — environmental factors, such as moisture and heat, can change the shape and resiliency of a pad to the point that it won't seal properly. Pads along the underside of your flute (the ones operated by levers like the trill keys) get more exposure to moisture while you're playing due to gravity, so they tend to wear out before the other pads — repair technicians call this group of pads the *water line*. Your repair technician can tell you when a pad needs to be replaced; you can replace a pad here and there during the clean-oil-and-adjust process, but replacing all the pads usually warrants an overhaul. (See the section "If your instrument needs an overhaul," later in this chapter.)

Spring wear

Your flute's springs, which make the keys pop back up after you depress them, or in the case of some keys, keeps them down until you press the lever that lifts them, can lose tension over time, at which point they'll need replacing. Another issue with springs is that they can occasionally pop out of their holders, the little hooks that hold them in place. If that happens, the key controlled by that particular spring will start flopping around like a wet noodle, not staying where it's supposed to be. Of course, having a key down when it's supposed to be up or vice versa greatly affects what's coming out of your flute (or not!), but luckily, this problem is easily fixed, and you can do it yourself if you're careful:

1. **Locate the popped spring.**

   It will be easy to detect — it's the metal piece that looks like wire sticking out from the rod, looking decidedly out of place.

2. **Gingerly, with a finger or other small nonmetal object, move the spring back behind the spring hook where it came from.**

   Just look at where the other springs are, and you'll easily figure out which hook is missing its spring, so you'll know where to put the stray, popped one.

   It's a rather delicate maneuver, but it's very do-able — just don't force anything!

If you're not sure what to do, take your flute in to your repair technician — he should be able to get that spring back in place in a matter of seconds.

If your instrument needs an overhaul

If most or all of your flute's pads are shot, and if it seems to go out of adjustment more often than it used to when it was new, your flute is probably ready for an *overhaul*. Regular maintenance helps increase the time between overhauls, but your flute will likely need an overhaul about every three to six years. If you have traditional pads, it'll be closer to the three-year mark. Synthetic pads last about twice as long, give or take.

If you tend to slam the keys down heavily when you play, the life expectancy of all pads will be shortened to some extent. Flute overhauls always include the installation of a brand new set of pads that you can wail on to your heart's content, if you don't mind shelling out the big bucks for more frequent overhauls.

The corks and felts that are attached to various parts of the flute's mechanism have a pretty long shelf life. They typically aren't getting as much finger pressure on them as the pads do, and their materials are more resilient, although the corks do dry out and compress over time. Nonetheless, these materials give levers their optimal height and they prevent key noise, so don't take them for granted. Your repair technician may replace a worn cork or felt here or there during your annual C.O.A., but replacing the whole set is reserved for the overhaul process.

Although the flute's metal parts are very durable, they can start to wear down after years of use. If you tend to grab onto the rods when you assemble or disassemble the flute (which you shouldn't — see Chapter 7) or if you drop your instrument (hey, it happens! I once had a clarinet player knock my flute over on stage during the intermission of a concert), your flute may have a bent rod, which really impedes the mechanism's performance. When a qualified repair technician does an overhaul, he inspects the rods thoroughly and checks tolerances between metal parts and any play between them. Then he tightens up the mechanism so that there's no stray movement when it's assembled. That way, the new set of pads can be installed reliably.

Here's what an overhaul typically entails:

- Correction of bent rods or other problems in the mechanism
- Tightening of the mechanism to correct stray movement (this process is called *swedging*)
- Adjustment of key height for optimal venting and intonation
- Checking for leaks in solder (on soldered tone holes)
- Replacement of all pads, corks, and felts
- Replacement of worn springs and pins
- Oiling of mechanism
- Replacement of headjoint cork
- Tenon adjustment to improve fit, if necessary
- Removal of any dents, tarnish, and dirt/dust buildup

Prices on flute overhauls vary widely — they run from around $300 to $1,000 and up, on average. Again, the price largely depends on what kind of flute you have, and how much work your particular instrument needs. Ask for an estimate up front — any repair technician worth his salt should be able to tell about how much work your instrument needs. However, sometimes unexpected problems do arise as the overhaul is in progress. In this case, the repair technician should call to notify you, give you a new estimate, and get your go-ahead before proceeding with further repairs. Make sure that your repair technician observes this type of notification process before any work is begun so that you aren't caught by surprise with a whopping repair bill when you go to pick up your instrument.

Flute 911: Finding a Good Repair Technician

An experienced, knowledgeable repair technician can be a lifesaver. The very best ones will be sensitive to your needs as well as your flute's. On the other hand, a clumsy, indifferent repair technician can be your worst nightmare and can even damage your flute. You want to choose your repair technician wisely because you're calling on this person to do extremely exacting work: Professional model flutes require working to tolerances of .001 inch — that's 1/1,000-inch margin of error. If you're like most musicians, you're pretty attached to your instrument — after all, it's an important part of your musical voice — so do your homework and ask a lot of questions before you leave your flute at any given repair shop.

Who says you can't teach an old flute new tricks?

Lots of folks have played the flute at one time or another. And of the former flutists I've met, a good many of them still have the flute that they played in high school, maybe 15 to 25 years ago (some even longer ago, but I'm not naming names). They've kept it in their closet or attic all these years, thinking that someday they would come back to it. If this is you and that day has come, the flute in question will need some work before you can think about playing on it, even if it was in great shape when you put it away all those years ago.

Your old flute's pads have probably dried out over time, and some corrosion may be present. At the very least, your flute will need a full re-pad, plus cleaning and oiling. Or you may be looking at a complete overhaul.

Consider the value of the instrument before you sink a whole lot of money into it — if it's a professional model flute, it's probably worth the investment, but if it's a student model, purchasing a brand new flute with all the current innovations may be a better investment than fixing up the old one. If that's the case, though, don't throw the old one out — if you ever want to try your hand at taking a flute apart and playing Dr. Frankenstein, an old student model is perfect for such experimenting.

The best way to find a capable repair technician is through word of mouth. You can contact the same sources I list for finding a teacher in Chapter 18: Ask flute club friends, duet buddies, high school band directors, music-store personnel, university flute professors, or any other flutists for recommendations.

In your quest for a repair technician, you're likely to come across a few different options:

- ✔ **The original manufacturer:** If you have a high-end professional model flute that was built by a relatively small company, your best option may be to send it back to the shop where it was made for maintenance. The people who know your instrument best are the people who made it, and some shops even offer free maintenance on their new flutes for a certain time period. The one drawback is shipping costs, if you don't happen to live in the same town where your flute was made. (Be sure to check with your insurance company to see whether or not you should buy shipping insurance for your instrument when you mail it.)

- ✔ **Independent repair shops:** These small shops sometimes run out of a small retail location, but quite often you'll find that the "shop" is an individual repair person working from home. If you find the right person locally, this option can be a great deal because you're cutting out the middleman and paying your repair person directly rather than going through a larger store or shop. You'll also find a number of independent shops nationwide that specialize in working on high-end flutes and ship the instruments back and forth with their customers — check the flute-related publications I mention in Chapter 18 for advertisements and listings.

✔ **Music stores:** Find out whether your local music store offers band instrument repair. As with all the other options, you definitely want to check with someone who has used the store's services to see whether the quality of their repairs is up to snuff. With a store, you have a comfort level with knowing that the store backs its work, but you're also paying the middleman here.

Generally speaking, I wouldn't take a handmade flute to a band instrument repair shop because these types of shops typically employ technicians who are trained to repair all the woodwinds from flutes to contrabassoons, and sometimes even brass and string instruments as well. They get a lot of traffic from local middle school and high school music departments, so they have to know a little bit about a lot of instruments, and depending on the time of year, they also have to turn them around quickly.

Sometimes, though, this option really is all you need for a student model flute. If you choose to use a music store's repair services, make sure that you know the person who repairs your instruments and talk directly to that person about your needs to ensure that you and your flute receive individualized attention.

✔ **Band directors:** High school band directors not only receive training in how to play every instrument they teach, they also learn how to perform minor repairs on all the instruments as well. Although most band directors don't hang out a shingle to advertise their instrument repair skills (and they're usually too busy for outside work anyway), you may be able to hit one up to repair a popped spring or a torn pad here and there. Just remember that their training isn't very specialized. However, if you need a bigger repair job done, your band director will likely be able to recommend the right person to do it.

Every repair technician or shop should have a repair warranty policy. Because pads and mechanisms can shift over the course of days or weeks after a repair, most shops offer you a period of time during which you can bring the instrument back and have it re-adjusted for free. Make sure that you check with your repair technician regarding specific warranty policies.

Part V
The Part of Tens

The 5th Wave   By Rich Tennant

"Okay – I'll front the band. But I want someone other than Dopey on flute."

In this part . . .

Just like the Grand Finale of a symphonic work, the Part of Tens covers many of the themes addressed in this book and brings them all together for you in new ways, making a crescendo toward a stirring and satisfying close that I hope will leave you with a greater appreciation for your instrument and the exciting possibilities open to you as you continue on your own musical journey. You discover some new and exciting ten-item compositions — lists of ten that are easy to review and come back to again and again as you continue to grow with your instrument and your new-found talents. I hope you discover something new every time you return to these pages, just as I do every time I play Beethoven's ninth symphony. It's not about the destination, it's about the journey. I hope you find yours to be as fulfilling as can be.

First, I tell you what *not* to do. For inspiration, I give you a list of top flutists you absolutely need to hear to believe. And finally, my list of ten different types of flutes introduces you to the world beyond the concert C flute.

Chapter 20

Don't Blow It! Ten Bad Habits to Avoid at All Costs

In This Chapter

▶ Steering clear of common pitfalls

▶ Staying away from faulty fingerings

*I*n my 20-plus years of teaching, I've seen countless students make many of the same mistakes over and over again — even the most experienced and seasoned students. Getting rid of these bad habits in your playing is much more difficult than never acquiring them in the first place. So if you want to save yourself a lot of extra work and aggravation in the long run, avoid sabotaging yourself from the very beginning by recognizing these ten all-too-common blunders.

Using Bad Posture

Shortening your neck, spine, and torso severely impacts your breathing. And making sound on the flute depends entirely on your breathing. If you're contracting your rib cage, sucking in your belly, or pulling your shoulders up, you won't be able to make a singing, open, beautiful sound — instead, you'll sound thin, stuffy, and shrill, or you may even have trouble getting a sound to come out at all. So take a look at the section on posture in Chapter 5 and always stay aware of your body's alignment when you play.

Time and again, I've been able to improve a student's sound almost instantly in lessons just by adjusting body alignment and reminding them of the basics of good playing posture. With good body awareness, you can do the same in your practice studio. Stay long, stay open, stay balanced, stay comfortable, stand straight — and play great!

Drooping Flute or Perfectly Parallel Flute

This one really goes hand in hand with my admonitions on posture, but it's a bit more specific. You want to keep as natural a body position as possible when you're playing. Giving in to gravity by letting the end of your flute droop toward the floor definitely isn't a natural or comfortable body position because you just end up shortening your torso and compressing your rib cage in the process, again impeding your breathing.

However, if you go the opposite route and incessantly work to keep your flute stick-straight and perfectly parallel to the floor, you end up sticking your chest out, thereby putting a strain on your upper back and shoulder muscles. Often, people who spent a little too much time in their school marching band gravitate toward the perfectly-parallel option, sticking their elbows way out away from their torsos — but even though it looks great to have a sea of uniformly straight flutes on the football field, it's fundamentally unsound from a playing perspective, and your band director is just going to have to deal with it.

Rolling Your Headjoint Inward

Covering too much of the embouchure hole with the lower lip is an all-too-common problem among flute players. If, upon checking your embouchure in the mirror, you find that you're covering more than half of the embouchure hole, you need to uncover so that you're only covering a third to half at the most. In lessons, I usually don't need to look at a student's embouchure to determine that he's covering too much: If the sound is muffled or pinched, or if he's having trouble with flexibility in jumping from one octave to the next, or if his intonation is tending to be flat, I can be pretty sure that he needs to uncover the embouchure hole to some degree.

Rolling the headjoint toward you makes you cover too much of the embouchure hole. If you're experiencing this problem, you're probably doing one of the following things:

- ✔ Your headjoint isn't properly aligned: Check to see whether the front edge of the embouchure hole is lining up with the edge of the first key on the top of the flute. (See Chapter 7 for more on assembling your flute.)

- ✔ Your head is bowing forward as you play, changing the position of your lips on the embouchure plate. Often, excess tension or fatigue from a particularly grueling performance or practice session or rehearsal is reflected in your playing in this way. Make a conscious effort to lift your chin up and off of your throat while lengthening the back of your neck. You need to remain constantly aware of your physical state and return to the fundamentals of sound playing, particularly when you start getting tired. Returning to the basics is your best wake-up call.

> ✔ You're not keeping your flute in balance. If you aren't using your chin, left-hand index finger, and right-hand thumb for leverage, the rods gravitate downward, making the flute roll toward you. Review your balance points in Chapter 7. You may also want to consider using a right-thumb balancing device like the Thumbport, which I also mention in that chapter.

Forcing Your Embouchure

When you're constricting your airstream too much, you're forcing your embouchure, which makes you sound harsh, buzzy, and out of tune and makes your notes prone to cracking. A lot of flutists start to force at some point, usually because they're doing too much with the embouchure muscles in order to try to get better control of the sound. In flute playing, as in life, things often work much better if you just let go.

If you're forcing your embouchure, you need to be especially aware of what your aperture is doing. Don't try to overcontrol by using a lot of muscle power in your top lip: Although it *feels* like you've got more control over the sound that way, you actually get more extraneous noise in your sound if you bear down on that top lip. Instead, think of gently guiding your airstream from the inside of the lip, the moist part, and let the outside part of the lip follow along instead of trying to lead. You'll be amazed at how much better you can sound by simply doing *less*. There's a decided Zen precept that exhorts us to "do by not doing." Do that!

Dropping Your Airstream

You'd be surprised how easily you can forget that your airstream is the most important factor in producing your sound. After all, without your air, there would be no sound at all. But many flutists don't support the airstream continuously all the way through a musical line. Technical passages suffer greatly when the airstream isn't properly supported. Once the fingers start flying, flutists often have small yet, noticeable gaps in their breathing because they're concentrating only on their fingers and not on other important factors, such as proper breathing and breath support. In slow passages, it's easier to concentrate on the airstream, but even then flutists still have a tendency to drop the airstream between notes.

Always be sure that you're exhaling smoothly and supporting your air all the way through a melody or technical passage, and you'll find that your intonation, sound, and technique will be much more consistent. Practicing fast technical passages slowly at first and working up to speed will give you firm and fertile ground in which to sow the seeds of airstream control and virtuosity. Just give yourself the time and conditions in which to grow properly as a player.

Not Tuning Carefully

In recitals, I regularly see this less-than-ideal scenario: Flutist and pianist walk onstage and take their initial bow with great aplomb, only to appear completely unnerved and confused by the tuning process. The pianist plays an A softly on the piano, and the flutist echoes it tentatively, playing a very quiet series of curiously apologetic-sounding short A's, as if tuning really wasn't allowed, and as if doing so properly would offend the audience in some way. Never mind them — by all means, tune! Instead of tentatively approaching your tuning A, just go for it. Try different dynamic levels, tune proudly, and let the audience know that you know what you're doing. Then nod confidently to your pianist and play on.

News flash: In order to tune properly, you've got to be able to really hear your tuning notes, which means you need to hold them out for a while, using a medium (*mf*) dynamic level. If you're tuning to a piano, remember that it can't sustain a note the same way the flute can. If the piano note fades before you're able to discern whether you're sharp or flat to it, ask for another A. Of course, checking your tuning A with the piano and/or your tuner before your audience arrives will give you a bit of a head start. But make sure that you still tune right before you play the first note of your performance, in case the warmer temperature in the packed hall has affected your instrument's pitch.

Flying Fingers and the "Death Grip"

Sometimes I use the phrase *flying fingers* to describe a well-executed fast technical passage. However, there's a big difference between fingers flying quickly and efficiently during fast passages, and fingers flying *up* while you're playing. Fingers flying up off of your flute are far less desirable because the farther your fingers have to move to come back down onto the key again, the less efficient your technique will be.

To make your fingers fly *fast*, don't let them fly *up!* Check yourself regularly in the mirror to make sure that your fingers are staying close to the keys as you play.

What I call the *death grip* is exactly the opposite of the fingers flying away from the keys: Some flutists grab the keys so tightly that they have trouble moving their fingers at all. Often, an inordinately tight grip by the player can be traced to the flute itself — that is, the pads not sealing properly over the tone holes: As the pads seal less and less well, the flutist instinctively pushes harder and harder on the keys in order to compensate. The process is gradual, so before you know it, it can get to the point where your flute is leaking like a sieve, and you're white-knuckling the instrument without even realizing it. Refer to Chapter 19 to find out about maintaining your flute so that you can avoid this issue.

If you're having trouble holding your flute using your balance points (see Chapter 7), you'll feel less than secure because the instrument will be moving around on you. Often, flutists compensate for this lack of stability by grabbing the keys more tightly than they should. This approach is another version of the death grip, also to be avoided because using too much pressure on the keys prevents you from developing a fast, efficient, fluid technique.

Using Only One B♭ Fingering

Many beginning and intermediate flutists are in love with their one-and-one B♭. They seem to have a phobia of the Thumb B♭ and B♭ lever fingerings and, consequently, never use them. (See Chapter 9 for more on the three fingerings for low and middle B♭.)

On the one hand, I can see the logic in only using one fingering: It's easier on your brain because you don't have to decide which fingering you're going to use. And the one-and-one fingering works in every situation: You never run into a passage where you can't use the one-and-one B♭. But using the thumb B♭ key and the B♭ lever when appropriate makes things a lot easier on your fingers and thereby facilitates smooth, flawless technique. Look for any opportunity to use your thumb B♭ key and your B♭ lever, get to know these fingerings well, and then enjoy the technical prowess you'll gain as a result!

Faulty Fingerings: Leaving LH 1 Down on Middle Register E♭ and D

In a slow or moderate passage, I can always tell by listening whether a flutist is using the correct fingering for the middle register E♭ and D. Countless flutists get into the habit of leaving LH 1 down on those notes, especially if they're in between other notes that already have LH 1 depressed, like C or E.

Unless you're playing a fast, technical passage, you really need to use the correct fingering, lifting LH 1 to vent those notes properly. Otherwise, your E♭ and D will sound very dull and stuffy, and they'll stick out as not sounding as good as the other notes you're playing.

When the music is moving along very fast, go ahead and leave LH 1 down if it makes the passage easier to play — if you're playing fast enough, the listeners' ears won't pick up the change in tone quality. But don't get lazy when you're playing a beautiful melody: In that case, use the right fingerings, allowing your middle E♭ and D to sing.

Watching That Wobble: Out-of-Control Vibrato

Nothing can get in the way of a melodic line like wide, erratic vibrato. Listening to a piece of music when the melodies are obscured by a huge wobble is really difficult; the vibrato then becomes more of a distraction than a decoration.

I once witnessed Marcel Moyse asking a flutist who was playing for him if she wasn't feeling well. She replied that she was feeling fine, thank you. As she continued to play, Moyse persisted, asking her whether she would like to lie down — before too long, the auditors and the student in question all realized that he was making fun of her rather obvious vibrato. That was a lesson she wouldn't soon forget!

Vibrato is one of many things that become second nature after a while. Once ingrained in your playing, vibrato can easily be overlooked. And while having a natural vibrato that you don't have to think about is fine, listening to yourself from time to time will ensure that your vibrato isn't becoming obtrusive.

For some reason, vibrato seems to be one of the things that's hardest to hear objectively in your own playing, but hearing your own vibrato accurately is a bit easier if you listen to a recording of yourself. Record your practice on slow melodies and listen to your vibrato carefully. Be especially aware of inadvertent accents you may be creating with your vibrato: If you hit the highest part of your vibrato amplitude at the beginning of a note, it can sound a lot like an accent, especially if your vibrato is on the wide side. Also, don't vibrate too far below the central pitch of a note; if you do, you'll likely lose necessary breath support at the bottom end of your vibrato, and your breathing muscles will start working more erratically, giving you an uneven vibrato. Keep your vibrato relatively shallow and fairly subtle, and, as always, stay conscious of your breath support to avoid falling into the wobble trap. (For more on vibrato, see Chapter 13.)

Chapter 21

Ten Flutists You Need to Hear

In This Chapter

▶ Getting to know some of the world's great flutists

▶ Listening to them on recordings, films, and in concert

The Check It Out! icon appears at the beginning of this chapter because you need to listen to all the flutists I mention here. Although they all play classical music, they represent a variety of flute-playing styles. Their various sounds and styles distinguish them from one another, but their playing exemplifies what's possible on the flute after you really master the instrument. Enjoy listening to these world-class flutists, whether it's on an LP, CD, or mp3, a movie soundtrack, or perhaps even live in concert. Get ready to be inspired!

You can find performance videos of most of the flutists I list here on YouTube (www.youtube.com) — just type the performer's name and the word "flute" into the search box. Some of the videos even show these flutists teaching masterclasses. Watching these videos is a great opportunity to not only hear great musicians play, but to take a look at their embouchures, fingers, and body alignment — consider these videos instant online courses in flute playing.

Julius Baker

For decades, Julius Baker (1915–2003) seemed to be *the* flutist and teacher in North America. He was the legendary New York Philharmonic Principal Flutist from 1965 until 1983. He taught at the famed Juilliard School in New York from 1954 until 2003 — just shy of a half-century of mentoring the country's top musical talent. (Jeanne Baxtresser and Paula Robison, also listed later in this chapter, were students of Baker's.) The man had quite an impact on the flute players of today — and that's not even mentioning his teaching at the Curtis Institute in Philadelphia or his stints with the Cleveland, Pittsburgh, and CBS Symphony Orchestras or his numerous recitals and masterclasses all over the globe. (See Chapter 18 for more on masterclasses.)

Julius Baker (www.juliusbaker.com) spent his college years at the Curtis Institute in Philadelphia, studying with the celebrated Philadelphia Orchestra Principal Flutist William Kincaid (1895–1967). Kincaid had studied in New York with the French flutist Georges Barrère (1876–1944). (See more on the flute and France in Chapter 3.) Baker's star quickly rose in the music world, and he was soon working in the best orchestras and with the most famous conductors of the day, Leopold Stokowski (1882–1977) and Leonard Bernstein (1918–1990) among them.

In 1966, *Time* Magazine described Julius Baker as follows:

"Baker . . . played the intricate trills . . . as casually as another man might whistle for a taxi. He is the supreme mechanic of his instrument, and he produces what is surely the most glorious tone that ever came out of a flute: big, round, cool, white, radiant as a September moon."

There's really no better way to say it: Baker had a singular technique that made flute playing look and sound easy, and a rich, singing tone that made everything he played sound beautiful. To hear him, pick up any recording of the New York Philharmonic made between 1965 and 1983 or look for his solo recordings.

Jeanne Baxtresser

Jeanne Baxtresser (1947–) studied at the Juilliard School in New York and followed her teacher, Julius Baker (see preceding section), as Principal Flute with the New York Philharmonic. Having previously held principal positions with the Montreal and Toronto Symphonies, Baxtresser (www.jeanne baxtresser.com) stayed on with the New York Philharmonic for 15 years before she left the orchestral world to pursue teaching full-time. She also taught at the Manhattan and Juilliard Schools during her years with the New York Philharmonic. As of this writing, she is Professor of Flute at Carnegie Mellon University in Pittsburgh.

Baxtresser's sound is powerful and full, and her technique is rock-solid, much like her teacher's. To hear her, get a hold of a recording of the New York Philharmonic made between 1984 and 1998 or check out her numerous solo and chamber music recordings. Also of interest is her book, *Orchestral Excerpts for Flute* (Presser), and the CD recording of the same title with Baxtresser herself playing the excerpts (Summit). This book and CD are must-haves for any budding orchestral flutist's library.

William Bennett

William Ingham Brook Bennett (1936–), affectionately known as Wibb, is based in London and teaches at the Royal Academy of Music there. He studied with Geoffrey Gilbert (1914–1989), the British flutist widely credited with bringing the French style of playing to England, Jean-Pierre Rampal, and Marcel Moyse. A true master flutist and teacher, he has enjoyed a stellar career as a soloist as well as a consummate orchestral musician. He has appeared as Principal Flutist and recorded with the London Symphony, the Academy of St. Martin-in-the-Fields, and the English Chamber Orchestra, among others, has toured across the globe, and has made countless solo recordings as well (most recently on his own label, Beep Records). In 1995, Her Majesty Queen Elizabeth II presented him with the Most Excellent Order of the British Empire (O.B.E.) for his disti nguished Services to Music.

Wibb (www.williambennettflute.com) is known for his exquisite musicianship, his perfect phrasing, and his signature resonant sound with seemingly infinite variations in tone color. (For more on tone color, see Chapter 12.)

Wibb is as renowned for his teaching as for his flute playing. College and professional level students flock to his masterclasses to experience his unique, at times eccentric, highly effective brand of coaching. (See Chapter 18 for more on masterclasses.) He has a special affinity for Moyse's melodic studies, such as the ones found in *Tone Development Through Interpretation* and *24 Little Melodic Studies with Variations.* (For more on melodic studies, see Chapter 17.)

Back when I was studying with him, my fellow students and I quickly learned that playing a melodic study for him in our lessons was not an easier alternative to playing our etudes and pieces for him, as we had hoped. He could easily spend hours on just one little melody, working on sound, tone color, phrasing, and many other musical details.

If, like so many millions of other people, you've seen the movie *Amadeus*, you've heard Wibb. He was Principal Flutist with the Academy of St. Martin-in-the-Fields when they recorded the soundtrack, and he has some prominent solos you can hear in the movie. Many recordings of the Academy of St. Martin-in-the-Fields and the English Chamber Orchestra made in the 1980s and 1990s feature Wibb as the principal flutist, and his numerous solo recordings are also readily available.

Sir James Galway

Sir James Galway (1939–) has played a very large part in creating a wider, more diverse audience for the flute. (See more about Galway's part in the flute's immense popularity in Chapter 2.) His jaw-dropping technique, huge sound, and winsome stage presence propelled him to superstar status after he left the Berlin Philharmonic to pursue a solo career. Known as "the man with the golden flute," he concertizes all over the world and teaches a week-long masterclass in Switzerland each summer. He received an O.B.E. in 1977 and was knighted in 2001.

Fun facts:

✔ Like Wibb, Sir James studied with Geoffrey Gilbert, Jean-Pierre Rampal, and Marcel Moyse. Wibb and Sir James met when they were students.

✔ Wibb recommended Sir James for his first gig, a second flute job with the Sadlers Wells Opera Orchestra.

To find a recording by Sir James Galway (www.jamesgalway.com), you don't have to look very far. His recordings are everywhere, and it's a pretty safe bet that you'll get a stunning performance no matter which one you pick. (See my list of essential Galway recordings in Chapter 2.) For a special treat, listen to Sir James performing in his principal flute position in the Berlin Philharmonic — he recorded with them between 1969 and 1975. But to really experience Sir James and his wonderful energy and stage presence, you've simply got to hear him live in concert.

Marcel Moyse

Of this list of ten flutists, four were students of Marcel Moyse (1889–1984): William Bennett, Sir James Galway, Paula Robison, and Carol Wincenc. Moyse has had an enormous influence on today's flutists, just by virtue of his teaching and his books. (Read more about Moyse's legacy in Chapter 17.)

Moyse's flute playing was, of course, masterful — he had a gorgeous, full, warm sound and played with an expressive, vocal style and facile technique. Listening to his recordings really tells you why he wrote all of those melodic studies!

Moyse's recordings aren't easy to find — he recorded chiefly between 1927 and 1938, and remastered CDs tend to go in and out of print — but a

CD called *The Recorded Legacy of Marcel Moyse* is available by mail-order through the Marcel Moyse Society (www.moysesociety.org). Moyse's playing is also featured on a more widely available series of historical recordings called *The Great Flautists* (Pearl), which also include recordings of Moyse's teachers, Philippe Gaubert (1879–1941) and Adolphe Hennebains (1862–1914). The Pearl label also puts out a compilation CD of Moyse's playing called *Flute Fantastique*.

Flute specialty retailers, such as the Carolyn Nussbaum Music Company (www.flute4u.com) and Flute World (www.fluteworld.com), which I also mention in Chapter 17, are more likely to have Marcel Moyse recordings and other hard-to-find flute-related CD's in stock than regular CD stores.

Emmanuel Pahud

Swiss flutist Emmanuel Pahud (1970–) burst onto the scene when he was appointed Principal Flute with the prestigious Berlin Philharmonic in 1993 at the tender age of 23. He was already quite accomplished, having won three major international competitions between 1988 and 1992. He had also held the position of Principal Flute with the Basel Radio Symphony Orchestra and the Munich Philharmonic, notable appointments all. Among his teachers were Swiss flutists Peter-Lukas Graf and Aurèle Nicolet, as well as French flutists Michel Debost and Alain Marion.

Not one to rest on his laurels, Pahud (www.fluteconnection.net/contfl/pahud.html) has recorded dozens of solo albums since he started with the Berlin Philharmonic. He even left Berlin for a year to teach at the Geneva Conservatory in Switzerland and to pursue an international solo career. Pahud re-joined the Berlin Philharmonic in 2002, though his solo career doesn't show any signs of slowing down. His substantial musicianship and dense tone color make his concert appearances and recordings a listening pleasure. He makes a point of working with other world-class musicians — many of the pianists and other instrumentalists he has worked with on his recordings have their own solo careers and are remarkable musical partners: Yefim Bronfman and Stephen Kovacevich, both pianists, and Trevor Pinnock, harpsichordist, just to name a few.

An especially interesting aspect of Pahud's flute playing is that he changes his playing style significantly when he's playing pieces from different musical periods. In Baroque and Classical repertoire he uses vibrato sparingly, an appropriate tribute to how musicians actually performed in the time of Bach and Mozart. (For more on vibrato in the Baroque and Classical periods of music, see Chapter 13.) When he's playing pieces by later composers, he cranks up the vibrato a notch or two, always tastefully and elegantly.

Whatever style of music he's playing, you're guaranteed a thoughtful yet virtuosic performance.

Emmanuel Pahud makes his solo recordings under the EMI label, which is widely available. Also check out Berlin Philharmonic recordings made from 1993 to present — he's playing principal flute on most of those, except for the year 2000, when he was teaching in Geneva.

Jean-Pierre Rampal

Jean-Pierre Rampal (1922–2000) enjoyed a wildly successful international solo career at a time when people didn't generally think of the flute as a solo instrument. (You can find out more about Rampal and the flute's popularity in Chapter 2.) Rampal raised the stature of the instrument by rediscovering long-neglected 18th century repertoire, performing it so impeccably and with such virtuosity that he quickly became a musical sensation. He also commissioned a number of new pieces, many of which have become staples of the flute repertoire.

Rampal studied first with his father, Joseph Rampal (1903–1983), who was the flute professor at the conservatory in Marseilles. (That's an amazing feat in itself — most children have trouble even taking driving lessons from their parents!) The young Rampal studied medicine for a while before deciding to pursue music. He then went to Paris to study with Gaston Crunelle at the conservatory there (his father's alma mater).

Rampal's recordings are readily available. (See my list of essential Rampal recordings in Chapter 2.) His sound was clear, transparent, and quintessentially French, and if you listen to some of his recordings of 18th century repertoire from the 1960s, you'll find that the clarity and speed of his articulation was nothing short of spectacular.

Paula Robison

In 1960, the famed conductor/composer/pianist Leonard Bernstein invited a 19-year-old flutist by the name of Paula Robison (1941–) to solo with the New York Philharmonic. She was a student at the Juilliard School at the time, where she studied with Julius Baker, and spent summers at the Marlboro Festival studying with Marcel Moyse. The special appearance with the New York Philharmonic was just the beginning of a stellar career: She went on to win the highly regarded Geneva Competition, and her career as a flute soloist was born.

From her very beginnings, Robison (www.paularobison.com) had been comfortable with the spotlight, having studied dance and theatre as well as music when she was a child. As a result, Robison has always had an unmatched flair on the concert stage. Not only does she play beautifully and expressively, she also moves so gracefully with the music that she enthralls concertgoers whenever she performs. She currently teaches at the New England Conservatory in Boston and has also taught at her alma mater, the Juilliard School.

You can still hear the recording that Paula Robison made with the New York Philharmonic (she had turned 20 by the time she recorded it). She plays the part of the bird (*Volière*) in Saint-Saëns's *Carnival of the Animals* (at breakneck speed, I might add), conducted and narrated by Leonard Bernstein. (Fun fact: Robison was given only one take to record that movement!) It's available on the Sony Classics label; the title of the album is *Children's Classics*.

The best way to experience Robison's musical gifts is to hear her play live. (I once had the pleasure of performing a flute quartet with her, and I can tell you first-hand that her unadulterated joy in making music is infectious both to her fellow musicians and to the audience.) But her recordings run a close second to her live performances. She has recorded on quite a few labels over the course of her career, most recently on her own label, Pergola Recordings.

Jim Walker

You've heard Jim Walker (1944–) play; you just may not know it. Have you ever been to the movies? To date, he can be heard on more than 500 Hollywood movie scores, including *E.T. the Extra-Terrestrial*, *Pretty Woman*, *Batman Forever*, *Titanic*, *Gladiator*, *The Princess Diaries*, *Mr. and Mrs. Smith*, and *Pirates of the Caribbean*. (For more about the flute's role in the movies, see Chapter 2.)

Walker studied with James Pellerite, Harold Bennett, and French flutist and conductor Claude Monteux (isn't there always a French connection?) and became the principal flutist with the Los Angeles Philharmonic after holding jobs with the U.S. Military Academy Band and the Pittsburgh Symphony Orchestra. L.A. turned out to be the perfect creative environment for Walker because it was there that he got into the studio scene and was able to nurture his love for jazz. In 1980, he founded a jazz/classical fusion group called Free Flight. A few years later, he left the Los Angeles Philharmonic, flying right into a solo jazz/classical and studio career.

Jim Walker's free spirit shows in his flute playing. He's got chops for days, sailing from the most difficult classical repertoire into scintillating jazz improvisation without blinking an eye. His recordings can be tricky to find, but flute specialty stores are a good source. You can also order directly from Walker's Web site at www.jimwalkerflute.com.

Walker teaches at USC and the Colburn School. You can even study with him online via Skype, which he has set up on his Web site.

Carol Wincenc

Winning the prestigious Walter W. Naumburg Solo Flute Competition in 1978 jump-started Carol Wincenc's (1949–) international solo career. Ebullient and energetic, Wincenc (http://carolwincenc.googlepages.com) has an engaging personal style. She has premiered numerous new works for flute and has been the driving force behind commissioning many of them. Her sheet music collection called *Valentines* (Carl Fischer) features 11 new pieces written especially for her by contemporary composers and includes a CD of Wincenc performing them. Wincenc's teachers include Robert Willoughby, Marcel Moyse, Moyse's student Charles Delaney (1925–2006), and Severino Gazzeloni (1915–1992). Wincenc now teaches at the Juilliard School and SUNY Stony Brook, following in the footsteps of yet another of her teachers, Samuel Baron (1925–1997).

Wincenc has premiered at least four substantial new flute concerti: *Flute Concerto* by Christopher Rouse, *Renaissance Concerto* by Lukas Foss, *Concerto* by Joan Tower, and *Klezmer Rondos* by Paul Schoenfield. She recorded the Rouse *Flute Concerto* with the Houston Symphony Orchestra (Telarc), the Foss *Renaissance Concerto* with the Brooklyn Philharmonic Orchestra (New World Records), the Tower *Concerto* with the Louisville Orchestra (d'Note), and the Schoenfield *Klezmer Rondos* with the New World Symphony (Polygram). Or, if you're less adventurous, you can easily find recordings of Carol Wincenc playing the more standard flute repertoire quite brilliantly.

In celebration of her 40th year on the concert stage, Wincenc commissioned six new works for flute by composers Jonathan Berger, Shih-Hui Chen, Andrea Clearfield, Jake Heggie, Thea Musgrave, and Joan Tower. She performed them all on a commemorative 2009–10 concert series in New York City. Clearly, flutists can look forward to many more important additions to the repertoire facilitated by this seasoned yet innovative musician.

Chapter 22

Ten Different Types of Flutes

Throughout this book, when I refer to the flute, I, of course, am talking about the Western Concert C Flute, which is the one that you most often see in the concert halls of the Western world. It's the one that sports the key system that Theobald Boehm invented (see Chapter 2) and has been around in one form or another since 1832. But up to this point, *Flute For Dummies* doesn't delve into the array of flute sizes in the Boehm family, or for that matter, the pre-Boehm historical flutes that are still in use today. There are also rich traditions in flute playing represented by a diverse and amazing world of instruments from cultures in every corner of the globe. I would be remiss in not introducing you to these truly magical world flutes. Enjoy!

In this chapter, you get to meet the whole flute family: from the piccolo to the contrabass flute, from the Baroque to the classical flute, and from the Celtic flute to the Japanese shakuhachi to the Chinese dizi. The variety and scope of these instruments — and the rich cultural history behind them — are truly beautiful to behold.

The Piccolo

The *piccolo,* shown in Figure 22-1, is the diva of the flute family — it's often the center of attention when playing in an ensemble. It's a tiny instrument that plays an octave higher than the concert C flute, which means you can often hear it above all the other instruments in a band or orchestra. When you play a piccolo, the notes in your part look exactly the same as they would for a C flute part, and you can use the same fingerings, but all the notes sound an octave higher than they would on the C flute. Piccolos come in metal (usually silver or nickel silver, more rarely in gold) or various types of wood, which creates a more mellow sound and is most often used in an orchestral setting.

The D♭ piccolo

Although they're rarely in use these days, you may come across a D♭ piccolo at some point. The D♭ piccolo is, of course, pitched in D♭ instead of the usual C. Because composers usually write pieces for band with flat key signatures, the piccolo used to be a traditional band instrument that made playing in flat keys easier. But it turns out that piccolo players can play in flat keys on the C piccolo just as well, so the D♭ piccolo went by the wayside. You may still see old band parts written for the D♭ piccolo, though. If you do, trade it in for a C piccolo part. Otherwise, you'll have to transpose the part in order to play in the right key.

Figure 22-1:
The piccolo.

The piccolo is the most common of what are called the *auxiliary instruments* in a band or orchestra's flute section, which means that if you play in an ensemble, you'll likely be called on to play a piccolo part at some point.

Other than the piccolo, the auxiliary instruments in the various woodwind sections are the bass clarinet and E♭ clarinet in the clarinet section, the contrabassoon in the bassoon section, and the English horn in the oboe section. Professional musicians who play auxiliary instruments often specialize in them — an oboist can specialize in playing the English horn, for example, and a flutist can specialize in piccolo playing.

The piccolo is a fantastic little instrument. Some call it the flutist's revenge: Because the piccolo is the highest-pitched member of any ensemble, its player never has any trouble being heard. The basic premise of playing the piccolo is easy to master; what's not so easy is playing it well — and in tune — at various dynamic levels. Quite a few piccolo-specific publications are available to help with this dilemma. One of the most useful I've seen is *The Complete Piccolo* (Theodore Presser Company), compiled and edited by Jan Gippo. It features contributions from several noted players and includes specific piccolo fingerings, historical perspective on the instrument, and a guide to repertoire. You can find much of what you need to tackle the challenges of this tricky little instrument that Trevor Wye has lovingly and appropriately called "the shrieking twig." (See Chapter 17 for more on Trevor Wye.)

Top picc's for the piccolo

Although the piccolo is most often heard in ensembles (*Stars and Stripes*, anyone?), it also has its own solo repertoire. My picks (picc's) for top three piccolo solos are

- *Concerto in C, RV443 (P79)* by Antonio Vivaldi (ed. Amadeus, Henle, or Schott). This concerto, originally for the recorder, is *the* essential piccolo piece. The first and third movements are highly virtuosic, while the slow middle movement is a beautiful little gem with plenty of opportunity for baroque ornamentation. You can hear this concerto and more piccolo concerti by Vivaldi and Telemann on an album called, aptly enough, *Vivaldi: Les concertos pour flûte-piccolo* (Calliope France). (The French title means *Vivaldi: The concertos for piccolo.*) This recording features Jean-Louis Beaumadier on the piccolo, with Jean-Pierre Rampal conducting the Orchestre National de France.

- *Piccolo Espagnol* by James Christensen (ed. Kendor Music, Inc.). This fun piccolo classic explores the full range of the instrument, with sensuous melodies in the low register, pulsing Spanish rhythms, and lots of fast scales up to the high B. Virtuoso piccoloist Laurence Trott recorded it on his album *From Rags to Riches* (Qualiton-Fleur De Son).

- *Concerto for Piccolo and Orchestra, op. 50* by Lowell Liebermann (ed. Theodore Presser). A dramatic and virtuosic new work for piccolo written in 1996 and recorded by Sir James Galway and the London Mozart Players, conducted by the composer.

Also check out the following repertoire to hear the piccolo in its full orchestral glory:

- *Symphony No. 9 in D minor, Op. 125* by Ludwig van Beethoven. Listen for the piccolo solo in the "Turkish March" section in the very last movement. It's a soft, rhythmic section that contrasts with the powerful choral music.

- *Overture to Semiramide* by Gioachino Rossini. The lightness, ease, and elegance with which a good piccoloist can play the solos in this famous Rossini Overture belies the extreme difficulty of the part. It's wonderfully effervescent music.

- *Symphony No. 4 in F minor, Op. 36* by Pyotr Il'yich Tchaikovsky. In this piece, the piccolo player sits on stage and doesn't play for the first two movements. Finally in the third movement, the piccolo comes in with a huge solo — and it's completely exposed as well as highly virtuosic! Pretty spectacular stuff.

The Alto Flute

You hear the *alto flute*, shown in Figure 22-2, occasionally in bands and orchestras, though composers rarely write a part for it. It's pitched in G, so it plays lower than the concert C flute by an interval of a fourth. The sound of a good alto flute is full, velvety, and delicious in the low register. The alto flute's third register can sound hollow and airy by contrast, and depending on the particular instrument, the high notes can go quite sharp. Usually when composers write for the alto, they keep the music in the instrument's low and middle registers.

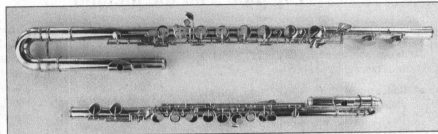

Figure 22-2:
The bass flute (top) and alto flute (bottom).

Because the alto flute is quite a bit bigger than the C flute, some flutemakers include a curved headjoint with the instrument to make it more comfortable to play. When you have an alto flute part, you play the notes written on the page, but they sound a fourth lower than the note you're fingering. (The composer has already factored in this difference.) If you're fingering a C, for example, it'll come out as a sounding G.

The Bass Flute

The *bass flute,* shown in Figure 22-2, is bigger and lower than the alto flute, is pitched in C, and plays a full octave lower than the concert C flute. Although this instrument is mostly seen in flute choirs and rarely makes a solo appearance, it's really satisfying to play. Maybe I'm saying that because I play so many high notes on a daily basis that it's refreshing to feel the vibrations of a low instrument in my hands, but the bass flute has a special sonic quality that's just otherworldly.

In 1976, composer/pianist Claude Bolling wrote an entire bass flute movement called *Versatile* in his *Suite for Flute and Jazz Piano.* Composers are starting to write more music for the bass flute, but solos are still few and far between.

The Contrabass Flute

The *contrabass flute* is pitched in C and is a full octave lower than the bass flute. Flute choirs, in order to sound more like real orchestras, need a stand-in for the string bass, which is where the contrabass flute comes in. The contrabass flute, shown in Figure 22-3, is made by Eva Kingma (www. kingmaflutes.com), a flutemaker based in the Netherlands who specializes in making low flutes.

The alto flute repertoire

Alto flute parts start to appear in music from the beginning of the 20th century. Three pieces in the standard orchestral repertoire showcase the alto flute with solos:

✔ *The Planets* by Gustav Holst. (Last movement: 7. Neptune, the Mystic)

✔ *Daphnis and Chloe, Suite no. 2* by Maurice Ravel.

✔ *The Rite of Spring* by Igor Stravinsky

In contemporary music, composers are taking advantage of the alto flute's sensuous low register more and more often. You hear it fairly regularly in movie scores — I think that trend must have started with those spy thrillers back in the 1960s and '70s, where the alto flute added just the right touch of mystery.

Figure 22-3:
The contra-
bass flute.

An impressive-looking instrument, the contrabass flute is played vertically (there's no way to hold that much flute sideways). The tube is usually about 9 feet long, and the top of the tube loops around and over sideways so that the embouchure is accessible to the flutist. (The loop at the top makes the contrabass flute look a lot like a big number four.) The instrument typically ends up being about 6 feet tall and usually comes with a special stand so that the player can adjust the exact height.

The contrabass flute doesn't play very loudly, but its sound is nonetheless intriguing. It's gaining some popularity as a solo instrument, especially in avant-garde music, usually with amplification in that context. Forward-thinking Swiss flutist Matthias Ziegler is pioneering this field, writing and performing his own music for low flutes with amplification. To expand your horizons, listen to clips from his 1999 album, *Uakti* (New Albion Records, Inc.), at www.matthias-ziegler.ch.

How low can you go?

As the popularity of the contrabass flute grows, flutemakers specializing in low flutes are responding by making more varieties available. I list a few of them here:

- **Contr'alto flutes:** Pitched one octave below the alto flute.

- **Subcontrabass flute in G:** Pitched one octave below the contr'alto flute, or a fourth below the contrabass flute.

- **Double contrabass flute in C:** Pitched one octave below the contrabass flute. (But at this point, wouldn't it be more logical to take up the tuba?)

The Flauto d'Amore

The flauto d'amore (Italian for "flute of love") is also called flûte d'amour (French for "flute of love"). They're pitched either in B♭ or in A, a whole step or minor third below the C flute, respectively.

This particular type of flute has its roots in the Baroque period and appears sporadically thereafter. Because its range is between that of the C flute and the alto flute, it provides the player with the dark tonal quality and super-responsive low register of the alto, but with a feel more like that of a C flute under the fingers for greater technical facility, and a good third octave.

All in all, it's a fun instrument to play, but unfortunately, there isn't a lot of music written for it — but the flauto d'amore repertoire of the Baroque and Romantic eras is definitely worth a listen, if you ever come across it.

The E♭ Flute

The E♭ *flute* is another rarity in the flute world. Also called the *soprano flute*, it's pitched in E♭, a minor third higher than the C flute. It's mostly played in flute choirs, but before the advent of the curved headjoint, teachers recommended it to beginning students with small hands. Sometimes, it's even substituted for the E♭ clarinet in school bands.

The Baroque Flute, or Traverso

Pre-Boehm flutes, born before Boehm invented the key system used today, are alive and well and still being played. (See more about Theobald Boehm in the sidebar in Chapter 2.)

The *Baroque flute,* shown in Figure 22-4, is so named because it was the flute in use during the Baroque period (1685–1750). It has six holes and one key. Its predecessor, the *renaissance flute,* has six holes but no key. The addition of that one key, which was the precursor to the D♯/E♭ key on the modern flute, allowed the flutists of the day to play in a wider variety of major and minor keys.

Figure 22-4:
A one-keyed Baroque flute (after Scherer) and an eight-keyed classical flute (after Kirst).

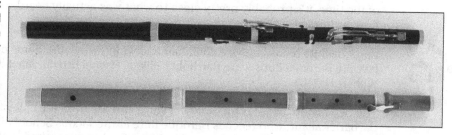

The Baroque flute is also frequently called the *traverso* — short for *flauto traverso,* which is what people called the instrument back in the Baroque era. *Flauto traverso* is Italian for "transverse flute," so called to distinguish it from the also popular but vertically held *recorder,* which was called *flauto dolce* (Italian for "sweet flute").

Baroque flutes were made of various types of wood, commonly boxwood or ebony, with ivory mounts placed where the joints fit together. Some Baroque flutists performing today play on the actual old flutes that were used back then, though they are, of course, quite rare. However, Baroque flutemakers take it upon themselves to painstakingly craft reproductions of the original Baroque instruments, using the same types of materials as were used in the originals, except for the ivory — they use a plastic resin instead. They also usually keep the instrument's pitch true to what it would have been during the time it was originally made — somewhere between A=392 and A=415, depending on the individual flute.

Baroque composers like Bach, Handel, and Telemann wrote their music with the one-keyed flauto traverso in mind, and as you can imagine, the traverso plays quite differently from the modern flute. The Baroque flute sounds softer and gentler — the wood gives it a mellow quality. On the modern flute, the ideal sound is to play all the notes equal in quality, but this ideal wasn't even a concept on the Baroque flute, because Boehm's system hadn't been invented yet. Some of the notes on the traverso sounded crystal-clear, and others, especially chromatic notes like B♭ and A♭, sounded muffled because of the complicated fingerings necessary to produce them. Baroque composers knew very well what these instruments sounded like in any given key, and they wrote their music accordingly. They might write a very sad piece, for example, in a minor key with lots of flats to promote a soft dynamic and a subdued tone color from the performer.

I love listening to Baroque flute performances, or any music played on early instruments or reproductions, for that matter. It's like taking a trip back in time to hear what the composer had in mind when he wrote the piece. And if the performance is well researched to conform to the performance practice of the time, it's probably pretty close to what was actually heard when it was first performed.

Baroque flute recordings are abundant and widely available. Some of my favorite Baroque flutists are Barthold Kuijken, Rachel Brown, Janet See, and Wilbert Hazelzet.

The two historical flutes pictured in Figure 22-4 are from the collection of Barbara Kallaur, who teaches Baroque flute at the Jacobs School of Music at Indiana University. French flutemaker Claire Soubeyran crafted both of these original instrument reproductions. The original version of the one-keyed box-wood Baroque flute was made by Scherer around 1720, and the original eight-keyed ebony classical flute was made by Kirst around 1790.

Four- and Eight-Keyed Flutes

In the middle of the 18th century, flutemakers started to experiment with adding more keys to the flute. The extra keys enabled greater technical facility in chromatic keys, so the new flutes in turn encouraged composers to write more technically challenging music. These flutes generally boasted a clearer, more assertive sound, and the extra keys enabled the player to create a more even tone quality from one note to the next.

Today's Baroque flutists use *four-* and *eight-keyed flutes* where appropriate — generally speaking, the later the music was written, the more keys the corresponding flute has. (This trend continued until Boehm invented the modern key system.) The later the music, the higher the pitch climbs to conform to the pitch of the respective musical period: These Classical- to early Romantic-era flutes typically play around A=430. (Figure 22-4 shows an eight-keyed flute.)

The Fife

The *fife* is traditionally a military instrument. It's a small transverse flute, customarily made of wood and pitched in B♭, C, or D, with six holes and no keys. The fife's penetrating sound made it a logical partner for the drums in rousing soldiers into battle during the American Revolution and the American

Civil War. You can still find fife and drum corps throughout the United States, most notably in Williamsburg, Virginia.

The fife's roots go all the way back to Medieval Europe — back then, the instrument was also commonly paired with drums with the purpose of giving signals for battle.

Though most people think of it as a historical instrument, the fife is also a useful tool for young beginning flutists. In starting a six-year-old on the flute, for example, it can prove difficult for the child to hold a concert C flute properly, even if it has a curved headjoint to help facilitate correct posture — sometimes the instrument is just too heavy for those small hands and arms. This is where the fife comes in. It's about the size of a piccolo, but has a lighter wall thickness, which means it's freer-blowing and therefore gives the student easier sound production. It's a simple instrument, without the added complications (and expense) of the Boehm system keys. It's the perfect training-wheel flute, because it requires the same type of embouchure as the concert C flute. And it's also available in the key of C, in plastic, for less than ten bucks.

World Flutes

Because the flute has been around for such a long time, variations of the instrument exist all over the world. I list some of the world flutes you're most likely to come across here. The flute, in all its forms, is more popular than ever — the world over!

✔ **Celtic flute:** This instrument is similar in structure and sound to the Baroque flutes and keyed flutes I talk about earlier in this chapter. Flutes played on Irish and Scottish folk tunes in Celtic bands are either original 19th-century instruments from the British Isles or reproductions of those flutes. They're available with one key, four keys, eight keys, or completely keyless and are traditionally made of wood. As with Baroque and other historical keyed flutes, the more keys you see on the flute, the easier it is to play in more major and minor keys.

Be sure to listen to recordings of Celtic flutists Chris Norman (*Man with the Wooden Flute*, Dorian Records) and Matt Molloy (*Matt Molloy*, Compass Records, or any recording of Molloy's phenomenal Celtic group, the Chieftains). You're in for a treat.

✔ **Pan pipes:** This row of pipes of various sizes banded together horizontally allows the player to switch pitches simply by switching pipes, no fingerings required. Think of it as a miniature organ, without the keyboard. You see a lot of pan pipes in Greek mythology, but today the instrument is popular in South America and Eastern Europe, although you still find it in various forms on just about every continent.

Romanian pan flutist Gheorghe Zamfir popularized the pan pipes in the 1970s with some amazingly virtuosic playing on the simple instrument. You can still find a good number of his recordings.

✔ **Native American flute:** These wondrous-looking and -sounding keyless wooden instruments have fascinated many people of all nationalities. The Native American flute is held vertically, and the player blows into the end, not across a hole, to activate the sound chamber inside. A *totem,* or carved wooden animal, sits right outside the sound chamber's opening, and you can move it to adjust the quality of the sound.

For a relaxing, spirit-soothing escape, listen to any number of recordings by famed Native American flutist R. Carlos Nakai. Or, for a completely different experience, listen to James Pellerite. An accomplished, classically trained flutist (he once played with the Philadelphia Orchestra and taught at Indiana University for many years), Pellerite switched from the concert C flute to the Native American flute late in life and never looked back. He has commissioned a number of classical pieces for the Native American flute with orchestra and recorded them with the Moravian Philharmonic on an album called *Visions, Dreams, and Memories* (Albany Records).

✔ **Dizi:** The history of the Chinese dizi flute goes back about 2,000 years. The dizi is a transverse flute that you can hold to the right or left side, depending on your preference. It's usually made from bamboo and has finger holes, but no keys. What sets the dizi apart from other types of flutes is its reedy, almost buzzy sound, which is due to the plant-based membrane covering an opening between the embouchure and finger holes.

✔ **Shakuhachi:** The Japanese shakuhachi is a vertical bamboo flute played by blowing across an edge at the top of the instrument. It's extremely difficult to get a sound out of a shakuhachi, so learning how to play one isn't a realistic task for the casual hobbyist. But the sound it produces is worth the effort: Beautifully dark and eerie, with characteristic slides and seemingly endless tone colors, the shakuhachi is the perfect vehicle for traditional Japanese music. (Some flutemakers are now making shakuhachi-style headjoints for the western concert C flute so that you can get the exotic shakuhachi sound on your own flute.)

✔ **Bansuri:** A low-pitched flute played in Northern India, the bansuri is a simple transverse bamboo flute with embouchure and finger holes. Paintings and sculptures featuring the Hindu deity Krishna often depict him playing a bansuri flute. The throaty, haunting sound of the bansuri is often heard in the *rāgas,* or sequences, of Indian classical music.

Part VI
Appendixes

"Does anyone else feel the flute and cello part is a bit too appassionato?"

In this part . . .

Appendix A includes six different fingering charts that you can consult regularly: a chart of basic fingerings for notes all through the flute's range, a chart for the alternate fingerings I get you started on in Chapter 15, a trill fingering chart to supplement the section on trills in Chapter 16, a specialized fingering chart for the C♯ trill key in case you have one (see more about the C♯ trill key in Chapter 3), and a tremolo fingering chart to supplement the section on tremolos in Chapter 16. These fingerings are all you need for most of the flute playing you're going to do. But just in case you haven't had enough of fingering charts after going through Appendix A (and in this case, I'm thinking you must have a bit of a fingering chart fetish, which isn't necessarily a bad thing), I include recommendations for entire books and Web sites dedicated to flute fingerings.

Appendix B tells you about the CD that accompanies this book. You find out which tracks correspond with which musical examples and step-by-step instructions. Click track countdowns have been provided to help you establish your tempo for each play-along track. The CD tracks are great learning tools that supplement the text in this book, so you'll want to make good use of them.

Appendix A

Fingering Charts

. . . .

I was going to call this appendix "Fun with Fingerings," but thought it wouldn't be serious enough. How dare anyone have actual fun while playing the flute? At any rate, here you find all (well, most) of the fingerings you'll ever need. (If you find yourself hankering for fingerings that I don't include here, which I don't envision happening anytime soon, you can pick up some of the fingering books I mention throughout this appendix.)

Reading Flute Fingering Charts

Follow these rules when working from all the fingering charts in this book:

- ✔ When a field is filled in, depress the corresponding key.

- ✔ When a field is left blank, *do not* depress the corresponding key.

- ✔ When a field is only half filled in, cover only about half of the hole in the top of the key. (These fingerings work only for flutes with open holes.)

- ✔ When a field is marked with an *x,* trill the corresponding key(s) by moving your finger up and down quickly.

Finding the Flute's Home Keys

If you read and follow my instructions in Chapter 7, you know about the flute's home keys. But Figure A-1 gives you a diagram for quick and easy reference.

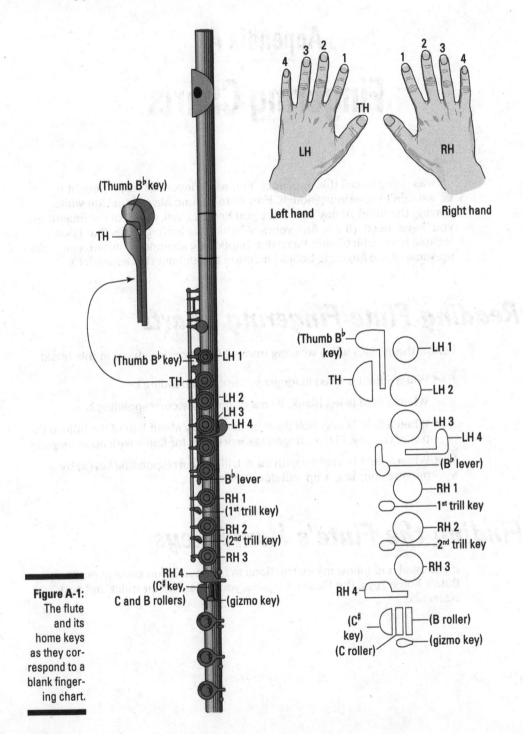

Figure A-1:
The flute and its home keys as they correspond to a blank fingering chart.

In Table A-1, I list which of your fingers corresponds to which abbreviation so that you can easily see which finger goes where in Figure A-1.

Table A-1	Numbering System for the Flute's Home Keys
Finger	*Abbreviation*
Left-hand thumb	TH
Left-hand index finger	LH 1
Left-hand middle finger	LH 2
Left-hand ring finger	LH 3
Left-hand pinky (G♯ key)	LH 4
Right-hand index finger	RH 1
Right-hand middle finger	RH 2
Right-hand ring finger	RH 3
Right-hand pinky (D♯/E♭ key)	RH 4

Using the abbreviations in Table A-1, look at Figure A-1 to determine which finger goes on which of the home keys on your instrument. Then refer to the blank fingering chart to the right of the picture that tells you the circles and squiggles that correspond to the keys.

Basic Fingering Chart

Figure A-2 is a basic fingering chart for all the notes on the flute.

For a truly comprehensive and ready reference to fingering charts for woodwind instruments, check out The Woodwind Fingering Guide at www.wfg.woodwind.org/flute. It's a great resource.

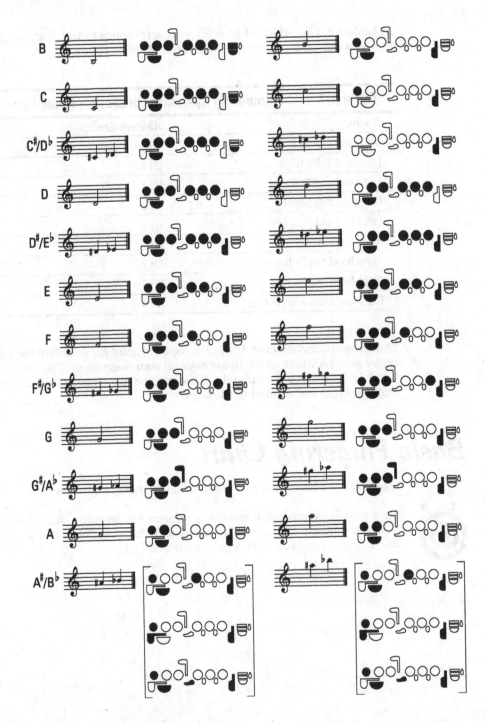

Figure A-2:
Basic
fingering
chart.

Alternate Fingering Chart

Figure A-3 is a chart of the alternate fingerings I find the most helpful. The column on the left features fingerings that correct notes that are typically quite sharp on the flute (especially if they're played *mf-ff*) by lowering their pitch. In the column on the right, I list fingerings that raise the pitch of notes that are typically flat on the flute, especially when played softly.

Play these notes using the indicated fingerings with your tuner to determine what dynamic level each fingering is appropriate for and don't be afraid to experiment on your own. For more about alternate fingerings, see Chapter 15. You'll notice that the note F♯ appears in both columns. These fingerings help stabilize the note as well as control its pitch. Because F♯ can be a tricky note at any dynamic level, it helps to have lots of options.

Alternate fingerings to lower sharp notes, especially when played at louder dynamic levels

Alternate fingerings to bring up flat notes, especially when played at softer dynamic levels

Lower part way only

Figure A-3: Alternate fingering chart.

If you're interested in more (much more!) about alternate fingerings, take a look at the book *Alternative Fingerings for the Flute* (Carolyn Nussbaum Music Company) by Nestor Herszbaum. Herszbaum has compiled more than 100 pages of alternate fingerings in this groundbreaking book. Knock yourself out!

Trill Fingering Chart

In Chapter 16, I introduce you to the fine art of trilling. In Figure A-4, I give you half-step and whole-step trills throughout the range of the instrument. I take you all the way up to the third octave C-D♭ trill.

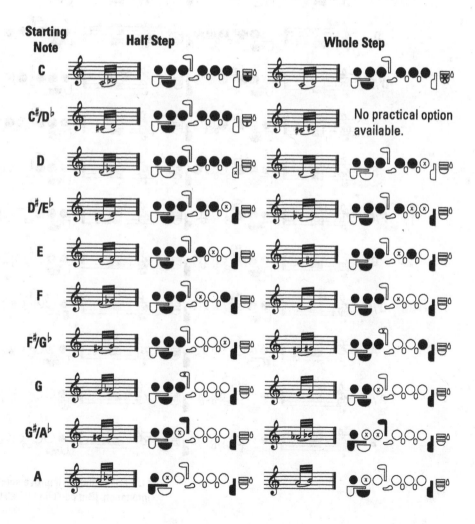

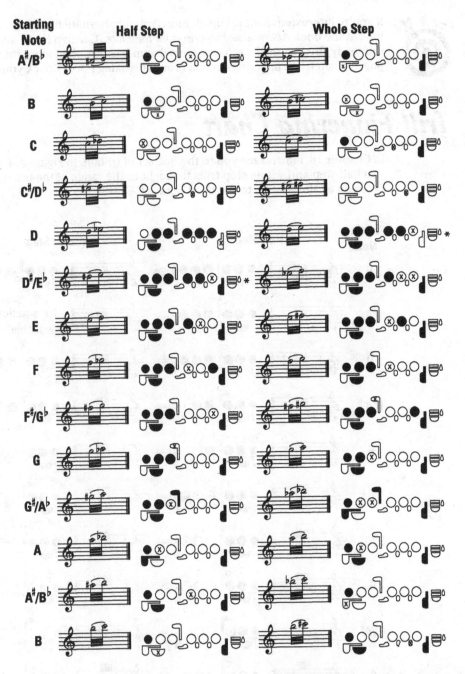

* Lift LH1 slightly to improve sound and
intonation. (But don't lift LH1 all the way!)

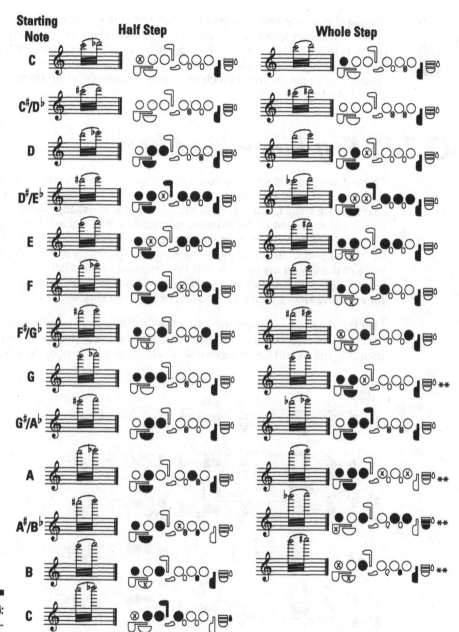

Figure A-4:
Trill finger-
ing chart.

** Requires quite a bit of air speed.

Trilling above those notes is possible, but not entirely practical — those trills never sound very good, and you almost never see them in music anyway. My policy is to leave them alone if at all possible. Notice that I put a footnote on some of the higher trills via a double asterisk: These trills require a lot of air speed. You've got to pretty much blow your brains out to get them to work. (But that's half the fun!)

C♯ Trill Key Fingering Chart

These fingerings will work for you only if your flute has a C♯ trill key. (If you don't have a C♯ trill key, reading this section may convince you to buy a flute that has one.) The *C♯ trill key* is an extra lever that is usually placed slightly above and to the left of the B♭ lever, as indicated in this chart. This little key is a great option to have. It gives you easier fingerings for several trills, as listed in the first part of the chart — the easy, clear high G to A trill alone is worth the price of the key, in my opinion. The last fingering on the chart gives you a high G♯ or A♭ that you can play very softly without cracking the note. (Don't use it for anything louder than a *pp*, though, or you'll go very sharp.)

I list the most useful fingerings using the C♯ trill key in Figure A-5, but you can also get some good tremolo fingerings by trying things here and there. As I mention, the C♯ trill key is incredibly useful. If you have it, be sure to use it!

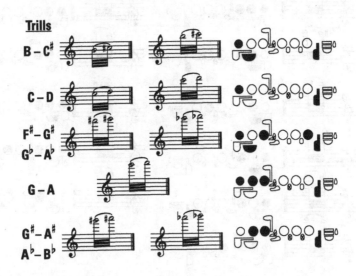

Figure A-5:
C♯ trill key
fingering
chart.

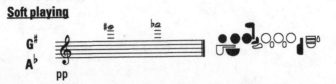

Tremolo Fingering Chart

The chart in Figure A-6 supplements my introduction to tremolos in Chapter 16 and includes tremolos in intervals of minor and major thirds, which will cover you for most of the tremolos you'll ever encounter.

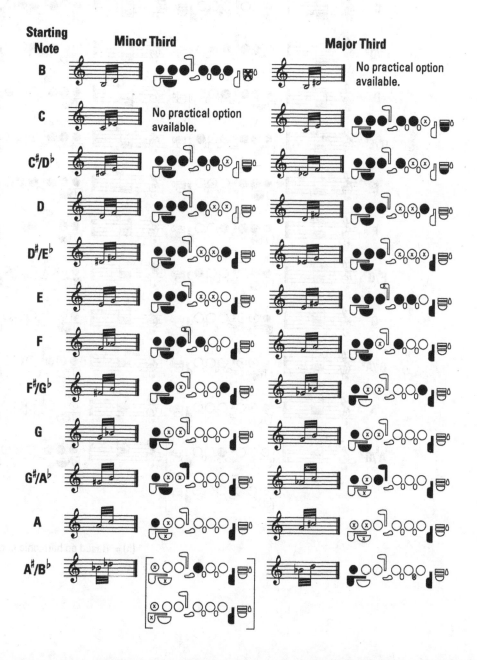

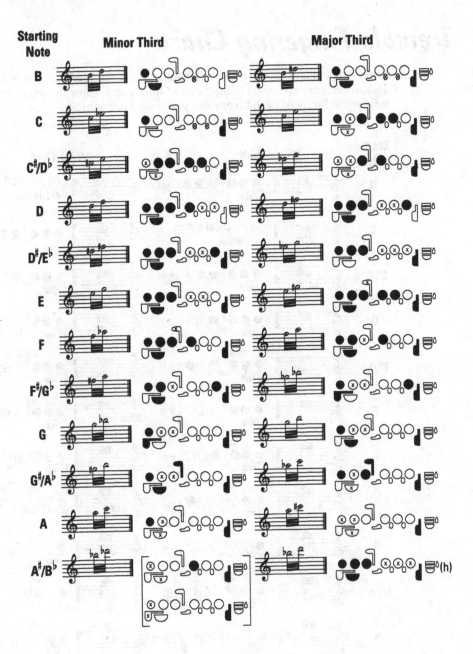

(h) = Based on harmonic fingering.

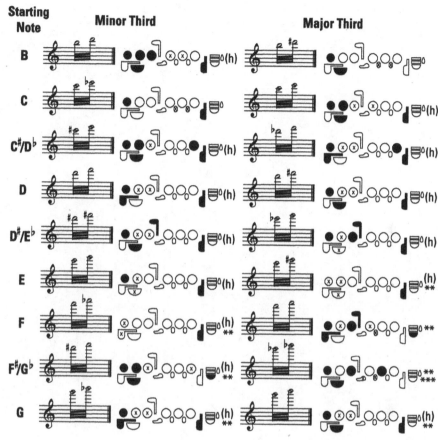

Figure A-6:
Tremolo
fingering
chart.

(h) = Based on harmonic fingering.

** = Requires quite a bit of air speed.

*** = Use your RH 3 finger (ring finger) on the RH 2 key.

If you come across a tremolo that spans an interval larger than a third, check the Woodwind Fingering Guide at www.wfg.woodwind.org/flute for a workable option.

If you'd like to add another reference book to round out your music library, you could purchase James J. Pellerite's book, *A Modern Guide to Fingerings for the Flute* (Zalo Publications). This book still sets the gold standard for flute fingerings decades after its first printing. It includes basic fingerings, alternate fingerings, trills, and tremolos in intervals from thirds all the way to octaves, and more — way more than you may ever need to know!

Appendix B

About the CD

The CD that accompanies this book is a fun and useful tool to help you in your practice studio. It gives you 94 tracks that correspond to various examples in the book. On some tracks, I demonstrate the examples by playing them for you, while other tracks provide a piano accompaniment for you to play with. All the CD tracks serve to further illuminate your *Flute For Dummies* experience.

If you're using this book as a method and working through it beginning to end, you can, of course, use the tracks in the order they appear in the book and on the CD. But if you have a little flute-playing experience, you can also peruse the track list and just work on the examples that interest you. You can find a wide variety of music, from traditional tunes to short classical pieces, all with one purpose: to help you become the best flutist you can be!

Referring to the CD

Every time you see the On The CD icon in this book, you'll find a track (or tracks) on the accompanying CD that corresponds to the section in which the icon appears. To use the CD, simply pop it into any conventional CD player, pick your track, and just listen to it or play along. Also feel free to import it into your favorite digital music application for playback on your computer or mp3 player. You may find that you have to retype the track names into your computer, but it's a small price to pay for the convenience of taking your reference tracks with you wherever you go.

You'll want to keep the CD with this book, not with your CD collection. Put it back into its protective sleeve in the back of the book after you're finished using it, and you won't have to go looking for it before your next practice session nor will you have to deal with any skips or scratches that could occur if your leave the disc out and unprotected. (Also, to that end, don't use your *Flute For Dummies* book or CD as a football, Frisbee, or doorstop, or you risk damaging the CD as well as the book! However, if you do feel compelled to kick the book around a bit to get out your frustrations about the flute — or me — be my guest. I'm just telling you now that I can't be held liable for any damage that you may incur during that process.)

For each new note you learn during the course of this book, a corresponding demo track on the CD features yours truly playing that note (without vibrato). You may or may not be exactly in tune with the pitches on the CD, but I'm sure you'll be able to tell whether you're in the ballpark. You may want to check a tuning note with your tuner and adjust your pitch to A=440 so that your pitches will match mine as closely as possible. (See Chapter 15 for more information on how to tune.)

Composer/arranger/pianist Cyndee Giebler and I perform together on the accompanied demo tracks. You can listen to us play first on the demo and then play along with her on the accompaniment track using the handy count-offs. (They sound like metronome clicks preceding each play-along track.) Or, if you prefer, you can take an intermediate step by playing along with me on the demo track before you venture out on your own with Cyndee. We hope you find these tunes and demonstrations helpful as well as enjoyable.

Using the CD

The CD included with this book will work just fine in any standard CD player. If you have a computer, you can pop the accompanying CD into your CD-ROM drive and use your computer's media player to play the CD. Make sure that your computer meets the following minimum system requirements:

- A computer running Microsoft Windows or Apple OS X or later
- Software capable of playing CD audio
- A CD-ROM drive
- A sound card for PCs (Mac OS computers have built-in sound support)

Discovering What's on the CD

Table B-1 is your comprehensive track list. Most of the tracks correspond to a specific figure in this book, so I list the figure numbers that correspond to each track number. In some cases, the tracks correspond to a more generalized description in the book (like a set of numbered step-by-step instructions) and not necessarily a particular figure, in which case you see n/a and the chapter number instead of the figure number.

Using the chapter reference and the description on the track list, you'll be able to quickly and easily determine what, specifically, a particular track is intended to demonstrate and where it's located within the book.

In the Demo/Accomp column, I tell you whether the track is a demonstration track or an accompaniment track. If it's a demo track, I'm playing on it, and you can listen to how that particular musical example or set of steps is supposed to sound. After you listen to it once, feel free to play along with me. If the musical example in question involves learning a note or notes, you can play along to make sure that you're getting the right note.

If a track is labeled Accomp, you'll hear only the keyboard accompaniment on that track, which also means it's time for your big solo! Check the number and note value listed in the count-off column. The number tells you how many clicks you'll hear before the music begins. The note value tells you what the rhythmic value of those clicks are. For example, on track 5, you hear four clicks that are each worth one quarter note beat. On track 31, you hear three clicks that are each worth one dotted quarter note beat, and so on. If you're not sure how to start, listen to the Demo track that comes right before the Accomp track. You'll hear the exact same number of clicks before the Demo track that I'm playing on, so you can either listen to that and go straight on the Accomp track or repeat the Demo track a few times and play along with me before you fly solo. Have fun!

In order to get as much material as possible onto the CD, I don't take repeats in the musical examples as a general rule. The track descriptions in Table B-1 tell you whether or not repeats are observed.

Table B-1		Contents of the CD		
Track Number	Figure Number	Description	Demo/ Accomp	Count- off
001	n/a Ch 6	Headjoint Sounds	demo	n/a
002	n/a Ch 6	Mini-flute/"Mary Had a Little Lamb"	demo	n/a
003	8-2	B/A/G	demo	n/a
004	8-3	"Mary Had a Little Lamb"	demo	4 ♩
005	8-3	"Mary Had a Little Lamb"	accomp	4 ♩

(continued)

Table B-1 *(continued)*

Track Number	Figure Number	Description	Demo/ Accomp	Count-off
006	8-4	F/E	demo	n/a
007	8-6	Melody/BAGFE	demo	4 ♩
008	8-6	Melody/BAGFE	accomp	4 ♩
009	8-7	D	demo	n/a
010	8-9	Melody/BAGFED	demo	4 ♩
011	8-9	Melody/BAGFED	accomp	4 ♩
012	9-1	B♭	demo	n/a
013	9-2	B♭ melody/*Ode to Joy*	demo	4 ♩
014	9-2	B♭ melody/*Ode to Joy*	accomp	4 ♩
015	9-3	A♭/G♭/E♭	demo	n/a
016	9-4a	G♯/F♯/D♯/intro	demo	n/a
017	9-4a	B♭/E♭/A♭ melody	demo	4 ♩
018	9-4a	B♭/E♭/A♭ melody	accomp	4 ♩
019	9-4b	F♯ melody/"Twinkle Twinkle Little Star"	demo	4 ♩
020	9-4b	F♯ melody/"Twinkle Twinkle Little Star"	accomp	4 ♩
021	9-5	Low C♯/C	demo	n/a
022	9-6	Low D♭/C/"My Country Tis of Thee/God Save the Queen"	demo	3 ♩
023	9-6	Low D♭/C/"My Country Tis of Thee/God Save the Queen"	accomp	3 ♩
024	9-7	Low B	demo	n/a
025	9-8	Low B Melody/"Exotic Tune"	demo	3 ♩
026	9-8	Low B Melody/"Exotic Tune"	accomp	3 ♩
027	9-9	Middle C	demo	n/a
028	9-10	Middle C Melody/"Frère Jacques"	demo	4 ♩
029	9-10	Middle C Melody/"Frère Jacques"	accomp	4 ♩
030	9-14	Middle D Melody/"On Top of Old Smokey"	demo	3 ♩.
031	9-14	Middle D Melody/"On Top of Old Smokey"	accomp	3 ♩.
032	9-15	D finger twister	demo	n/a

Track Number	Figure Number	Description	Demo/ Accomp	Count- off
033	10-1	Slurring exercise (no repeats)	demo	n/a
034	10-2	Tied notes/Fauré *Fantasie*	demo	8 ♪
035	10-2	Tied notes/Fauré *Fantasie*	accomp	8 ♪
036	n/a Ch10	Tonguing exercise	demo	n/a
037	10-3	Staccato/"Row, Row, Row Your Boat"	demo	4 ♩.
038	10-3	Staccato/"Row, Row, Row Your Boat"	accomp	4 ♩.
039	10-4	Legato/"Row, Row, Row Your Boat"	demo	4 ♩.
040	10-4	Legato/"Row, Row, Row Your Boat"	accomp	4 ♩.
041	10-5	Köhler *Etude*	demo	n/a
042	11-1	slur low to Middle D and E♭	demo	n/a
043	11-2	E-octave	demo	n/a
044	11-3	Harmonics	demo	n/a
045	11-4	Octaves	demo	n/a
046	11-5a	Gluck *Aria*	demo	4 ♩
047	11-5a	Gluck *Aria*	accomp	4 ♩
048	11-5b	Gluck *Ballet (no repeat)*	demo	3 ♩
049	11-5b	Gluck *Ballet (no repeat)*	accomp	3 ♩
050	11-5c	Gluck *Air de la Naïade*	demo	3 ♩
051	11-5c	Gluck *Air de la Naïade*	accomp	3 ♩
052	12-1	Marcello *Largo*	demo	3 ♩
053	12-1	Marcello *Largo*	accomp	3 ♩
054	12-2	Marcello *Cantabile*	demo	3 ♩
055	12-2	Marcello *Cantabile*	accomp	3 ♩
056	n/a Ch12	Harmonic C/C/G	demo	n/a
057	12-3	Mozart *Là ci darem la mano*	demo	n/a
058	12-3	Mozart *Là ci darem la mano*	demo	n/a
059	12-4a	Handel *Sonata in F Major* 1st movement	demo	3 ♩

(continued)

Table B-1 *(continued)*

Track Number	Figure Number	Description	Demo/ Accomp	Count-off
060	12-4a	Handel *Sonata in F Major* 1st movement	accomp	3 ♩
061	12-4b	Bach *Sonata in E♭ Major* 2nd movement	demo	6 ♪
062	12-4b	Bach *Sonata in E♭ Major* 2nd movement	accomp	6 ♪
063	n/a Ch13	Measured vibrato	demo	n/a
064	n/a Ch14	Harmonic G/D	demo	n/a
065	14-1	Slurring into high notes	demo	n/a
066	14-3	Doppler *Fantasie Pastorale Hongroise* — harmonics	demo	n/a
067	14-4	Prokofiev *Classical Symphony* excerpt	demo	n/a
068	14-5	Tchaikovsky *Piano Concerto #1* excerpt	demo	n/a
069	14-6	4th octave C#/D	demo	n/a
070	14-7	Dropping high notes/ harmonics	demo	n/a
071	14-8a	Gounod *Petite Symphonie*	demo	n/a
072	14-8b	Saint-Saëns *Romance*	demo	4 ♩
073	14-8b	Saint-Saëns *Romance*	accomp	4 ♩
074	15-3	Bizet *Minuet from l'Arlésienne*	demo	3 ♩
075	15-3	Bizet *Minuet from l'Arlésienne*	accomp	3 ♩
076	n/a Ch16	Double tonguing	demo	n/a
077	16-1	Andersen *Etude*/double tonguing	demo	n/a
078	16-2	Gariboldi *Etude*/double tonguing	demo	n/a
079	16-3	Bach *Sonata in C Major* 2nd movement/double tonguing (no repeats)	demo	3 ♩
080	16-3	Bach *Sonata in C Major* 2nd movement/double tonguing (no repeats)	accomp	3 ♩

Track Number	Figure Number	Description	Demo/ Accomp	Count- off
081	16-5	Andersen *Etude*/triple tonguing 1	demo	n/a
082	16-6	Andersen *Etude*/triple tonguing 2	demo	n/a
083	16-7	Ravel *La Valse*/flutter tonguing	demo	n/a
084	16-8	Counting out trills	demo	n/a
085	16-9	Trill fingerings/dotted rhythms (no repeats)	demo	n/a
086	16-10	Mozart *Andante in C*	demo	4 ♪
087	16-10	Mozart *Andante in C*	accomp	4 ♪
088	16-11	Ganne *Andante et Scherzo*	demo	n/a
089	16-12	Tremolos	demo	n/a
090	17-1	Wibb's harmonics (first 12 measures of A and B sections)	demo	n/a
091	17-2	Chromatic long tones	demo	n/a
092	17-3	Bizet *Carmen Entr'acte*	demo	n/a
093	17-4	Faure *Pavane*	demo	n/a
094	17-8	Andersen *Etude*	demo	n/a

Troubleshooting

If you have trouble with the CD-ROM, please call the Wiley Product Technical Support phone number at (800) 762-2974. Outside the United States, call (317) 572-3994. You can also contact Wiley Product Technical Support at http://support.wiley.com. John Wiley & Sons will provide technical support only for installation and other general quality control items.

Index